Lewis's Laws of Mail Order Advertising

Three Laws of force-communication cover every medium except direct response:

The First Law:

Effective advertising is that which reaches, at the lowest possible cost, the most people who can and will buy what you have to sell.

If that Law is a truism to you, hurrah! Too many communicators stop at "the most people." Shooting for mass instead of selective coverage will cost someone a lot of money.

The Second Law:

In this Age of Skepticism, cleverness for the sake of cleverness may well be a liability, not an asset.

It isn't cleverness that can hang you. Cleverness related to product or service is what we do for a living. But cleverness designed to make a reader or viewer say, "How clever that writer is!" is a disservice to what we're selling and to the person who is paying us.

The Third Law:

$E^2 = 0.$

This simplest of equations means simply that when you emphasize everything you emphasize nothing. A laundry list of "147 Reasons Why You Should Buy Now" is weaker than one powerhouse reason, reinforced by ancillary reasons.

For direct response, we add ——

The Fourth Law:

Tell the reader or viewer what to do.

Subtlety doesn't work. You have to induce action from a single exposure. Don't just describe. Get the order.

Also by Herschell Gordon Lewis:

How to Make Your Advertising Twice as Effective at Half the Cost

How to Handle Your Own Public Relations

The Businessman's Guide to Advertising and Sales Promotion

More Than You Ever Wanted to Know About Mail Order Advertising

(as coauthor)
Symbol of America: Norman Rockwell

Direct Mail Copy that Sells

Direct Mail Copy that SELLS!

Herschell Gordon Lewis

Prentice-Hall, Inc.
Englewood Cliffs, New Jersey

Prentice-Hall International, Inc., *London*
Prentice-Hall of Australia, Pty. Ltd., *Sydney*
Prentice-Hall Canada, Inc., *Toronto*
Prentice-Hall of India Private Ltd., *New Delhi*
Prentice-Hall of Japan, Inc., *Tokyo*
Prentice-Hall of Southeast Asia Pte. Ltd., *Singapore*
Whitehall Books, Ltd., *Wellington, New Zealand*
Editora Prentice-Hall do Brasil Ltda., *Rio de Janeiro*

Library of Congress Cataloging in Publication Data

Lewis, Herschell Gordon
  Direct mail copy that sells!

  Includes index.
  1. Advertising, Direct-mail.   2. Advertising copy.
I. Title.
HF5861.L475   1984   659.13′22   84-3273

ISBN 0-13-214768-8
ISBN 0-13-214750-5 {PBK}

10 9 8 7 6 5 4 3

Printed in the United States of America

Foreword

by Henry R. Hoke, Jr.

The technique of communication is changing.

Some "communicators" wonder why their golden copy doesn't sell as well as it used to. Some old-timers who resist change just because it *is* change don't recognize the difference between "vintage" writing, marking them as anachronisms, and contemporary writing.

If we look back to the 1940s, the 1950s, the 1960s, and even the 1970s, we see at once the evidence of change: hairstyles, fashion, the language in movies, acceptance of technological miracles, implicit distrust of politicians, blurring of the lines distinguishing the average person from what we now call the "upscale buyer."

One reason we haven't been so quick to see changes in what Herschell Gordon Lewis so aptly calls *force-communication* is that until now, we've had few rules for writing. Teachers of the noble art of copywriting might say, "Be friendly," or, "Be personal," but codifying the process of asking someone who never heard of you to buy something has awaited the arrival of someone with the courage, the imagination, the technical knowledge, and the communications skill to write them down for us. Once they're written, we finally can advance our creative thinking into the mid-1980s alongside other evolutionary trends.

The moment—and the person—is here.

As the publisher of *Direct Marketing* and *Fund Raising Management*, I never cease to be amazed at the unending stream of writings from the world's best copywriters. But how much is there to say? How much can actually be new?

Plenty. From the "pen" of the indefatigable Herschell Gordon Lewis.

Herschell is indeed a rare bird among writers. I deal with writers all day, every day. Typically, they're jealously protective of their pet devices; they're at least mildly introverted; some have diffculty with fast-paced conversations or speechmaking.

The author of this book couldn't be more different. He takes no proprietary position on the rules of effective copywriting he shares with us. He's an accomplished tennis player and scuba diver. He's one of the best speechmakers in our business.

He also is one of the highest-paid, most-respected, best-known direct response copywriters in the world. Herschell's clients are everywhere—throughout the United States, in many countries of Europe, and even in some of the exotic lands with hard-to-spell names. "I spend most of my time banging the keys of my word processor," he told me once. "I don't dare get stale, and that's what happens if you pontificate without getting your own hands dirty."

In my opinion this is a remarkable book—a milestone, if you will. For the first time a successful writer gives us hard rules for writing, rules we have no trouble translating in terms of our own projects.

I'm pleased and proud that some of the information in this book first appeared in the pages of *Direct Marketing* magazine. And I commend this book to you if you have any interest in what makes mail order buyers buy. You'll find no hedging here. Herschell Lewis practices what he preaches in straightforward, no-nonsense, easy-to-understand writing.

One last point: If you disagree with what's in this book, contact Herschell, not me. You'll probably find him on the tennis courts at Jacaranda Country Club in Fort Lauderdale, making handwritten notes between games. On second thought, contact both of us . . . if Herschell's ideas tickle your fancy.

Author's Preface

On the same page, in an advertising/marketing magazine, were three news items that gave me the willies:

1. "Oldsmobile will change its ad theme for 1984, with 'There is a special feel in an Oldsmobile' replacing 'Have one built for you.' "
2. "America West Airlines breaks its initial ad campaign. Themed, 'Owned by the people who serve you,' newspaper ads will run in five cities. Radio supports in three markets."
3. "Dodge broke the first 1984 model car advertising with spots for its Daytona Z on ABC-TV. 'Dodge introduces a new legend,' says the spot."

Envisioning the meetings, the brain-wracking, and the number of initials on copy-sheets before these campaigns broke, I was chilled.

Why? Because in a copywriting class, these noncommunicative, nonmotivating campaigns might get a "C" if the instructor is particularly benevolent. They typify an approach to force-communications in which bulk space and time-buys serve as crutches for imaginative sterility. None of the three ideas could survive the first slashing blue pencil of a marketer who sells by direct mail.

Direct mail ads have to kill with one blow. If they don't motivate, they're *hors de combat*. They can't wait for an "awareness buildup" or complain, "It would have worked if we'd had network TV saturation."

No, direct response isn't a playground for poseurs, would-bes, or charlatans. As often as not, your piece of copy goes head-to-head with another approach written by a hungry competing writer who wants to taste the blood of two victims—

the person whose name is on the envelope, and you. List selection and name alternation being what they are, you can't cover failure with a lame excuse. Your message pulled better than the other one, or it pulled worse. What a classic and easy way to keep score.

For some years I've earned my living as a direct response writer. In the old days, when I had a conventional advertising agency, I'd have seen nothing awry with a campaign built around a neutral-gear slogan such as "There is a special feel in an Oldsmobile" or "Dodge introduces a new legend." I'd have taken credit for any increase in sales and put the blame for declines where it belongs—on the car, not the campaign. But now I know these nonarguments for what they are— holding actions. They neither make nor break the product's success; they just hold the product name in suspension so public awareness doesn't drop to zero.

Let's suppose your neighborhood car dealer wants to get you into his showroom. He sends you a piece of mail. Would you waste the time and gasoline if his message to you were this dully sell-puffed megalomaniacal line?

> Dear Mr. Jones,
> There is a special feel in an Oldsmobile.

Or would you respond better to specific benefit to you?

> Dear Mr. Jones,
> Your 1982 Datsun is worth $7,000 on a new
> Oldsmobile—
> if you come in this week

or,

> I have a free AM/FM signal-seeking radio for you.

The point of this book you have in your hands isn't that so much advertising is poor; no, no—the point is this:

WRITING EFFECTIVE ADVERTISING IS EASY IF YOU KNOW AND FOLLOW THE RULES.

What rules? They're in this book. Some are irreverent, but all are pertinent.

I'm firmly convinced of two marketing facts:

1. Writing copy that sells is no accident.
2. Without copy that sells, you're at the mercy of what the competition does.

Those facts alone should make this compendium of disrespectful comments a good working manual for you. To sweeten the pot even more, I'll add this claim to the mix:

This book is geared to the Age of Skepticism, the times we live in *now*. It isn't history and it isn't theory. It's a way to survive by knowing more about human motivation than the fellow at the next word processor. In my opinion any book written during the 1970s is ancient history and its rules are valuable only as curiosities.

Do you agree? I hope you'll read the book through before making your final decision. Thanks, my friend.

Herschell Gordon Lewis

Acknowledgments

I'm indebted to Mr. Henry R. Hoke, Jr., the genial publisher of *Direct Marketing* and *Fund Raising Management*, not only for giving me a forum for some of the ideas in this book but also for writing the introduction.

Similarly, Mr. Charles Tannen, publisher of *Catalog Age*, gave me the opportunity to try out my notions about catalog writing in the pages of his magazine before exposing them to you.

I'm grateful to Paula Nelson for organizing and retyping much of the material, and to my favorite proofreader, Ruth Moffett, for helping me to keep these words reasonably literate.

Principal credit for the book's appearing at all goes to my wife and partner, Margo, on whose judgment I increasingly rely and on whose shoulder I increasingly lean.

Contents

1

The Challenge:
The Age of Skepticism—
and What to Do About It

Marketers were spared the Stone Age. They matured during the Iron Age, became bewildered during the Atomic Age, and are wildly competitive during the Electronic Age.

The mid-1980s pose what could be a brick-wall obstacle: the Age of Skepticism.

This is the Age in which nobody believes anybody, in which claims of superiority are challenged just because they're claims, in which consumers express surprise when something they buy actually performs the way it was advertised to perform.

Some of the direct mail old-timers blind themselves to this evolutionary horror. They wonder why their copy doesn't pull, why their letter that worked so well in 1974 doesn't convince the readers in 1984, why their claims aren't believed. "What's the matter with those people out there?" they wonder.

I don't dare suggest the answer is simple. Far from it. What *is* simple is the recognition of change. Farmer Brown no longer buys the Brooklyn Bridge; instead, he crosses it in his new Mercedes.

Treating buyers as though they're yokels is not only out of fashion; it's downright stupid, especially since *implicit in any marketing problem are the seeds of the solution to that problem.* Since we can solve the problem, why ignore it?

1

Cleverness for the Sake of Cleverness—NO!

Lewis's Second Law of Mass Communications should be carved on your forehead in blood, if you're locked in the unholy battle against the forces of skepticism.

Although you just read it, I'll repeat this Law because it's a key to dominance in today's marketplace:

IN THIS AGE OF SKEPTICISM, CLEVERNESS FOR THE SAKE OF CLEVERNESS MAY WELL BE A LIABILITY RATHER THAN AN ASSET.

What makes me so sure we're in the Age of Skepticism? And if we are, what makes me so sure we don't want the reader or viewer to say, "How clever whoever wrote that is!"

My certainty stems from the three ghastly reactions organized society has aimed at our promotional messages:

1. I don't trust you. Why should I?
2. I'm surprised when something I buy actually performs the way it was advertised to perform.
3. Others make the same claim you do; ergo, most of you are lying.

Neither you nor I nor anyone who communicates from an ivy-covered tower standing tall in the pleasant green forest of direct response should accept responsibility for having this monster in our midst. We didn't turn King Kong loose; it was those other guys. They came up with television commercials that insult the viewer's intelligence and strain their willingness to believe. They're the ones who want to win those strange awards given to writers who spend thousands of dollars showing off their own cleverness instead of the advertiser's wares.

TV: Guilty by Reason of Insanity

I'll buy that.

TV, the instant sophisticator, has sped up by 50 years the date that inevitably would come—when the targets of our spewing rhetoric would rise up and force us to mount a logical, thoughtful, sincere sales argument. What a sad day this is!

TV has sped up this sociological inevitability:

As Familiarity Increases, Dignity Begins to Shred.

Who has greatest visibility in our society? Politicians. Who is most ridiculed? Politicians. In pre-television days, even Millard Fillmore was safe from the sea of placards that now greets not just Ronald Reagan but any celebrity—Howard Cosell, Bo Derek, Carl Sagan.

Television is guilty and we in direct response are innocent on another count: A multiplicity of similar claims breeds confusion. With separation of 15 minutes or less between claims for superiority by a dozen brands of detergents, motorcars, toothpastes, or dog foods, the befuddled viewer must sink into Reaction 3: "Others make the same claim you do; therefore most of you are lying." Since direct response is one-on-one, we fall victim to that reaction only because we're there when the general state of mind exists—the bystander being shot by police chasing a robber.

When the target of our advertising message begins to compare what is with what was supposed to be, the very comparison means we might as well have mailed a Corvair brochure to Ralph Nader; our recipient is *skeptical.*

Our job, as communicators, is to prevent that reaction in the first place. We must climb Mt. Olympus and not be judged with "those people" who generate, aggravate, and bring to a boil the latent skepticism that shouldn't be allowed out of the box. We must say to the prospect, "We aren't like them. We're like you."

I'm not complaining that the Age of Skepticism exists. No, I'm pointing out how direct response communicators not only can survive but can turn the Age to their advantage!

12 + Rules to Save Your Copy's Life

I like orderly presentations. The only orderly way to present the formulae for overcoming the Age of Skepticism is by listing rules for smothering skepticism. As I write this I can think of a dozen rules; you might, as you grunt and heave in the gladiatorial arena of mail order selling, add more.

The first rule is the big one; the others are refinements. You can't follow all the rules in a single selling argument: you'd seem hysterical and incoherent. But if you ignore Rule 1, you surely will sell a lot less merchandise in the mid-1980s.

Rule 1: If You Make a Claim, Prove It.

What a difficult rule this is! It means doing some homework. You have to sell hardware (fact) rather than software (puffery). This means you can't in the foreseeable future use the word "Quality" in a headline. In the Age of Skepticism, *quality* doesn't hack it. It's a "me" software pitch, not a "you" hardware pitch.

Example:

At Ford Motor Company, quality is more than a
priority . . . Quality is Job One!

Analyze that for a moment. It's useless rhetoric. An entire creative team has substituted a repeated software word for a genuine idea. A rhetorical duck blind has replaced a cogent competitive selling argument.

Another example, from Snap-On Tools:

Some Things Last . . . Quality Endures.

In what way is that a selling argument? In what way does the statement generate a state of mind which might result in positive action?

One of the best examples of excellent use of Rule 1 is a mail order ad which runs regularly in sports and in-flight magazines. The headline:

Golf Pros Banned From Using New
"Hot" Ball; Flies Too Far

I don't know who wrote that ad, which is full of specifics overcoming any skepticism about that strong grabber of a headline, but I wish I had.

Compare the muscle of that headline with typical pro-shop brand golf ball ads.

Rule 2: Don't Lie.

It's confounding that anyone believes it's logical and sound business practice to lie in a letter or brochure and then, at the moment of truth—the order form—unmask with a "Yes, but . . . " disclaimer. Some in our business say they get orders that way, but I'll bet they get tons of white mail (complaints and hate letters), few reorders, and less response than they'd have were the message less shady. I wouldn't rent their lists, by the way.

An example: I have a "Dear Executive" letter addressed to me by *HFD*, a publication. The letter says, in its first indented paragraph:

> If you will return the enclosed card, we will enter a *free trial subscription to HFD* in your name. So, during the coming weeks you may enjoy the industry's only weekly newspaper without any obligation on your part.

Oh, yeah?
Here are the options on the enclosed order card:

– Yes. Please enter my one-year subscription and bill me for $21.95 after my subscription begins.
– I prefer a two-year subscription for $32.95.
– I prefer a three-year subscription for $42.95.
– Canada: One Year—$60.00
– Please tell me more about your discount group subscription program.

And that's it. No "free trial subscription." Out of pique more than curiosity I went back to the letter. I knew what I'd find, and, yes, it was there, carefully buried three paragraphs from the end: "If after a few issues, *HFD* disappoints you, just write 'cancel' on the invoice you'll receive and return it to us. There will be no cost, no obligation. And you keep all copies sent."

Okay, now I understand it. Why didn't you tell me in front this is a standard magazine subscription pitch? Why masquerade as a "free trial subscription"?

Is puffery parallel to lying? Almost; but it's desperate,

which is worse when uncovered. There's a whole chapter coming up about that.

Rule 3: Tie Your Claims to Credible Testimonials.

Some adpeople applaud the Muhammad Ali roach killer TV commercials. How many know the brand name?* When attention is drawn to the celebrity rather than the product, it's a violation of Lewis's Second Law:

IN THIS AGE OF SKEPTICISM, CLEVERNESS FOR THE SAKE OF CLEVERNESS MAY BE A LIABILITY, NOT AN ASSET.

Telcom Research of Teaneck, New Jersey, released a report that should have had more attention in advertising trade publications. The report underscored what happens with improper use of celebrities:

1. Some "star presenters," such as Frank Sinatra for Chrysler, draw attention away from the product.
2. Humor at the expense of a product (the ill fated "Drink Schlitz or I'll Kill You" campaign) hurts the product's image.

So why do they do it? They keep score another way: the number of people who remember seeing it, not the number of people who responded to it. We can't do that. Someone else may write a less memorable masterpiece of prose that pulls two orders for every magnificent one of ours.

That second conclusion of Telcom Research brings us to another rule.

Rule 4: Don't Clown.

Want to be safe? Don't make jokes. One exception: follow-up literature explaining a goof of which the buyer previously was unaware. But if you're answering a complaint, *no humor*.

Don't have the reader say, "What a clever fellow that writer is. By the way, what was he selling?"

---

*D-Con.

Rule 5: Imply Bulk or Community Acceptance.

"Everyone's doing it." That's what moves mountains that otherwise labor and bring forth a mouse. Take a look at the products for sale openly, over the counter, that a few years ago were shocking or sold surreptitiously. What made the change? The suggestion of bulk or community acceptance.

There's power in being able to father this reaction: "Gee, if all those people think that way . . . ."

Then, after legitimizing it and varnishing over the strangeness—

Rule 6: Personalize.

When you write a letter that says, "Only you . . . ", you've told the recipient that to you he isn't a unit, an anonymous number in a computer, a faceless organism with a zip code.

You also project an attitude of friendliness. Friendliness is less common than it used to be, and one reason is the psychoanalytical approval of egocentricity—the "Me" generation spreading its plague of "I'm the focal point of the universe, and if you can't accept your assigned position in orbit around me, then the heck with you, Buster."

This attitude was obvious in the renewal notice from the club of which I'm a member. The letter was four paragraphs long. The first paragraph had the happy news that dues were being increased, "in order that we may maintain the quality that we think you deserve." Then, to drive home the nail, the second paragraph:

> Upon receipt of your renewal statement, please send us your check or money order for the full amount. Partial payments, cash, or credit cards will not be accepted. All dues are payable by (Date). This will insure the renewal of your membership without interruption.

What did I do to warrant such cold and distant distrust? I pay dues and charges on time. I play on their tennis team even when I should be smacking away at the typewriter. I entertain in their clubhouse. If that's the way they feel about me, the heck with them, Busters! (I rejoined, of course, but the golden glow is tarnished.)

Even the giants stumble, victims of the "Me" generation. Omaha Steaks ran an ad with this as the complete
headline:

> "I'm Norma Jean Knollenberg, Incentive Sales Manager
> for Omaha Steaks International. CALL ME . . . TOLL
> FREE!

Okay, the second pair of quotation marks was omitted.
That isn't the problem. Norma Jean Knollenberg is a reasonably
attractive young lady, but why should I phone her when no
one has given me a reason? Let's read the first paragraph of
text; maybe the reason is hidden there:

> Let me explain a few of the many successful incentive
> programs we've custom designed for companies all
> across the nation. Programs that truly have motivated
> people. Programs that have helped companies break
> records and surpass goals.

Nope. The "We" ("Me") approach says *we've* motivated
people, but they don't motivate me. The combination of a weak
software pitch and egocentricity which leaves me, the possible
buyer, out of their considerations, doesn't chip a grain of sand
out of the barrier erected by the Age of Skepticism and those
who maintain it.

How long has it been since you wrote a letter that began
"Dear Sir:"? Eons, I hope. My wife got one, from Research Institute Recommendations. Whatever may have happened in
our depersonalized society, including this letter, my wife is no
"sir," thank goodness. I'm hard pressed to think of a less personalized greeting.

Rule 7: Be Positive and Specific.

One clear, firm statement is stronger than many paragraphs of writing around the point. You know that; I know
that. Why do we flood the reader with weak, overwritten arguments when instead we could pierce him with the needle-spray
of a fine-tuned message?

If we're to be positive and specific, that means burying
in an unmarked grave *however, needless to say, input, viable,*

truthfully, frankly, I mean, I'll be honest with you, and *impact* as a verb. It means using contractions, since *don't* is stronger than *do not* and *I'm* is stronger than *I am.* It means shaving off the pomposity of *for* as a substitute for *because* and never again writing or saying *indeed.*

I'll have more—much more—to say about this in chapter 4.

Being specific, if you think it through, is a first cousin of giving the reader an understandable benefit. One of the best examples of specific copy I've seen lately is a space ad for binoculars. You and I have seen ads for binoculars for years, but they're usually "8 × 16" equation-type ads we don't completely understand. This one, from Professional Shopper of San Francisco, has as specific a headline as any ad for binoculars could wish:

> You can look the sparrow
> straight in the eye from 250 feet
> and you can see it blink.

That's positive. That's specific. To me, that kind of copy suggests a unique selling proposition that dissolves skepticism long before we get to the toll-free phone number.

You'd think classified ads would adhere implicitly to this rule, because specificity is implicit in word count. Not so. Here, in their entirety, are two of 20 classified ads I might have chosen from one representative publication—a mail order tabloid called *Better Living*:

> *More Money Now.* $10 report. 98-01
> 67th Ave., 11G, Queens, NY.
>
> *Business & Sports* instructional cassette
> tapes. (3) brochures, $1. Write: Attitude
> Plus, P.O. Box 295, Dept. AB, Staten Island, NY 10302.

What, you may ask, is wrong with those? First, would *you* send $10 for a "report" as underdescribed as that first one, especially to an address that doesn't even include a zip code? The second is so general that we can only take a wild guess what our dollar will bring. I didn't decoy these ads; they may have pulled thousands of orders, but I doubt it.

I doubt, too, that copy as Spartan as this will pull many orders:

> 8″ × 10″ Gold on Parchment Paper—
> limited edition. Personal Creed, Life's Clock, etc.
> Each different. 6-$9, 12-$17 ppd. AnQ Enterprises,
> P.O. Box 643, Martin, TN 38237.

The rule is simple: If you don't have the budget to tell the reader what you're selling, advertise in a less expensive publication. Oddly, this classified ad has two *surplus* words, "Enterprises" and "P.O." The space used for them might have been dedicated to words of reader interest.

Rule 8: Cut Down the Puffery.

David Ogilvy, who first codified rules of advertising copy,* said it first and best: Puff is no substitute for fact. Using hardware to sell, instead of software, is the best way to follow Ogilvy's advice while the Age of Skepticism is upon us.

Using copy such as, " . . . the greatest artist who ever lived," or, "This is the finest cordless phone you've ever used," is a waste of the typesetter's time and your (or your client's) dollars.

Use *great* only when referring to size; use *fine* only when referring to thinness; use the *-est* suffix only when you can satisfy yourself that you're adhering to Rule 1. Never use a comparative such as *better* or *more valuable* unless you complete the thought: better or more valuable than what?

Never say *The number one* . . . anything unless you explain how whatever it is *is* number one. Watch the adjectives: that's where puffery breeds!

Rule 9: Don't Assume Your "In" Terminology Is Familiar to the Public.

The image of the fellow who says "Vegas" instead of "Las Vegas," "Eldo" instead of "El Dorado," and "L.A." instead of "Los Angeles" is the barely successful comedian who

---

*David Ogilvy, *Confessions of an Advertising Man*, Atheneum, 1963.

appears on late-night television shows, taking the microphone off its stand and talking a little too loudly, working a little too hard: "I drove my Eldo from Vegas to L.A. . . . " Is this the image a responsible wordsmith wants to project?

Write within the experiential background of the reader, not yourself. Regardless of personal prejudices, you can't make a mistake keeping your dignity.

Technical copy also falls victim to this malady. The writer, steeped in corporate lore, assumes everyone shares his knowledge; instead of explaining, he writes for a readership already familiar with the product. This tactical mistake eliminates possible buyers who feel inadequate. So, unless you're writing material for Don Rickles, don't let your copy make the reader feel inadequate. It'll cost you! In fact, *reverse* inadequacy can be a winner:

Rule 10: Showing Innocence or Artlessness Can Prove Your Sincerity.

We see many mail order ads, especially those selling self-help books, that say, "Gee, mister, I don't know much about the technical end of this, but it seems to work. I'm a nice guy, and life is short, so I'll share it with you while I can."

In a single issue of a publication called *American Business* were four such ads. One was headed, "Too Busy Earning a Living to Make Any Money?" and started:

> You think you've got problems?
> Well, I remember when a bank turned me down for a
> $200 loan . . . .

The second ad shows its innocence and artlessness in this headline: "You don't know me, I realize . . . But, I want you to have this before it's too late." Then the utterly sincere, carefully unsophisticated body copy:

> Hello . . . My name is Bud Weckesser. I'm 47 years old
> and own a small company in Dunkirk, New York. Our
> phone number is . . .

The third isn't quite so innocent and childlike, but the tone of ordinary-guy-to-ordinary-guy is maintained by this headline (a near miss, since the word *thriving* is out of key with the rest): "We will guide you *step by step* into your own thriving business." Then this wonderful byline: "a true story by Bob Ferrel."

> This is not a business for a lazy man. But if a man is ambitious and will work to deserve those nice things in life we all want, this business is made to order for such a man . . . .

Did you catch that phrase, " . . . those *nice* things in life"? *Nice* isn't a masculine, *Popular Mechanics* word; but in this Duraclean ad, it underscores the innocent, non-macho friendliness, which soothes away the skepticism.

The fourth ad is in the same pattern, although it has a slickness that borders on the objectionable. There's a "bored professional copywriter" feeling to the headline: "HOW YOU CAN BEAT INFLATION AND LIVE LIKE A MILLIONAIRE." But the body copy is carefully wide-eyed:

> Some people will not only survive during these hard economic times, they will enjoy great financial prosperity. Are you going to be one of us?
> My name is Dan Collins. I remember a short time ago when I was worse than broke . . . .

An archetypical example of Rule 10 is the excellent space ad headed, "The $12,000 Secret of an Ohio Housewife." The opening paragraphs of text act as a blotter, soaking out the reader's skepticism:

> Have you tried to make an honest dollar at home lately? My wife and I did. And, we found ourselves flooded with bogus envelope stuffing schemes, "party plans," and a variety of other non-profit balderdash. It was a sour experience. Then, several years ago at a bridge party, one of the guests began discussing a very different and special home "money project." The secret was literally whispered across the table . . . . "

Rule 11: Tie Newness to an Established Base.

Whatever you're selling isn't just new. It's newer than something. This doesn't mean you must find a comparative for an innovation that isn't directly comparable to something already existing. Whatever the field of interest, you can always use the "touchstone" method of comparison: "Just as (WHATEVER) was new then, so (THIS) is new now." Compare the breakthrough with another event or product your buyer knows about.

Don't confuse a claim of newness with *parity advertising*, in which the only claim you're able to make is that no competitor is better: "If you can find a better or newer (Whatever), buy it." Or, "No other financial institution gives you a higher rate of interest." This is cheating; validated claims of newness aren't. (More to say about this, later.)

Rule 12: Don't Make Something Big Out of Something Little.

I admit, this is my all-time personal pet peeve. I'm glad to report direct response is far less guilty of this copywriting sin than other, more glamorous media. We don't usually outrage the thoughtful message recipient's sense of proportion or glorify paranoid lunacy as do the acting corps in television dramatizations:

> When he told me my coffee wasn't strong enough, my day was ruined!
> The most important shower of my life, and you switched deodorant soaps!
> The fight of the Century: Borateem Plus versus Chlorine Bleach.
> Call the police. Your hands are a crime.

To me, this sophomoric mistake is founded on the sandcastle thinking that *attention* is a substitute for *approval*, and that's why direct response has less of this than any other medium. When we do lapse into the slough of thinking that "noted" parallels "sold," we can easily insult our would-be buyer: Our one-to-one message can't cop out, as television can, with an "it's entertainment" excuse.

So:

These are the rules that come to mind. Others are half-formed, like the pods in *Invasion of the Body Snatchers*, rules such as:

Rule-to-Come 13:

It's okay to talk down to the reader if you do it personally and with the appearance of helpfulness.

Rule-to-Come 14:

Admit an Achilles heel.

Rule-to-Come 15:

Tell the reader, early, something he or she already knows.

Battling with prospective buyers is an exhilarating football game in which the defense, committed only to protecting that dollar-spending goal-line, constantly shifts to block our runs, intercept our passes, and, heaven help us, sack our quarterback. But we're the pros. As Knute Rockne would have exhorted his warriors before they barreled out for the second half, "Get out there and fight!"

With what? The four great motivators, of course. Chapter 2 tells you what and how.

2

The Four Great Motivators of Today

Some of the old duffers along Retirement Row may remember when an advertiser could motivate prospective buyers with a simple announcement of goods for sale.

Many of us recall when Sex and Status were *the* powerful motivators.

Ah, but we've slid into the Age of Skepticism. Safety lies in one of these four great motivators for the mid-1980s:

Fear

Guilt

Greed

Exclusivity

Fear: Best of the Four Great Motivators

Of the four, Fear is the most potent. It's the direct lineal descendant of the best of the old motivators, more so even than Exclusivity.

(What are we afraid of? Failure. Not being accepted. Being taken advantage of. Missing an opportunity. Physical ailments.)

In a skilled surgeon's hands, Fear cuts through the layers of fat around the reader's brain, jabbing and needling until, trembling with the unquenchable desire built on frustration, the recipient of your Fear message grabs his pen or his phone to soothe his fever.

TO	UNITED AIRLINES TRAVEL CARD CUSTOMERS	FROM	CREDIT CARD MARKETING DEPARTMENT

SUBJECT Protection of your credit cards IMPORTANT	DATE FOR IMMEDIATE RELEASE

MESSAGE

Dear United Travel Cardholder:

Lost and stolen credit cards are a very real problem today. Here at United, we can attest to how inconvenient it can be if your credit cards are lost or stolen.

For instance, if you lost your United Airlines Travel Card or one of your other cards, would you know what to do? Even worse, what if you suddenly discovered that your entire wallet, with all your credit cards, was missing. . .lost or stolen?

Who would you contact to cancel the cards? Where would you call? Would you have to repeat the procedure for each and every card (assuming you can remember all the various cards and charges you carry)? What would you be liable for?

The cost — the time and trouble and aggravation you'd face -- would seem endless. But things could be even worse. Some of our United Airlines Cardholders who have called to report lost or stolen cards have been stranded out of town without cash or credit cards and with no way to get home. Naturally, we are concerned about this situation.

Therefore, through arrangement with the nation's leading credit card protection agency — the Credit Card Service Bureau — you are now eligible for a special protection plan. . .one that guards against the fraudulent use of your credit cards, should they be lost or stolen. (Not just your United Airlines Travel Card, but all your immediate family's credit cards, store charge plates, etc.)

71B

Figure 2.1 This credit card protection mailing, which overstates the problem the typical cardholder would have if his cards were lost or stolen, exemplifies *fear* as a motivator.

Selling *use* (benefit), not product or abstract concept, is implicit in any solid Fear sales argument. Advertisers for a protective device had thought they were selling *use* with this copy:

Now you can disable any attacker from up to 10 feet away.

They weren't. *Use* and *product* were intermixed, and the drama a writer can create by striking fear into the heart of the reader lay in a different copy direction. How much more forceful this version is:

You're walking home, as you've done for years. As you approach your front door, the horror that "can't happen here" strikes: You feel something pressing into your back, and a voice betraying desperation and toughness says, "Don't turn around."

With several Fear-inspiring photographs, an alarm system uses the scalpel:

If it were your family . . .
Could you have saved them?

One of the best uses of Fear I've seen recently is the opening of a letter from *Boardroom Reports,* selling subscriptions:

Dear Business Colleague:
Do you believe—do you truly believe—that your customers, that your suppliers are all 100% honest and "on the level"?

See how easy it is? You don't have to moan, "The goblins will get you if you don't watch out." You don't have to groan, "There ain't no Santa Claus." You just have to scare them *a little,* with what appears to be logic but is actually emotion—like castor oil hidden in a chocolate soda.

A Dangerous Weapon, Not for Beginners

Fear is a loaded gun for insurance, financial, and self-improvement offers, plus the area of its overuse, fund raising. Genius lies in using it for other businesses.

But in amateur hands, slashing away blindly with Fear can be laughable.

This was driven home to me when I saw a space ad in a magazine aimed at planners of sales meetings. This writer took his lance of Fear in hand and promptly fell off his horse:

RENO DARES YOU!
. . . To take advantage of the Greatest Convention Bargain ever offered . . .
FREE

> In today's uncertain economy, the bottom line for
> holding a convention is the cost. With that in mind the
> City of Reno "dares you" to take advantage of the
> greatest convention bargain ever offered . . . .

Instead of degenerating into Greed, Reno would have been better off not playing the dangerous word-game and *starting and staying* with a coherent Greed theme.

Certainly Fear combines well with the other motivators. In fact, the blend with Greed or Guilt often is more palatable than an entire sales message based on Fear alone, which can be too thick to swallow. But trying to skew a sales argument into a Fear channel can make a mess. We'd be better off with good old dependable Greed, which never misses if it's halfway comprehensible to the reader.

Mixing Fear with Exclusivity, the fourth great motivator of the 1980s, was the downfall of this letter from a company selling home security systems by mail:

> Dear Homeowner:
>
> You're an intelligent individual who has achieved
> success by objectively weighing the facts and making the
> right decisions.
>
> In this letter, I'm going to show you how you can better
> protect your home and family from crime and I'm going
> to tell you how you can save substantial money doing it!
>
> YOU'RE A MEMBER OF A SELECT GROUP
>
> You're receiving this letter because you have *more to lose*
> than the average person! It's a fact that burglars seek out
> homes of people who have achieved a higher standard
> of living. Homes like yours . . . where they can expect to
> find higher-priced stereos and televisions, sterling silver,
> and expensive jewelry . . . .

The letter starts with phony stroking and shifts suddenly but belatedly into high gear. Read it again, *starting* with "You're receiving this letter" (I know *receiving* is a weakener, but that isn't the point here), and you'll see how "blah" the original opening is and how the first two sentences and the meaningless subhead tie the argument to a stake until Fear finally cuts it loose.

AMERICAN BANKERS LIFE
ASSURANCE COMPANY OF FLORIDA

600 Brickell Avenue, Miami, Florida 33131 (305) 374-2244

Dear

Before I began writing this letter, I re-read the article by Ray Porter which I'd clipped and intended to save.

The article tells the full story of our THRIFTGARD PLAN so much better than I can that I decided to copy it and send it to you. So if you're easily bored and are willing to read just one enclosure in this mailing, drop this letter and read the reprint of Ray Porter's article instead.

If you're still reading, it means you aren't easily bored and have a profound interest in your family's future. I congratulate you, because not everyone plans for the future.

No, too many of us drift along, thinking, "Everything will always be all right," and then, wham! If and when tragedy strikes, it's doubly unfortunate, because financial problems can hit a struggling family when they're least able to afford it - and when, suddenly, they realize you're no longer there to handle things.

I'm really not interested in discussing the old-fashioned type of life insurance with you. You probably have a local agent who handles this for you.

Instead, I want to tell you about a special kind of protection. You qualify because you have a credit card from SOUTHEAST BANK and a good, solid record of payments on that card.

Think back to the last time you took out an insurance policy.

Undoubtedly you had to take a physical examination to qualify. Undoubtedly someone asked a lot of questions about the kind of work you do, what personal activities you have, and whether you participate in any sports that particular company doesn't regard as safe.

Those questions and exclusions are logical for a regular, standard life insurance policy. But <u>we don't ask those questions. We don't ask you to take a physical examination (unless you have a negative medical history). We don't have a single occupational exclusion on our THRIFTGARD policy.</u>

We obviously aren't selling you life insurance as you've known it. Rather, we have the kind of coverage for you we feel you'd choose for yourself: coverage which gives you the most protection during the years when you most need it - then gradually tapers until you're 64 years old. By the time you're 64, this policy will have served its purpose. Your children will be through school and your family will be reasonably secure.

Figure 2.2 Power in this letter is doubled, because immediately after hitting the reader with *exclusivity* in the third paragraph, the writer uses *guilt* as the key selling argument in the fourth paragraph.

A heavily produced mailing for an encyclopedia would have benefited from an injection of Fear. You can see how they fumble the motivational ball. Our team can pick it up, but we already have lost interest in the game:

> Dear Friend:
>
> We believe you are a person who wants and needs to stay well informed. You probably read the most important books; subscribe to the best magazines. But are you as well informed as you'd really like to be? Are you as well informed as you *need* to be in today's world?
>
> In these rapidly changing times, it's difficult to be knowledgeable in *every* area. Why, until a few years ago, Zimbabwe or Beijing couldn't be found on any map . . . and Camp David was just the President's vacation retreat.
>
> To get information on these, and thousands of other really current topics . . . .

Coupled with this letter is Eggheaded brochure cover copy:

> BROADCAST INFORMATION
> IS FAST . . . BUT FLEETING.
> NEWSPAPER INFORMATION
> IS CURRENT . . . BUT TRANSIENT.
> MAGAZINE INFORMATION
> IS RECENT . . . BUT SELECTIVE.
> *NONE* OF THESE SOURCES ARE
> ENOUGH TO SATISFY YOUR
> NEED TO KNOW.

Suppose you're a live prospect for an encyclopedia. Mightn't you think, "This is over my head"? It's hard, slogging through this rhetorical maze. What if the writer had stuck that knife of Fear into you, right off: "When the people you're with ask you what you think of Zimbabwe, do you have any idea whether it's a place, an event, or a person? While you're thinking that over, take a look in your most current reference book and see whether the Chinese capital is spelled 'Peking' or—as it's spelled in an *up-to-date* encyclopedia—'Beijing.' " Impaled, the reader can't move freely. He's stuck.

Some Fear pitches skirt dangerously close to the chasm of reader insult. You can pull out *all* the stops only if one of two circumstances exists:

1. The apparent relationship between you and the buyer is cemented firmly in place, or you want the reader to think you feel it is; or
2. The potential buyer-universe is small and no other logic has budged this group.

This mailing, even including the "Dear Client" greeting, exemplifies the first circumstance:

Dear Client:
Smart collectors don't buy every plate that comes along.
But I'm afraid you've passed up some excellent
opportunities that I've called to your attention over the
months, and you are now in danger of losing your
priority status with the Bradford Exchange.

This one is a hard-boiled version of the "Frankly, I'm puzzled" letter:

Dear Friend (I hope you're still my friend),
I can't for the life of me understand why you asked for a
copy of our catalog.
I've sent you, in fact, *two* catalogs. Unless our computer
is completely wacko, all those pretty pictures,
sensational prices, and money-back guarantees haven't
meant a thing to you.
I don't want to be dramatic and say, "This is your last
chance." I must be realistic, though, so if you don't
order *something* from this current catalog, the
businessman in me will override the nice guy in me, and
we won't be able to send you any more catalogs (which
means no more pretty pictures, no more sensational
discounts, and no more opportunities to inspect
anything you buy in your own home without risking a
dime).

Fear for Them = Power for Us

As we writers begin to play with Fear, we become bolder and bolder. It's as though we're testing our powers. The might of Fear as a motivator can cause us to feel invincible, and we move into the thunderbolt-throwing posture whether our message belongs there or not. Here's the four-step evolution of the headline on a space-ad:

The first headline: *Are you heavier than you want to be?*

The second headline: *Are You Too Fat?*

The third headline: *Are You Carrying a Time-Bomb Around With You?*

The fourth headline, great-grandson of "Do You Make These Mistakes in English?" and "They Laughed When I Sat Down at the Piano": *Behind Your Back—Do They Call You Fatso?*

I said earlier that *being taken advantage of* is one of the circumstances we fear. That's why politicians spray Fear at us. The attacker uses Fear—"Had enough? Or will you sit numbly while your pocketbook gets thinner and the fat cats at City Hall get fatter?" and the incumbent reverses that same Fear— "We've made a start, but if you don't let us finish the job, you deserve the disaster that can hit this city."

The magazine *Telemarketing* uses this variation of Fear on its order-card:

YOU WILL
SUBSCRIBE . . .
If your career & the
survival of your
company is
important to you!
Enter your
subscription
TODAY.

(Why the ampersand? "&" is too corporate-title to strike fear.)

An advertising agency specializing in direct selling sent this 100 percent Fear letter to prospective accounts:

MEMO TO: DIRECT SELLING EXECUTIVES

Here's a repulsive checklist.

– It costs too much to recruit sales people.
– The only people who answer the ads are the ones who want free samples.
– Nobody wants to make calls anymore.
– Some other company's wild claims, even though untrue, outpull yours.
– Once you've recruited someone, he or she quits and you don't even know it for weeks.
– The manager/district/area method is breaking down on all levels.
– Turnover is three hundred percent a year or more.

How many of these problems do you have?

CHANCES ARE, YOU HAVE ALL OF THEM . . . .

If you wonder how the letter ends, don't worry. Help is on the way. And that's the core of the first of three rules of Fear-Use in Direct Response. Here they are:

The Three Rules of Fear

The First Rule of Fear:

THE READER ALWAYS MUST KNOW THAT YOU HAVE THE SOLUTION TO HIS PROBLEM.

The Second Rule of Fear:

UNLESS YOU WANT A WEAKER MESSAGE, WRITE A DIRECT CHALLENGE, NOT A "WHAT IF" SUBJUNCTIVE.

An example of Rule 2: "What will you do when . . . " is a direct challenge; "What would you do if . . . " is the subjunctive version.

The Third Rule of Fear:

DON'T LOSE YOUR NERVE HALFWAY THROUGH AND BEGIN POLLUTING YOUR FEAR WITH LIGHT-HEARTEDNESS.

Your very decision to use Fear as a motivator puts you in a game of Chicken with the reader. Don't brake halfway through.

The Other Great Motivators

Guilt, Greed, and Exclusivity are dynamic motivators in the Age of Skepticism because they penetrate the shield of apathy raised against an outside opinion commenting on "what *I* want to do."

Is the concept obscure? I hope not, because it's a *positive inversion* of the negative rule that *you can't motivate someone who doesn't know you to buy by angering him.*

Guilt is as easy to generate as this:

Dear Former Subscriber:
It hurts to lose an old friend.

Greed is as easy to unlock as this:

Special extra discount applies only to preferred buyers who qualify for this priority invitation.

Exclusivity is as easy to create as this:

Quite frankly, the American Express Card isn't for everybody.

Sometimes, when the sun shines on your destiny, you can think of ways to combine two of the four great motivators. Careful! You *could* have the most dynamite-laden message since "Do you make these mistakes in English?"—or you *could* generate two vibrating messages that cancel out each other. Remember the Third Law ($E^2 = O$): Don't dilute a potent sales argument.

Greed, Guilt, and Exclusivity are all Herculean as selling arguments, but Fear is the strongest, because it's the one motivator that can cause the reader to lose sleep.

For example, share this Fear with me:

You're writing direct response copy, as you've done for years. As you approach your sales argument, the horror that "can't happen here" strikes: You feel something pressing into your ear, and a voice betraying desperation (and toughness) says, "Don't bother finishing that copy. We're mailing something else."

EXPRESS CHECK

NATIVE SUN

REF CODE NS-83-19
CHECK VOID 5/16/83
CHECK NUMBER 198
EXT. CODE

Pay SIX THOUSAND AND..........00 Dollars $6000.00
TO THE
ORDER
OF

MR H G LEWIS
9748 CEDAR VILLAS BL
FT LAUDERDALE FL 33324

Non-negotiable,
non-transferable
unless signed by an
authorized Native Sun
representative.

⑈:0000678946: 12345678⑈

EXPRESS MESSAGE

*QUICKLY...*tear off the above check and call 1-800-328-1590 to find out if you have won $6000.00!!!!

Enclosed you will find a sealed envelope. Whatever you do... do not open this envelope...until you are in the presence of a Native Sun awards director. Tampering with the envelope immediately voids this offer. Your specific award is determined by the contents of the envelope.

One of the nine Vacation Time Awards listed below is yours. The awards have been divided into three groups. To discover which awards are in your group call immediately and give your *Express Check* number. Then call to schedule your appointment to visit and inspect Native Sun and to receive your award.

- $6000 Cash • Microwave Oven • $2000 Cash
- Honda Moped • Home Stereo • Color Television
- Gas BBQ Grill • $1500 Cash
- Home Video Game (connects to your TV)

You must bring the sealed envelope and the *Express Check* with you.

Call immediately 1-800-328-1590 Monday through Friday 10 a.m. to 9 p.m., Saturday 10 a.m. to 6 p.m.

Call us today... Remember, do not open the envelope.

Figure 2.3 This mailing piece, typical of time-sharing resorts, shows the potency of *greed* as a motivator.

AMERICAN EXPRESS TRAVEL RELATED SERVICES COMPANY, INC
AMERICAN EXPRESS PLAZA, NEW YORK, N.Y. 10004

Diane Shaib
Vice President
Marketing

H. G. Lewis
Communicomp
P.O. Box 15725
Plantation, FL   33318

Dear H. Lewis:

Quite frankly, the American Express Card is not for everyone. And not everyone who applies for Cardmembership is approved.

However, because we believe you will benefit from Cardmembership, I've enclosed a special invitation for you to apply for the most honored and prestigious financial instrument available to people who travel, vacation and entertain.

The American Express Card is the perfect example of the old adage, "You get what you pay for."

For example, you get the unique benefits of a worldwide network of offices of the American Express Travel Related Services Company, Inc., its affiliates and Representatives. "Homes away from home" you can turn to for personal attention and a wide range of services that make traveling more enjoyable and worry-free.

The Card guarantees your <u>personal</u> check for up to $250 when you are a registered guest at participating hotels and motels in the U.S. and Canada ($100 abroad). You can even cash a personal check for up to $1,000, $200 in cash and the balance in Travelers Cheques, at most Travel Service Offices of American Express Travel Related Services Company, Inc., its affiliates and Representatives worldwide. Just present the Card and your personal check. (Subject to cash availability and local regulations.)

And now you can obtain last-minute or emergency travel funds through a network of automated American Express Travelers Cheque Dispensers in selected major U.S. airports. These Dispensers allow you to obtain from $100 to $500 in Cheques in 60 seconds or less virtually 24 hours a day, 365 days a year. All new Cardmembers receive full information on how to enroll to use this new convenience.

Cardmembership includes $100,000 accidental death and dismemberment insurance automatically every time you or your family travels by common carrier on land, sea or air when

(over, please)

Figure 2.4 One of the best known direct mail promotions of the 1980s is this credit card mailing from American Express. The author, who has had an American Express card for almost 20 years, gets several of these each year, reminders that *exclusivity* is one of the great motivators during the Age of Skepticism. (They're also reminders that oversell cancels exclusivity.)

Figure 2.5 What one reader may regard as nonsense, another may regard as a logical appeal to *exclusivity*. An example is this insert in a packet of mailed offers. The sales argument: "Look like you own a sports car!" (A parallel: sand to rub in your eyes, with the line, "Look like you have cable TV!")

3

Emotion vs. Intellect—
A TKO in the First Round

Those who keep score report that direct marketing is a $150 billion business. That's an impressive number unless you compare it with the federal deficit.

What if—*what if*—a simple technique of word selection could increase dollar volume by 10 percent? That would tack an additional $15 billion onto the total without any additional cost other than the cost of this book.

In my opinion 10 percent is a modest expectation; but since the pump primer is so basic, so easy, and (to me) so obvious, I'll keep the goal reasonable.

The Prelude

This $15 billion suggestion isn't some new technique for list selection. It isn't an analytical term like *psychographics* or *videotech*. It's based on an absolute rule of human psychology:

WHEN EMOTION AND INTELLECT COME INTO CONFLICT, EMOTION ALWAYS WINS.

As unyielding as that rule is, I'll stick by it with no qualifiers, no "except . . . ," no "if you . . . " or "but you must . . . " followers. The rule stands, Gibraltar on the stormy seas of I-guess-this-should-work direct response copywriting.

Yes, you can prevent the conflict altogether; it's easier in copywriting that in life. As communicators, we're primitive psychologists, pygmy poseurs in a Freudian Valley of the Giants. But, dear friends, we're supposed to be players, not umpires; we're force-communicators, not analysts. Our job is to interfere with the reader's natural skepticism and force that person—our subject—to lift a pen or the phone and respond to our message.

We don't want that individual, reading our words, to lapse into analysis of how he or she feels about what we're selling; if we get that type of reaction, we'll *reduce* the $150 billion by 10 percent or more. No, no! If we're analyzed, we've failed. Even if the order or donation comes in, it's not because our message was properly coded to zap the reader's brain.

The value to us as salespeople (sorry, writer/introverts—that's what we are) of knowing the dominance of emotion over intellect is our own prior knowledge of word use. That's how we become giants on the earth.

The Solid Gold Rule

This isn't a puzzle. I'll give you the $15 Billion Rule in the next paragraph; you'll see at once why the prelude was necessary.

REPLACE INTELLECTUAL WORDS WITH EMOTIONAL WORDS AND YOU'LL SELL MORE BECAUSE YOU'LL TRIGGER AN EMOTIONAL RESPONSE.

See how our crassly commercial Rule snuggles up against the cosmic psychological Rule?

Don't worry about losing your dignity by using this Rule. Dignity without sales is the Emperor's New Clothes.

Better than that: in some cases, put-on intellectualism is a deliberate ploy to generate the *emotional* reaction, "Gee, this message is intellectual, and it's aimed at me!" We don't need gutter language to benefit from an emotional reaction; the only subordinate rule we need as an ally is one every writer has tattooed on the tips of his typing fingers:

WRITE WITHIN THE EXPERIENTIAL BACKGROUND OF THE READER, NOT YOURSELF.

I'm not outraged when I read an ad or mailed package reflecting stuffed-shirt intellectualism, the way I **am** when it

Carriage Hill Collections

Dear Collector:

    For most of us, the possession of rare and beautiful objects brings pleasure to life. This pleasure increases if the objects appreciate in value as time goes on and confirm our good taste.

    The Children of Mary Cassatt is a collection of just such objects. They are rare, beautiful, and quite likely to increase in value.

    Let me explain why.

    The Children of Mary Cassatt is a series of four fine china plates from Pickard. Each plate in the series is being produced in a limited edition of 7,500.

    Carriage Hill will have an allocation of plates from these editions, but I doubt if they will last for long. One look at this series' remarkable qualities will show you why.

    To begin with, The Children of Mary Cassatt marks a very special union of two great names -- Pickard China and Mary Cassatt.

    Pickard is the studio that has been recognized as the finest maker of limited editions for the last three years in a row by the National Association of Limited Edition Dealers and the last five years in a row by the readers of Plate Collector magazine -- and won every major industry award for quality, craftsmanship and artistry. Mary Cassatt is the Impressionist who was America's first major woman artist and who is today recognized as one of the greatest painters this country has produced.

    This combination of Pickard craftsmanship and Cassatt artistry makes this a series that a great many collectors will be proud to own -- and therefore anxious to acquire.

    Artistically, this series is Cassatt at her best. The first issue in the series, "Simone in a White Bonnet", shows you

(over, please. . .)

Figure 3.1 Does a quiet, intellectual argument sell better than excitement? Usually not. That should distress the writer of this letter, whose use of *the possession of* when he could have used *owning, objects* when he could have used *works of art,* and constructions such as *quite likely* and *allocation* starts this letter off in so low a gear the generation of excitement may not be possible later on (the letter is four pages long).

shows no command of decent grammar. Rather, as the subscription mailings say, "Frankly, I'm puzzled."

I no longer think intellectualized ad writing is at the opposite pole from ungrammatical writing, the result of too much education instead of too little. That's due to the peculiar mix I've seen: People who write intellectual copy are even more likely to suffer from insecurity and fear of rejection than are we proletarians. Intellectualized words, in writing and conversation, become buffers against the fear of appearing unlettered or uninformed. Maybe that's why so many textbooks are impenetrable fortresses of pedantic jargon.

Examples from the Mailbox

In consecutive mail deliveries I had by-mail offers whose letters opened this way:

> This is to notify you that you have been selected to
> participate . . .

and . . .

> I'm writing to alert you to an exceptional opportunity
> that exists for you right now . . .

The offers, coincidentally, were parallel. My reactions weren't. The first example is cold, once-removed, the kind of letter I might expect from a hostile lawyer. The second is personal, warm, and, yes, leaning toward the *emotional* rather than the *intellectual*.

An even better example of a cold, once-removed letter is this subscription letter from an antiques magazine. The form itself is antique; except for the topical references it might have been written at the turn of the century:

> Dear Madam or Sir:
>
> Americans seem especially wistful about the absence of
> excellence today. Because we live in an age in which
> craftsmanship seems to be a depleted cultural resource,
> we remember a time when trains were punctual, when
> household appliances lasted and workers worked, when
> manners were civil and marriages endured, when wars
> were just and honor mattered, and when you could buy
> a vine-ripened tomato . . . .

Want to grab me by the emotional gorkles? Then change *the absence of excellence today* to *the way excellence has disappeared,* *punctual* to *on time,* and *endured* to *lasted,* and you're halfway there: you've warmed up the approach by using emotional instead of intellectual words. Not that I'd ever respond to a letter with that "Madam or Sir" greeting.

I continue to think it's a tactical mistake to send a message that has the recipient reacting as a *reader* instead of a *participant.* The first impression I had of this next letter was that someone had a neatness complex, because the letter was carefully word processed to be flush right as well as flush left— another tactical error if you're trying to personalize; the content matched:

> Dear Collector:
>
> For most of us, the possession of rare and beautiful
> objects brings pleasure to life. This pleasure increases if
> the objects appreciate in value as time goes on and
> confirm our good taste . . . .

The implicit gap between writer and reader isn't bridged here; it's widened, because the writer's formality, exemplified by words such as *possession, pleasure to life, appreciate in value,* and *confirm.* The writing becomes a treatise, not a communication. The writer has forgotten that *without an emotional base the reader can't become involved.*

How might one brighten that opening? I'm not overwhelmed by the word *objects* but I'll leave it in the copy to avoid the accusation of unfair restructuring:

> Dear Fellow Collector:
>
> If you're like I am, owning rare, beautiful objects brings
> you great pleasure. Think how much *more* pleasure we
> feel if those objects prove us right by increasing in
> value . . . .

Time-sharing condominia fill the mails with outrageous offers of free goodies. Here are two openings—to which might you respond?

Number 1:

> Dear Vacationer,
>
> We have great news for you. You're already a winner.
> Here's how you claim your award:

Number 2:

YOUR NAME HAS BEEN SELECTED BY COMPUTER
TO PARTICIPATE IN A PRIZE-AWARD PROGRAM IN
WHICH PRIZES ALREADY HAVE BEEN ALLOCATED.
TO RECEIVE YOUR AWARD YOU ARE REQUIRED TO
PHONE FOR AN APPOINTMENT BEFORE THE
EXPIRATION DATE ABOVE YOUR NAME.

If you chose the second approach, I opine you'd give
the salesperson a hard time, cold-bloodedly claim your prize,
and leave as you came—without ever considering buying what
they're selling. They deserve you, because the letter eliminates
empathy. (One qualifier: If the advertiser's image benefits from
*de*personalizing, the computer look is preferable.)

One more example, and as you read this opening of a
subscription offer from a "remarkable national magazine on
technology and its implications" (ugh!) visualize getting it in
the mail. At what word or phrase would you quit reading, even
though you're still in the first paragraph?

Are you concerned about the implications of
technological change—economic, social, cultural,
political? Do you want to understand more about the
promise—and the problems—of emerging new
technologies? Do you want to be more fully aware of
your options—as a scientist, an engineer, an executive, a
public policy decisionmaker, or a private citizen?

It's hard to think of another string of questions it's as
easy to say, "No!" to.

What, Never? Well, Hardly Ever

Seeing a confusing ad for Saab ("The most intelligent
car ever built") with this headline—

ONE CAR YOU CAN BUY WHERE YOUR EMOTIONS
AREN'T COMPROMISED BY YOUR INTELLECT.

—triggered the realization that intellectual words *can* make a
point. I myself, writing about replicas of antique pistols, used

Figure 3.2 This puzzling headline attacks but fails to solve the Emotion *vs.* Intellect question. Opinion: the writer of this headline had his emotions compromised by his intellect.

the intellectualized word *firearms* instead of *guns* because I thought the word better justified the price. I've used *motorcar* instead of *automobile* to sell expensive cars, and I've used *colour* instead of *color* and moved periods and commas outside the quotation marks to give a Continental look to copy.

No, that doesn't violate the rule, because the intention is to generate an emotional reaction by intellectualizing, not to wear a frock coat to sit in the bleachers at the ball game.

For three areas of direct response sell, I wouldn't even go that far. In my opinion it's a kamikaze mission to attack these three groups with any variation from a straight, hard, emotion-based selling argument:

1. Senior citizens
2. Children
3. Fund-raising targets

What's a "safe" emotional approach to these groups? If I'm forced to generalize, I'd lay out these equations:

Senior citizens = *bargain*
Children = *gratification*
Fund raising targets = *status/guilt*

Approaching any of these groups, beware of suggesting that what you're selling represents change. Innovation, yes, but *change* is an emotional threat. Tie newness to an accepted base, and the threat dissipates in the foggy mists of the Age of Skepticism.

An Emotional Word Primer

Not being Mr. Chips, I'm distressed at giving away information it took me half a lifetime to compile. Proof of the power of emotion over intellect is my decision to do it, for a purely emotional reason: I'm more concerned about your rejecting the concept if I don't give you examples (my emotional reaction) than I am about my private right to hard-earned knowledge (my intellectual reaction).

Technology Review

MASSACHUSETTS INSTITUTE OF TECHNOLOGY

Cambridge, Massachusetts

Are you concerned about the implications of technological change -- economic, social, cultural, political? Do you want to understand more about the promise -- and the problems -- of emerging new technologies? Do you want to be more fully aware of your options -- as a scientist, an engineer, an executive, a public policy decision-maker, or a private citizen?

Let me send you a sample copy of TECHNOLOGY REVIEW, the remarkable national magazine on technology and its implications, edited at M.I.T. for specialists and general readers alike. We're certain you'll find it interesting and informative. Essential reading for the times we live in.

Dear Reader:

How can the United States regain its technological lead in an increasingly competitive world? How can we as a nation -- industry, government, organized labor -- work together to upgrade the skills of American workers?

How damaging are government-erected barriers to the free flow of scientific and technological information? And do such barriers serve their intended purpose?

Why might it be disastrous to the environment <u>not</u> to proceed with the development of nuclear power?

How might the new communications technologies -- cable TV, video cassettes and discs, home computers -- change the very fabric of American society?

Will microelectronics technology make commuting to the office a thing of the past for information workers?

Who commits computer crimes? Who pays? Why might computer

over please...

Figure 3.3 How easy it is to say *no* to every question in the opening paragraph of this letter, which winds down tortuous rhetorical streams for six pages! Arguing that a publication with this title should use "dignified language" misses the point of why emotion outpulls intellect—which has nothing to do with dignity.

The following words are alphabetized in the "intellectual" column, but not categorized. The hundred or so examples aren't supposed to be a jim-dandy reference guide; they're supposed to show you how easy it is to shift word choice in favor of emotion.

Some of these aren't exact synonyms? Hah! That's an intellectual objection. Our job is to get those people to lick the envelopes or lift the phones so we can add that $15 billion to the total.

Take a look at your next piece of copy. Making equivalent substitutions, mail two versions, identical except for the emotional or intellectual words. Analyze the response.

Then let's talk.

Emotional Word	Intellectual Word
speed up	accelerate
applause	accolade
there's more:	additionally
help	aid
let	allow
joke	anecdote
expect	anticipate
beat up	assault
smart	astute
over	at an end
good looking	attractive
eager	avid
good for	beneficial
dare	challenge
round	circular
fight	combat
finished	completed
worried	concerned
about	concerning
build	construct
write you	contact you
bag, bottle, jar	container
brave	courageous
hurt	damage, harm
death	demise

hope	desire
tough	difficult
small	diminutive
eat	dine
see	discern, perceive
explain	disclose
give	donate
old	elderly
marvelous	exceptional
test	experiment
ease	facilitate
hungry	famished
tired	fatigued
afraid	fearful
faithfulness	fidelity
gun, shoot, bullets	firearm, fire, ammunition
because	for
lucky	fortunate
hopeless	futile
dress, suit	garment
enjoyment	gratification
hurry	haste, hasten
giant	huge
funny	humorous, amusing
sick	ill
right now	immediately
tell	inform
bright	intelligent
I'm sorry	I regret
has	is provided with
kidding	jesting
big	large
find out	learn
make	manufacture
has to	must
doesn't have to be	needn't be
idea	notion
naked	nude
seen	observed
stubborn	obstinate
leave out	omit
maybe	perhaps
danger	peril

sweat	perspiration
medicine	pharmaceuticals
happy	pleased
rear	posterior
save	preserve
stop	prevent
buy	purchase
favorable	propitious
get	receive
asked for	requested
answer	reply
send it back	return it
pick	select
take care of	service
if you decide	should you decide
dirty	soiled
find the answer to	solve
horse	steed
dull	stodgy
belly	stomach
hit	strike
since	subsequent to
enough	sufficient
better than	superior to
late	tardy
end	terminate
news	tidings
use	utilize
rich	wealthy
we want to	we would like to
in the world	worldwide
young	youthful

4

How to Be a First-Rank Wordsmith in the Next Ten Minutes

If I were a soldier of fortune, my life would depend on my wits and my weapons.

I'd buy the best guns, keep them oiled and ready, and load them with the most foolproof ammunition. In my profession as for-hire gunslinger, a jammed or misfiring weapon means I'm dead.

Okay, I'm not a gunfighter. I'm a writer. Does the difference in professions entitle me to sloppiness and shoddiness? Words are my bullets, and if I'm firing wet and rusted ammunition—or worse, blanks—from a sand-filled barrel, I'm just as dead; another hired Hessian has written words that outpulled mine.

Wordsmith, Heal Thyself

With that admonition as a frontlet between thine eyes, read the first two paragraphs of a "Copy Strategy" proposal sent to a mail order company by an advertising agency which earns its living advising others how to prepare a readable, interesting, coherent presentation:

> In analyzing the advertising (and follow-up materials) of the (NAME OF PRODUCT), the problem of course, is to determine which appeal or appeals come closest to hitting the "hot button" of the prospect. Whether

(COMPANY) has hit the hot button is yet to be determined.

Actually the "Ad Rankings" is non-determinative. There is not enough arithmetic to come up with definitive conclusions. Most mail order men are suspicious of figures that whisper.

Except for a missing comma, the grammar isn't what's wrong with this memo. No, it's the stultifying, passive-voiced "is yet to be determined" and "definitive conclusions" that betray this memo writer. He or she has lapsed into governmentalese, a sure indicator of uncertainty. In the Age of Skepticism, uncertainty and lack of specificity are weakeners that sap vigor out of the selling argument. The use of nonmotivating words when motivating words are at hand is a more serious offense, because thoughtlessness in word selection is inexcusable for a professional wordsmith.

Figure 4.1 This is one of my all-time favorite pieces of copy. It's a simple little half-page ad, about nothing very much; but I admire the writer. Think for a moment: How would *you* have sold these golf balls?

Most of the examples I'll give you aren't horrible; they're simply weaker than they should be. Come to think of it, presenting a selling argument that's weaker than it should be is indeed horrible.

A Potpourri of Weak Words

Here's an easy one: what's wrong with, "It has the famous UL label"?

Right! *Label* is a blah word. The UL *emblem* has some selling power.

Another, selling a collector's plate: "Quantities on hand are limited."

If your vision is keen today, you see two words that cancel each other out—*quantities* and *limited*. The very word *quantities* denies a limited edition. How much more logical it would be to say, "Our allotment is limited," suggesting that you and your customers both are on the dole.

"Not Just a Doll!" a headline trumpets. I'd word that, "More Than a Doll!"—a more positive keep-reading incentive.

How often have you seen, or written, "Convenient postage-paid envelope"? If from now on you switch to "postage-free envelope," you have a free trigger word.

"We hired the famous artist . . . " begins a tedious paragraph of letter copy. Think for a moment: Is a famous artist for hire, the way you hire a mover or a carpenter? No! "We *commissioned* the famous artist."

The famous artist was victimized even more in this same mailing. One intricate sentence began, "The reason for the great span of time involved . . . " After asking myself why the word *involved* was involved at all, since the construction is better without it, I realized that *great span of time* is a mismatch with the replication of a work of art. Instead, *lengthy preparation time* would have suggested people instead of cosmic eras.

"Once the fine detail has been obtained . . . " the letter rambles on. *Obtained?* Why not *achieved?*

"They have responded to his paintings with enthusiasm . . . " *Enthusiasm?* That word is weak and inactive compared with *accolades*.

What seems to happen with writing like this is that the writer has no concluding idea and runs out of steam at the end of each thought. Weakness seems to hit those prepositional phrases at the end of sentences the way a boll weevil hits an unsprayed field of cotton.

"This wooden racquet . . ." somehow reminds me of Pinocchio. In describing tennis racquets, *wood* is preferable to *wooden*. If we know that, why didn't the writer?

(Less objectionable is the word "racquet," grammatically correct but at variance with the more commonly used, if technically incorrect, "racket.")

We all have seen and used "This is the information you requested" hundreds of times. I don't use this any longer, because I've concluded that *requested* and *received* are two words with the impact of a wet dishrag. Instead, I now write, "This is the information you asked for."

Receive is a dangerous word. I know it's sometimes unavoidable, but it now has negative overtones since newspapers insist on using it: "He received his fatal wound . . ."

While we're on crime, *burglarize* is weaker than *break into*. Somehow *burglarizing* doesn't seem as vicious a crime as *breaking into* someone's home.

More: *Talented workers* don't justify as big a consumer expenditure as *gifted artisans*. A watch shouldn't be described as *inoperative;* instead, *it won't work.* "This is your last *chance*" suggests Las Vegas; why not use the more motivational *opportunity? More cost-effective* is the way the Pentagon would present *cheaper* or *less expensive.* Why say, "24 inches in length," when you can say "2 feet long"?

"It was determined" reads like something out of Kafka. "We decided" accepts responsibility and adds authoritative stature.

Even government workers hate official language when it hits them in a mailing piece. "Probably you are wondering why I am communicating with you at this time" is just about as pompous and amateurish an opening sentence as anyone can fashion. It holds three separate deficiencies: (1) It's just as easy to make "you" the first word; (2) contractions are more personal; (3) *communicate* isn't called for here. A simple retread: "You probably wonder why I'm writing you." *At this time* should be blue-pencilled forever.

We have the benefit of a lifetime of reading and

evaluating; we know that a pretty woman is more sensuous than a pretty girl, who in turn is more sensuous than a pretty lady. We know that a perfume has a *fragrance,* which smells better than a *scent* or an *aroma.* We know that starting a sentence with *however* instead of *but* erects a barrier between us and the reader. Why do we lapse into weakness when strength is at hand?

Some quickies: Precious *stones* aren't as precious as precious *gems. Art work* isn't as valuable as *work of art. Yellow* isn't as inviting as *golden.* A *dozen* doesn't seem to be as many as *a set of twelve.*

A final ugh: "Enclosed please find our latest brochure and price list for your perusal." In the same mailing was, "Allow me to introduce you to the world's most beautiful golf equipment." See the weakness? The word *beautiful* is meaningless here, since golfers want a lower score, not beauty.

Interested in seeing more examples? Read your mail. Regrettably, they'll be there.

The Law of Conditional Declension—
Rifle Bullets, Not Spitballs

If you don't write direct response copy for a living you may neither know nor care that copy beginning, "What if I told you that . . . " is weaker than a more dramatic (and shorter), "What if . . . ", or that either of these openings is crippled compared with straightforward exposition ("You'll find $35 a week missing from your pocket unless you . . . ").

Nonspecifics melt the steel out of selling arguments. "There are many features which suggest a host of new uses for your home computer" is a wet dishrag next to "With 96K of memory you'll balance your checkbook two seconds after you make the last easy entry—and have enough juice left to balance the checkbooks of everyone on your block."

Low-powered words are weak, and even as we write, "Soon you should be able to . . . " we know it's implicitly weaker than "Soon you can . . . "

There's a rule covering this (p. 48). If I were pedantic I'd call it the *Law of Conditional Declension*—which in English means:

Figure 4.2 Can you think of a better way to describe the power of a pair of binoculars? Although slightly copy-heavy, this sales argument is effective, without using terminology the reader doesn't understand.

46

ROBERT H. KLINE
President

UNITED STATES HISTORICAL SOCIETY
ADVISORY COMMITTEE

VIRGINIUS DABNEY
Chairman
/
MERRILL LINDSAY
Author/Historian
/
GREGORY PECK
Actor/Producer
/
ERICA WILSON
Designer

Dear Friend:

Let me pose a question to you:

Suppose you decided to undertake the monumental project of presenting to the world an exact image of a distinguished American -- one who lived before we had photography. How would you make the key decisions?

Using Benjamin Franklin, for example --

Did he, as so many contemporaries did, wear a wig, or did he style his own hair?

Were his hands large or small?

What color were his eyes?

Was his head unusually large for his body? Average, smaller than average?

Were his legs straight, knobby, heavily muscled, flabby?

Why do we care so much about Benjamin Franklin? And why should such questions arise now? The answers are exciting, in both history and art.

<u>The Spirit of America</u>

More than any other individual before or since, Ben Franklin represented the spirit of America. The man whom a newspaper in 1776 called, "the genius of the day and the great patron of American liberty," the man who at the signing of the Declaration of Independence said, "We must all hang together or most assuredly we shall all hang separately," the man who coined such homilies as "A penny saved is a penny earned" and who earned immortality as the discoverer of electricity...this rare man was above all the supreme American patriot.

First and Main Streets · Richmond, Virginia 23219 · (804) 648-4736

Figure 4.3 This letter is a "grabber." It involves the reader in the vendor's own research. Before you know it, you're reading the sales argument. (The letter is a four-pager.)

THE MORE CONDITIONAL THE STATEMENT, THE WEAKER IT IS.

You want strength in your copy? Change conditional statements to straightforward ones. Change hypothetical circumstances to real ones. Change generalizations to specific examples.

A hidden benefit of this Law is its ability to work for you as well as against you. Want to subordinate some elements to others? Want to bring in some negatives? They can be handled easily by a gear shift into the conditional mood.

The Power Filters

Moving right along, we see in an increasing number of ads and mailing pieces grist for another easy-to-implement rule. What's wrong with this phrase?

"As I explained before . . . "

If your blue pencil leaped to your fingers and your reflexes automatically began crossing out the phrase, you have it. The rule:

SURPLUS WORDS ARE WORD POWER FILTERS, REDUCING IMPACT.

Examples? "Such" has no place in this sentence—"It will bring you such wealth." "But" should butt out of "But you see, it's as easy as that." And "If you have any interest whatever . . . " is beyond redemption; the whole thought stinks.

If you have any interest whatever (only kidding!) in the *specifics* of word usage, you'll brandish your creative scalpel and sutures to reconstruct this opening of a sales letter:

If you are the type that likes to wake up singing . . .

I don't mind the "If"; I mind the "type," and I'm annoyed by being a "that." By categorizing me, this writer has killed the fragile "Only you . . . " potential of his message. I'm one of a mob, and there's *zero* personalization in our relationship. I'm not a "that," either, I'm a "who," and by betraying his contempt for me—I'm a faceless unit in the marketing mix—the writer has alienated me. Why couldn't this letter begin: "If you like to wake up singing . . . "

You may not see immediately the parallel between that example and this one, a space ad for a tennis racket: "Oversize frame and tension-stringing provide extra power."

The word "provide" takes power *out*. ("Tension-stringing" is unexplained, and whatever it is, throwing it away suggests the writer doesn't know what it is either.)

We see art objects advertised as "manufactured." Even automobiles aren't "manufactured" these days, they're "built." "Manufactured" suggests mass production, a psychological no-no. An art object is *crafted*, suggesting loving one-at-a-time care.

"You will possess . . . " reminds me of *The Exorcist*. What's wrong with the word "own"?

Every Word Affects Impact

Even the harmless, unnoticed articles of speech figure in our calculations. You give and you take away when you write, "You are one of a handful who can own . . . " because you ignore the positive difference substituting *the* for *a* would make—"*the* handful" don't just exist, they're chosen.

Let's build (not "manufacture") that into another copy rule:

WHEN YOU HAVE A WORD CHOICE, USE TERMS AND PHRASES THE READER REGARDS FAVORABLY UNLESS YOU'RE USING FEAR AS A MOTIVATOR.

The telephone company obviously knows this rule. They sent me a letter with envelope copy which, although flawed by telling me too much, had a word I thought was excellent:

How much does it cost to visit by phone?
Take the quiz inside and find out.

Bell might have said, "Take this test." They might have asked, "Can you answer these questions?" Instead the writer used the excellent word "quiz." Why is it excellent? Because when one compares the three words—*test, questions,* and *quiz*—only *quiz* is fun. The others are work.

We may not want the strongest word. For New Year's Eve we prefer *revelry* but for a computer game we probably feel safer with the milder *good time*.

BECAUSE WE'RE THE NEW KID ON THE BLOCK

WE HAVE TO BE BETTER.

For years, you have known Forest Lawn Memorial Gardens as the finest cemetery in Pompano Beach. For years, we have helped thousands of Broward County families select and plan their memorial estates. But for years you have had only one funeral home in Pompano Beach. Now, there is a new kid on the block . . . FOREST LAWN FUNERAL HOME NORTH.

As a funeral home/cemetery establishment, Forest Lawn offers many outstanding advantages:

JON C. THOMAS, II

- ONE CENTRALIZED FACILITY where you can select your burial property or above ground mausoleum crypts and arrange a LOW COST, INFLATION-PROOF funeral plan for a wide range of services from direct cremation to a traditional funeral . . . ALL IN ONE PLACE . . . a short distance from your home.

- ONE CENTRALIZED FACILITY available to all faiths, providing complete funeral and burial services at one location, or if you prefer, coordinated with a service at your house of worship . . . the choice is yours.

- ONE CENTRALIZED FACILITY eliminates the need for expensive funeral coaches, flower cars and escorts, sparing your family and friends the anxiety of driving in a controlled funeral procession in South Florida traffic.

- ONE CENTRALIZED FACILITY means lowered cost . . . and those savings are passed directly to you.

To find out more about how Forest Lawn Cemeteries and Funeral Homes are better, just call my Dad, Jon C. Thomas at 523-6700, or return coupon below and he'll rush you all the facts. And as an added bonus, we will provide you with a complimentary copy of our Estate Planning Guide.

---

send to:

FOREST LAWN
cemeteries and funeral homes

200 NW 24th Street
Pompano Beach, FL 33060

( ) I want more information about Forest Lawn Funeral Home

( ) I want more information about cemetery property
( ) North ( ) Central ( ) South

NAME_____

ADDRESS_____

CITY/STATE/ZIP_____

PHONE #_____

Figure 4.4 This ad would place high on any "Bad Taste" award. Before reading it, decide what they're selling. A cemetery? They're kidding! (Unfortunately, they aren't. The second option in the coupon is unrelated to the selling argument, but compared with using the owner's child in this ad, it's a minor gaffe).

The Hamilton Collection
Joyfully Announces
The Heralds of Spring
An Original, Limited-edition Songbird Collection—
Fine Art Sculptures by the Renowned Richard Palmer

Rise up, my love, my fair one,
and come away.
For lo, the winter is past, the rain
is over and gone;
The flowers appear on the earth;
the time of the singing of birds
is come...

The Song of Solomon 2.10-12

Figure 4.5 Whoever the "renowned" Richard Palmer is (no identification is furnished in this eight-page brochure), he, like the rest of us, would be jarred by the word "joyfully" used in this context. More puzzling is the quotation from the Bible, apparently thrown into the mix only because the word "birds" appears in it.

Use words that match or generate a mood. "Sea" is more romantic than "Ocean." "Swimsuit" seems trimmer than "bathing suit." "Fashionable" seems old-fashioned compared with "high fashion," and "stylish" is out of style.

The Key to the Padlock of Skepticism

Before I remind you of the next rule, try this quiz (not "test"). How would you edit this sentence?

"Huckleberry Finn" is the most American of any work of fiction ever written, and Samuel Clemens is America's most beloved fiction writer.

We agree if you share my view that *personalization* is the key to salesmanship. I'd make these quick changes:

"Huckleberry Finn" is the most American story ever written, and Samuel Clemens is our most beloved author.

How many mailings come to you with copy like this?

Looking through the enclosed brochure is like taking a journey through the pages of . . .

The difference between *enclosed brochure* and *brochure I've enclosed* is the core of the next rule:

PERSONALIZING MELTS SKEPTICISM AND APATHY.

In my opinion art suffers from prosaic word use more than any other area of direct marketing. I object to the phrase "art works" when the writer means "works of art." "Art works" suggests a struggling, not particularly talented student. I object to "Three remaining paintings in this series . . . ." when the writer had the option of using *future, forthcoming,* or even *additional,* all of which are stronger than *remaining,* which has the overtone of something abandoned or second-choice. And we don't *give* an honor to the artist, we *bestow* it.

Our *job,* then, is to *avoid* using the word "job" in an art description. It's no more difficult to use the word *task* when we write, "The delicate *job* of transferring this art . . . " and we lift the subject one plateau above bricklaying.

An artist's
loving tribute
to the magic
of little girls

Figure 4.6 Look what happens when the copywriter and the artist don't discuss the project with each other. The copy has nothing whatever to do with the illustration. Incidentally, if the artist was trying to imply that the "loving tribute" is based on getting up in the morning, he should have set the alarm and the clock time to the same hour; as it is, we see the clock an hour and 20 minutes after rise-'n'-shine time.

Recognizing our dedication, we no longer write, "You can obtain it right now." *Obtain* is lobster-like awkward. If we dislike *get* because it seems common and guttural (sometimes an advantage!), we have *acquire*, which imparts value to whatever it is we're obtaining.

One more rule before we all go racing back to our dictionaries and word processors:

WRITE IN COLOR, NOT BLACK AND WHITE.

The best example I have in my file is a mailing from a company that normally sells cheese but has moved into the art field. This company is offering four original etchings. These are the titles:

House
Sheep
Pig
Cows

I can't think of more naked and undignified titles, and the argument, "That's what they are," doesn't sell me. *We're supposed to be the romanticists, and abdicating our creative thrones opens our magic kingdom to pretenders who write even worse than we do.*

I admire the writer who replaced "Gets rid of layers of built-up fat" with "Washes away years of built-up fat." I'd hire the writer who, instead of suggesting my garden hose leaks, warns me it "dribbles water all over your Adidas."

My absolute current favorite is the writer for a company named On The Run who wrote this sentence about a diver's watch:

A push of a button sets into motion a fiercely talented stopwatch.

Not one writer in a million would think of "fiercely talented," especially to describe a stopwatch. It says to the outside world, "Not all writers are cliché artists."

But too many are. Did a writer *think and choose* before immortalizing this thoughtless headline?

Presenting a grand tribute to the world's favorite funnyman, Bob Hope

Grand?

Even Less Excuse in Ads Than in Mailers

There's less excuse for ineffective copy in an ad than in a mailing.

Why? Because an ad usually has far fewer words, and each of those words has greater visibility.

I'm not excusing *any* thoughtless, uninformed, or ridiculous use of words, in any circumstance in which a professional writes the copy and another professional makes the decision to use it, change it, or reject it. I do say space ads have fewer words, and we don't know who's reading those words. These two factors alone should make us cautious.

That's why I was surprised, reading a heavily produced ad for expensive timepieces, to find this:

Gents' two-tone bracelet watch, $850.

"Gents"? There's a 1930s term, smacking of old barber shops, spats, and galluses. We walk the tightrope over a grammatical chasm, with fogey talk on one side and hipness on the other. "Gents" is even beyond the far end of fogeyism, and I don't doubt that many, who might consider this item, may have had their desire blunted by the generation gap an antique word created.

Know Your Reader

The same difficulty beset the writer of this noncommunication from a communications company:

We are taking the liberty of enclosing a copy of an article featured in the *Wall Street Journal* which is self-explanatory.

Is one word of this sentence necessary? The approach is like an old steam locomotive, trying to get underway from a standing start, with rods and wheels spinning and sliding until finally the monstrous machine can gain some.traction.

So we come to the *Rule of Contemporaneous Transmission:*

UNLESS THE WRITER HAS A KNOWLEDGE OF THE BACKGROUND OF HIS TARGET READER, COPY CAN BE A HORRIBLE PSYCHOLOGICAL MISMATCH.

Figure 4.7 This ad is a classic example of making a wild promise in the headline, then trying to con the reader into thinking the promise has been kept. Are any of the "reasons" genuine?

Figure 4.8 This ad has been running for years, and with good reason: It combines exclusivity with a painless introduction to fine art. Opinion: a superior piece of copy, worthy of running for many more years.

A different problem besets the writer of this ad, which intends to generate inquiries for a handsome mailing package describing executive homes:

> A most unusual home with excellent financing that must
> be seen to be appreciated.

Sure, we can't see financing. The writer compounds his crime by giving us nothing else *to* see. There's no touchstone. *Why would anyone respond?* What's the motivator? The lapse into the nondescriptive phrase *most unusual* is the giveaway: the writer hasn't any idea what the homebuyer wants.

Nor did the writer of this mail order insurance ad use many of the psychological clubs in the rhetorical golf bag:

> We're "picking up the slack" on senior citizens'
> insurance!

Okay, suppose I'm 82 years old and terrified every time I cough. I'd respond better to a motivator than I would to a piece of loose self-puffery. Here's an idea: Stop after you read this paragraph and spend 60 seconds thinking of better headlines for senior citizen insurance. Ready?

Yours are probably better than these three I noodled out over the one-minute span:

1. Over 65 and worried about hospital costs? Forget it!
2. Just because you're over 65 . . .
3. Who pays when Medicare and Medicaid won't? We do.

These, and yours, were the result of a near-zero information base. Imagine what power we could turn on if we knew as much about his particular policy as the original writer did!

Compare that with the strength and force of this computer letter, which unfortunately didn't come to my own mailbox:

> Congratulations. Our computer has discovered, from a
> search of various mailing lists, that you are a passionate
> lover of lusty literature. As such, you have won the right
> to join the Erotic Art Book Society, America's most
> stimulating book club—for only $1.

I admire someone who uses words professionally. Look at these: *passionate lover, lusty literature, most stimulating book*

SYDNEY DATAPRODUCTS, INC.

Thank you for your recent inquiry through CREATIVE COMPUTING about
our exciting new game EVOLUTION.

SYDNEY is a major developer of innovative packaged software for both
mainframe and micro computers.

We are assembling a catalogue of products and expect to have this
available in the near future. In the meantime here is a short list
of software products available now.

EVOLUTION   (Commodore 64, IBM-PC, Apple II Plus)

 - Suggested retail price $ 39.95
 - Dealer price (2-99 units)   25.00
 - Distributor price (100+ units)   16.50

Custom Drapery and Interiors Business Systems

 - Suggested retail price $5000.00
 - Dealer price   3000.00

Real Estate and Analysis Systems

 - Suggested retail price $1895.00
 - Dealer price   1140.00

Commercial Drapery Estimator

 - Suggested retail price $1095.00
 - Dealer prices to be determined

We have the exclusive world wide rights to use the comic strip
characters from the Wizard of ID and B.C. for games and education
packages and expect to release two or three high quality products
each year for Coleco, IBM-PC, Apple II Plus and Commodore 64.

Again, thanks for thinking SYDNEY. We look forward to doing business
with you. If you would like any further information on any of these
products please do not hesitate to contact us.

Yours sincerely,

Carolyn Frost
Carolyn Frost
Marketing Manager

444 CAMINO DEL RIO SOUTH, SUITE 129, SAN DIEGO, CA 92108   619-298-5886

Figure 4.9 The most ghastly aspect of this letter is that it's the answer
to a serious inquiry, for which the advertiser paid hard dollars. Try to
find one sentence in the letter which addresses the inquiry—about the
"exciting new game EVOLUTION."

Figure 4.10 Wrong words can cause the wrong targets to read an ad. This one isn't aimed at people whose incomes embarrass them; it's aimed at those whose *lack of* income embarrasses them.

club. Without calling the recipient a lecher, the writer has made his point. It's a difficult job, handled well.

Less fortunate was this thoughtless line from a collectibles mailing:

> Redoute is acknowledged as "the Raphael of roses"—
> one of the greatest rose artists of all time.

This copy lapses back into selling *software* (puffery) instead of *hardware* (facts). It doesn't convince us. We're in the Age of Skepticism.

We want to know who "acknowledged" him before we in turn acknowledge the writer's assumptions. Another problem here: Dumping on us a conclusion *requiring* an information *base* not one percent of the recipients can have, and the use of that sadly deficient descriptive word *greatest*, both contribute to the wet-sponge impact.

Does that mean we need far-out terms to draw the reader into our webs? Certainly not. Labored writing is worse than thoughtless writing. Here's an example of a simple line of copy, with only one two-syllable word, that helps make a sweepstakes mailing a winner:

> Let me show you how to enter and win . . .
>   Lee Rogers, President
>   American Holiday Association

How much stronger and more credible this is than the words "Enter and win" without the one-to-one psychology! The same mailing overcomes a nondescript, nondescriptive corporate name by putting this return address on the outer envelope:

> Prize Award Headquarters

Mutually Cancelling Words

Ever since the poet Algernon Charles Swinburne befuddled his readers with the phrase *brown bright nightingale,* writers have deliberately or carelessly strung together mutually cancelling words. Today we're at epidemic proportions. I'm looking at a description of some art objects: "This nostalgic, new series . . . " *Nostalgic* means old. *New* means new. Why put the two together, muddying the word image?

Here's another: "A small crowd saw the event." Who was in that crowd? A group of large midgets? Why use *small* and *crowd* together?

Yet another: "Never have you seen a deeper, richer white." *Deep* doesn't ruin the word *white*, but it brings us to a stop. Our brains won't juggle the two words together. Even the cliché-thought, "You've never seen a more dazzling pure white" is better, because the words aren't in a descriptive battle. ("Never have you seen" has to go!)

Long ago I came to the conclusion that, as one Mr. Malaprop put it, "If Norman Rockwell were alive today, he'd turn over in his grave." Rockwell seems to be the target for more semi-pro writers than any other subject. This mailer combines three classic copy failures: (1) a logical gap; (2) an unconvincing nonargument; and (3) a deadened conclusion. Here's the first paragraph of body copy from the brochure:

> Any set of fine porcelain collectibles is eagerly anticipated by collectors everywhere. When such a set features the brilliantly evocative art of Norman Rockwell, it is an event of truly unusual importance . . . and when such a set is so remarkably low in price, it is a dramatic announcement, indeed.

Let's count.

(1) A logical gap: "Any set of fine collectibles is eagerly anticipated by collectors everywhere." How can collectors anticipate this until they know it's coming, by which time it isn't anticipation but reality? The rhetoric is just words strung together.
(2) An unconvincing nonargument: " . . . it is an event of truly unusual importance." That word *truly* is the dashboard indicator—the writer is out of gas, and as the empty verbal juggernaut wheezes to a stop he tries to push it a few more feet with *truly unusual importance.*
(3) A deadened conclusion: " . . . and when such a set is so remarkably low in price, it is a dramatic announcement, indeed." Indeed? The heck you say. It might be a bargain, but the word *dramatic* is entitled to a little drama.

Let's form a rule here, out of reader fatigue if for no other reason:

> DRAMA IN WRITING IS IMPLICIT, OR IT DOESN'T EXIST AT ALL. LABELLING ISN'T PARALLEL TO COLORFUL WRITING. CLAIMING "DRAMA" OR "EXCITEMENT" IS AN UNINSPIRED AND PUNCHLESS SUBSTITUTE FOR USING WORDS TO PROVE THE CLAIM.

Accentuate the Positive

Some words have no sell in them. *Strictly* is one of those. Aside from the old-fashioned images it calls up ("strictly fresh meats"), it's the type of word Mrs. Meany would use in the orphanage. So when a writer refers to Gorham China Company's "strictly limited edition," we feel as though we've been put into the classroom of an unpleasant teacher.

Stringently is another word we can do without in direct response. Those who know what it means react negatively; those who don't associate it with strings.

"We stripped our warehouse . . . "; "Your service is our endeavor . . . "; "Our supply is severely limited . . . " Words such as *stripped, endeavor,* and *severely* suggest a negative state of mind.

A master fund raiser can use negatives to pry dollars out of our pockets. For ads and mailings selling protective devices, insurance, some types of financial services, professional newsletters, and inflation or recession fighters, a skilled wordsmith can use negatives as paladins to *fear,* the crown prince of motivators in the Age of Skepticism.

For the journeyman whose use of negatives is inadvertent, words with happy faces are safer because as word-swords they have only one edge and are less likely to carve up the user.

In One Sentence . . .

Since words are our only weapons in the battle of wits with readers, let's keep our arsenal sharpened and polished. Otherwise we lose the battle by default to "those people" whose marketing inventiveness often is limited to criticizing ours.

We've Made A Case For You.

No matter who you are, Hazel makes your kind of case: slim or husky. Leather or vinyl. Brief or not-so-brief. For top management or the top route salesman. In fact, Hazel is America's only complete line of cases for business, arts, and pleasure. Made with integrity and designed for individuality for almost a century. At fine office supply dealers, department and specialty stores nationwide.

Hazel

America's Case Maker.™

Figure 4.11 Instead of a play on words, the writer might have given us a reason to fill out the coupon. The first words of body copy are as unconvincing as they can be—"No matter who you are, Hazel makes your kind of case."

5

The Magic Word
that Can
Make You Rich

About two thousand years before a televised husband/ wife confrontation, in which we see and hear the cosmic accusation, "The most important conference of my life and you switch deodorant soaps!" another classic confrontation occurred.

A man named Pontius Pilate, Roman governor of Judaea, brought himself not only dubious immortality as a statesman but a permanent niche in the mass communications hall of fame for this question, reported in John 18,38: "What is truth?"

For direct response writing, Pilate had a point. What *is* truth? Does the concept have any validity as a selling argument in the Age of Skepticism?

We're all corrupted by television, and corruption skews our sanity. We excuse, on grounds of attention getting, outlandish selling arguments that, head-to-head, we'd dismiss as childish non sequiturs. Some of us forget the only way we taste blood in direct marketing—*persuading someone to buy*.

Old Pilate understood better than many of us who earn our livings as communicators the significance of a magic word:
Verisimilitude.

Apparent Truth

The power pulsing within the magic word is this: verisimilitude *isn't* truth; it's *the appearance of* truth. We've all learned, as we replace original idealism with cynicism, that the "whole" truth not only doesn't make us free; it isn't a particularly shrewd way to sell. But *the appearance of* truth—ah! The Kingdom of Heaven! Instead of being strapped to a cold metal table of facts, we have soft cushions of quasi-facts on which we lean.

Selectivity underlies the First Great Rule of Verisimilitude:

> **THE CORNERSTONE OF SUCCESSFUL DIRECT RESPONSE COPY ISN'T TRUTH, BUT HAVING THE READER REGARD WHAT YOU WRITE AS TRUTH.**

See the difference? All the truth in the world won't sell for you unless the message recipient believes it's true. The writer is Peter Pan, and unless the reader believes, Tinker Bell—what you're selling—will drop dead.

The truth may set you free, but too much of it, *unselected,* is like drinking champagne from a tennis shoe just after a tough match—you've won the match but lose the celebration. An example:

> These aren't Givenchy or even Calvin Klein fashions. The label isn't fancy. But these are good, solid, middle-America fashions, and they'll never take you off the deep end.

Figure 5.1 Here's an example of verisimilitude. This "check," included in a mailing for Corning Ware, is convincing not only because of its format but because of the amount—$86.05. The amount is so odd one thinks it *has* to be true.

We wish the writer had kept the typewriter in check. "I'm sorry, but . . . " may be true, but it has no sell. The "deep end" thought would have been a sound copy platform, but why must we denigrate the product? My opinion is a basic one: The writer had a comparative contempt for his product, and some of that contempt leaked out.

How do we achieve the appearance of truth? If you haven't achieved the nirvana of automatic verisimilitude, you'll be pleased to learn it's as easy as establishing a personal writing discipline based on *logic*—or, to keep our own sales argument coherent, *the appearance of* logic.

This leads us to the Second Great Rule of Verisimilitude:

CONSISTENCY PREVENTS THE BUILDUP OF SKEPTI-CISM, WHICH ERODES VERISIMILITUDE.

Want a few examples? Read (and reread until you see the flaw) this paragraph from a catalog selling gemstones:

> The natural inclusions, or imperfections, are typical of emeralds, and do not detract from the value. Emeralds have more inclusions than other stones—which explains why a perfectly clear emerald is priceless.

Once you understand what the writer has written here, you're bound to say, "You're full of it, Buster," because the two sentences are mutually contradicting. If inclusions don't detract from the value, then how can emeralds without inclusions be worth more? All the rest of the selling argument, which might be powerful, dies because we reject an obvious contradiction, an inconsistency.

Truth Alone Is No Defense

Suppose the writer says, "But it's true. 'Detracting from the value' isn't parallel to 'why a clear emerald is priceless.' " Our answer: "Your argument is full of it, Buster." The sales argument itself is an absolute denial of *both* the First Two Great Rules of Verisimilitude, and that's suicide in a competitive marketplace.

Some examples of inconsistency are so laughable one wonders whether anyone bothered to look at the first draft before copy was approved. I treasure a mailing from a company called Hanley Associates, addressed to me and marked "PERSONAL AND CONFIDENTIAL." Inside was a letter, with this greeting: "Gentlemen:"

Consistency disarms skepticism in the name itself of an auto rental company called "Rent-a-Wreck"; but someone slipped up in the name of a mail order clock offer. The letterhead, in a continental-type script, says, "Jean Roulet." The address is full of French words ("UBS La Chaux-de-Fonds"), but the product is called "The President Clock"—about as French as Ronald Reagan. *L'horloge presidentiele* wouldn't win the Verisimilitude of the Year Award, but it surely is a more credible product name, consistent with the ostensible source.

The Consistency Rule suggests tying together logical threads. If you claim an extraordinarily low price and you offer no choice of color, you build verisimilitude by combining the two points:

"Sorry, no choice of color at this low price."

Obviously, verisimilitude is based on the use of fact. When the factual presentation is *unfactual*, the vendor would have been wiser to omit all reference. Sometimes factual error results from a too-casual approach to fact checking. A letter selling demitasse sets with miniature rose motifs begins, "A few months back I received an invitation to visit with Howard Walters, President of the American Rose Society." Sure enough, an endorsement enclosure has the name typed below the signature: "Howard Walters." Verisimilitude disappears, though, when we read the handwritten signature above the typed "Howard Walters." The signature reads clearly, "Harold Goldstein."

A parallel example of left hand not knowing what right hand is typing is a mailing whose letter says, "Just for agreeing to try this offer, we'll send you a *free mystery gift!* It's *yours to keep*—absolutely free—no matter what you decide. . . ."

Oh, boy! A mystery gift! I love surprises, but my pleasure was cut short as soon as I turned to the brochure. In it was a picture of the Mystery Gift with the cutline, "KEEP THIS FREE CHRISTMAS ORNAMENT." Mystery solved. Verisimilitude dissipated.

Figure 5.2 Bald commercialism is annoying, and this ad points up how commercial the Olympics have become. We accept the first sentence of body copy as a confusing lie. The oddest part of the ad is that it ignores the many positive sales features of this electronic typewriter.

Match the Reader's Background

When facts don't match the reader's experiential background, your verisimilitude is in trouble.

So we have difficulty with this headline, because we know aloe vera as a shampoo:

$$$$ MIRACLES$$$$

keep coming when you sell my 100% pure "Herb Healing"

ALOE VERA JUICE!!!!

It sells—sells—sells like liquid gold

Somehow we can't avoid the image of ingesting shampoo.

The same problem attends an ad headed, "Flapper Earns Big $." A drawing of a mechanical bird has this subhead:

XMAS$$

BONANZA!

IMAGINE: FIVE OR SIX TEENAGERS

EACH EARNING YOU FROM $100.00

TO $700.00 PER WEEKEND

The copy-heavy ad explains the arithmetic: the mechanical bird retails for $6.95; distributor cost is ("as low as") $2.60. "They line up to buy."

What's wrong here is the incredible numbers. Even if they're true, they aren't believable. Remember the First Great Rule of Verisimilitude—the cornerstone of successful direct response copy isn't truth, but having the reader regard what you write as truth. This ad reaches beyond the reader's experiential background. Assuming a median figure, five teenagers averaging $400 would net the distributor $2,000 per weekend. We just don't believe it; if the projection is reset to $50 to $150, the profit seems realistic; credibility returns; verisimilitude works for us.

That example exemplifies The Third Great Rule of Verisimilitude:

**STAY INSIDE THE READER'S EXPERIENTIAL BACK-
GROUND. MAKE INCREDIBLE CLAIMS CREDIBLE BY**

ACKNOWLEDGING THEM AS INCREDIBLE, THEN EX-
PLAINING WHY THEY'RE TRUE.

Disarming the reader comes naturally to the direct mail writer who knows the reader is armed. A company called Creative House disarms our skepticism about prices, in a space ad for attaché cases at a discount. Instead of ignoring the Third Great Law with workmanlike but uninventive headlines such as "Amazing Low Prices!" or "While They Last!" this company dispels our skepticism with a headline our experiential background accepts:

IMPORTER'S CLOSE-OUTS!
LEATHER ATTACHÉ
CASES (1982 Series)

A near-perfect headline, without a single trick word! Verisimilitude is as near as your own sense of logic.

Equally powerful is this opening sentence from a subscription letter for a publication called *Undercurrent:*

Dear Fellow Diver:

Join us, won't you, for a few choice words about
defective equipment, phony diving resort claims,
underwater death traps, and other assorted menaces to
your health and bank account.

We already saw in chapter 2 that fear, properly exploited, is a potent motivator; but the energy bursting from this first sentence isn't a *fear* energy, it's *verisimilitude* energy, with words dead center in a scuba diver's experiential background—"defective equipment," "phony diving resort claims," "death traps." How much stronger this is than the usual rhetoric about scenic diving sites!

"I Don't Believe You"

Why feed the reader's implicit skepticism?

When I read brochure copy like this, I realize that laziness, however passive an antagonist, is another enemy of verisimilitude:

Jessica DeStefano

The list of juried shows, awards, and one-woman
exhibits credited to Jessica is far too lengthy to list.
Simply put, she is one of America's best-loved sculptors
whose work is eagerly sought by museums, galleries and
private collectors.

    We can't believe this dull puffery because the rhetorical
meal gives us no facts to chew. Compare the nonspecifics with
the verisimilitude-generating specifics of this section of a letter
from a company in the same business as the one selling the
works of the sculptress whose list of credits "is far too lengthy
to list":

So we completed arrangements to buy some china and
glass to offer ACC members. On the Monday before the
Thursday on which Braniff filed bankruptcy, we'd
mailed a check in payment. Ironically, on Wednesday of
that same week, Braniff rebooked us on an American
flight to New York because they said their planes were

Figure 5.3 The number, visible through a die-cut window, brings verisimilitude to this otherwise pedestrian envelope.

grounded in Dallas due to bad weather. I missed being
on one of their last flights on their final day of operation.
But because of the bankruptcy action, we were left in
limbo for weeks as to whether we would, in fact, get the
china and glass we had paid for . . . .

Here's another fine use of verisimilitude, lifted from a
letter printed on the inside cover of a stamp catalog:

We have been on Nassau Street since 1952, when my
father-in-law purchased SUBWAY STAMP SHOP from
Henri Baer. We are not a "here today–gone tomorrow"
company located in some post office box. Our shop at
111 Nassau St., NYC, is open Monday through Friday,
9:30 AM–5:30 PM. We look forward to meeting our
customers and hope you will stop by and visit us
whenever you come to New York.

Compare the verisimilitude bursting from every syllable
to your reaction if the copy had read something like this:

We have been in business a long time, and we intend
staying in business an even longer time. We are not a
"here today–gone tomorrow" company located in some
post office box. We are determined to bring to our
customers the finest quality merchandise from the four
corners of the earth.

My point: A claim doesn't create the feeling of truth unless that claim is tied to a fact acceptable to the reader.

The key, translating that point to the Fourth Great Rule
of Verisimilitude, is that last kicker phrase—*acceptable to the
reader*. So we formulate the Law:

**USE FACT TO MAKE A POINT, NOT JUST FOR THE
SAKE OF USING FACT.**

And we tie the Fourth Great Rule to the last, the Fifth
Great Rule of Verisimilitude:

**EVIDENCE IS MORE CREDIBLE THAN AN UNEX-
PLAINED STATEMENT OF POSITION.**

So "My friend Roger told me" is better than "A friend
told me"; "List price $14.95, our price $8.75" is better than

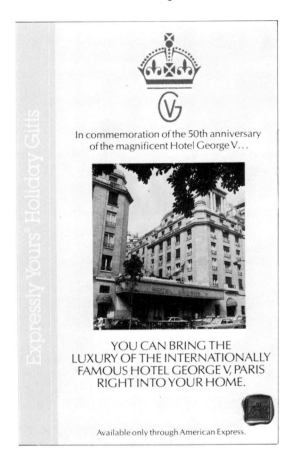

In commemoration of the 50th anniversary
of the magnificent Hotel George V...

YOU CAN BRING THE
LUXURY OF THE INTERNATIONALLY
FAMOUS HOTEL GEORGE V, PARIS
RIGHT INTO YOUR HOME.

Available only through American Express.

Expressly Yours® Holiday Gifts

Figure 5.4 Does this advertiser seriously expect us to believe we're being offered whatever is inside this folder (a bathrobe) "in commemoration of the 50th anniversary of the magnificent Hotel George V"? A more credible sales argument: "For the first time in 50 years..."

"What a bargain at $8.75!"; "This check ($86.05) is valid only toward the purchase of one set of IM–#20 CORNING WARE cookware" is better than "$86.05 Off on CORNING WARE cookware"; and "Ms. DeStefano won the coveted Schletke Award" is better than "The list of juried shows, awards, and one-woman exhibits credited to Jessica is far too lengthy to list."

When you apply the Fourth and Fifth Great Rules, don't forget the Second Great Rule—consistency. The last proofreading before setting type should have the dedicated purpose of checking all factual claims for consistency. I'm looking at a brochure that lists the color choice for the product: "White, red, and green." Now, here's the order form. Uh-oh! "Red and green available in 42" length only." Verisimilitude, I mourn your mortal wounding at the hands of the careless, the lazy, the uninformed, the pompous, and the regurgitators of undigested fact.

These scoundrels can wound verisimilitude; cheating, handled without finesse, and lying, with or without finesse, can kill it.

The Difference Between Cheating and Lying

When a copywriter hits his keys in desperation, he can start to lie. Lying in Copy is inexcusable; whether discovered or undiscovered, it damages all of us in this business.

Cheating, though, *might* be despicable or *might* be a wonderful way to sell product or raise money without damaging anyone.

The gulf separating lying from cheating is as simple as this direct marketing rule:

A LIAR IS A SCOUNDREL WITHOUT REDEMPTIVE QUALITIES AND SHOULD BE DISAVOWED BY EVERYONE IN THE BUSINESS; A CHEAT IS A SALESMAN, WHO MAY BE A SCOUNDREL, MAY BE MISINFORMED, OR MAY SIMPLY BE TRYING TO WIN FAVOR WITH THE READER. CONCLUSION: SCURRILITY ISN'T ABSOLUTE IN CHEATING AS IT IS IN LYING.

Lies generally are less thoughtful and more desperate than cheating. This space ad is an example:

Tonight at midnight, history will be made when the
National Monetary Center opens its vaults and releases
to the public some of the last surviving ORIGINAL, U.S.
GOV'T. MINTED MORGAN SILVER DOLLARS IN
EXISTENCE IN ALL THE WORLD.

How do I know it's a lie? Because the ad appeared in a monthly publication. "Tonight at midnight" blends the occult with the fantastic, but one thing for sure: it isn't true. The enigma of this ad is that it's a well-written, hard-boiled ad into which the writer has thrust this incredible interjection. Why do it?

A parallel space ad doesn't lie; instead, it cheats:

(Headline) 1 oz. Silver Ingot $4.95—.999 pure

(Coupon) Please rush my 1 oz. .999 pure silver ingot and my new subscription. Enclosed is $28.95.

In between these two mismatched dollar-numbers is the tie between the "grabber" headline and the ugly-truth coupon. If you want that ingot for $4.95, you must subscribe to the monthly newsletter for $24.00 a year. You may not admire the copy platform, but you can't accuse the copywriter of lying.

A coupon ad in *Newsweek* calls attention to Brother Industries, Ltd., of Nagoya, Japan. The coupon is tied to this headline:

If it's the "Official Typewriter of the
Los Angeles 1984 Olympic Games"
you know it's quality,
you know it's *brother*.

Now, come on. I know that Eastern is the "Official" Airline of Disney World, even though the planes have to land in Orlando. But awarding the title "Official Typewriter"? Does that mean it won some sort of event, leaving IBM and Royal gasping as it cleared the bar at 15.8 characters? The coupon offers no help, only a bland and inscrutable face: "For more information."

Brother is cheating by inventing validity for its purchased credential. Every word of the ad is true; every word of the headline is inconsequential. A *Newsweek* reader knows there was no such scenario as the delivery to Nagoya of an unexpected "official" letter from Olympic officials, who, together with Consumer's Union, had tested all typewriters and made this gold medal conclusion. In this case the cheating is of dubious value in mounting a coherent sales argument.

The First and Second Rules of Cheating

To us, it has value of another sort. It helps establish the First Rule of Cheating:

TO BE ACCEPTABLE FROM ANY VIEWPOINT, AN AD THAT CHEATS MUST BE UNASSAILABLE FACTUALLY.

And the Second Rule of Cheating:

TO BE COMPETITIVELY PREFERABLE, AN AD THAT CHEATS MUST BOOST THE PRODUCT OR SERVICE BEYOND THE ABILITY OF A CONVENTIONAL SALES ARGUMENT TO DO SO.

The De Lorean Motor Club of America sent me a mailing offering me the "official De Lorean Motor Club" jacket. This was their sales incentive:

Retail price $60.00; Members price $45.00.

Who, I wondered, would want a jacket with that legend on it except a member? Who, for that matter, would even see this offer, since the jackets are the "official" ones offered only by the Club to its members, unless that person saw the same mailer sent to me? Was this artificial "members price" (where's the apostrophe?) a lie or was it cheating? Did it matter? Sure it did, and the extent of damage a taradiddle like this can cause becomes clearer later on in this chapter.

I didn't buy the jacket, nor the "official" sweater, nor the "official" T-shirt (which has a tacky John Travolta overtone anyway). But I did come out of the encounter with the First Rule of Lie-Avoidance:

A LIE VISIBLE TO THE TARGET READER IS A SYMBOL OF A WEAK IMAGINATION.

Lies Hover Like Flies When Competing Products Are Similar

Collectibles are afflicted with image sameness, which makes them particularly vulnerable to lying and cheating. A mailed invitation to own a collector's plate had a heading I've come to detest, since two automobile manufacturers exhibited their imaginative sterility by using variations of it:

If you can find it at a local dealer, buy it.

The copy proceeded:

Dear Friend:

This is about a scarce new piece of art.

It is a beautiful $19 plate showing a little boy on a rainy day.

Demand is big enough that it has been projected to reach a value of $1,000 in our lifetime.

But reservations are already hard to find.

Reservations are very hard to find in U.S. stores and almost impossible to find overseas. If you can find a reservation at a local dealer, buy it.

Or mail the enclosed form for your reservation. But do it now since time is important.

Let's analyze: "Scarce" and "new" don't go together. We suspect a lie. Who projects that $1,000 value? The person writing the letter? This technique worked five years ago, but collectors have grown up enough to ask for credentials. The statement is impenetrable, so we can't tell if it's a lie or not. We label it cheating.

Reservations are almost impossible to find overseas? Ah—that's *clever* cheating. The statement undoubtedly is true. I'll bet not one dealer in Albania has this item. In fact, if no marketing has been done outside this country, reservations probably are totally unavailable overseas. As a marketing technique, this statement rivals the old "Unique Selling Proposition" of Rosser Reeves, former head of Ted Bates Advertising. But because it's awash in the milky weakness of the less-effective cheating arguments, this gem is dulled. So:

With this example, we have the Third Rule of Cheating:

SURROUNDING A THOUGHTFUL CHEATING ARGUMENT WITH WEAK AND THOUGHTLESS CHEATING ARGUMENTS SAPS STRENGTH BY THINNING THE BASE OF READER CREDULITY.

The Thin Line Between Lying and Cheating

All this nit-picking may spray a veil of confusion over the hairline separating the top edge of lying from the bottom edge of cheating. This example may clarify:

One of the major credit card companies just mailed an offer for a bronze sculpture. The sculpture is a limited edition, and the description of the limitation cheats:

Your Advance Reservation must be postmarked by September 9 . . . . At the final closing date, the edition will be closed forever, never to be offered again . . . .

Verisimilitude isn't killed off; this cheating is reasonably well done. The Advance Reservation date is specified, but it isn't the closing date, which isn't mentioned. For all we know, it could be the year 2001. But the average reader will slide by this omission, cushioned on the air pillow of rhetoric, believing in the congruence of the advance date and the ultimate date.

In the very next paragraph, cheating turns to lying:

In addition to its status as a one-of-a-kind original, "Mare and Colt" will possess a wide range of important qualities . . . .

If this example were in chapter 4 I'd attack the copywriting—"possess a wide range of important qualities" isn't the *ne plus ultra* of imaginative word usage; but here, we're talking about lying and cheating. Calling one piece within a limited edition "a one-of-a-kind original" is a deliberate misuse of the word "original"—ergo, a lie. Ungood, professionally and ethically.

On the brochure, the representation is:

An Acquisition Opportunity In Original Art.

Here we're cheating, not lying. The truth is bent to fit a convoluted shape but it's not broken. The sculpture *was* originated for this particular limited edition. The writer can milk the word "original" because each sculpted piece is cast individually.

The difference between the lie in the letter and the cheating in the brochure is just enough to show how the same type of sales argument might fall into either category. In fact, it's so close we begin to wonder why the writer chose to test the reader's naiveté instead of writing inside the just-as-easy, *unassailable* cheater's argument such as, "Each one is hand cast, with the tiny but unmistakable differences from any others that are hallmarks of an original work of art . . . "

You can see it: integrity seeps back into the sales argument when we don't lie. It's Humpty Dumpty resurrected from his crash onto the hard ground of self-destructive falsehood.

Some samples are far clearer-cut. A coupon ad in a trade magazine has this copy:

> We're Winslow and Rothschild, the biggest name in
> apparel marketing.

Only two possibilities: Winslow and Rothschild are telling the truth, in which case they *are* the biggest name in apparel marketing (could it be?); or they're playing a game of Russian roulette, lying instead of puffing and hoping no one will call their hand.

Does the Benefit Exist?

Cheating to present a benefit that exists is good sales technique; cheating to present a benefit that doesn't exist is a lie.

We can have fun with cheating; we can't have fun with lying. As cheating approaches the border, it becomes more and more uncomfortable, because of the Fourth Rule of Cheating:

> **AS CHEATING MOVES TOWARD LYING AND BE-TRAYS A LACK OF INTEGRITY, EFFECTIVENESS AMONG THE BEST BUYERS VANISHES IN DIRECT RATIO.**

Under this rule, "Retail price $60.00; Members price $45.00" is less effective than "A $60 Value for $45," because the latter gives no ammunition to the potentially hostile reader. "Broadcasts Up to 1,000 Feet, Depending on Terrain" will generate less returned merchandise than "1,000-Foot Signal."

Ah, but we don't need samples; we don't even need to think twice. We'll all do fine if we paste onto our mirrors the Ultimate Rule of Lie Avoidance:

> **LYING ISN'T NECESSARY. IF IT EVER BECOMES NEC-ESSARY, LET'S ALL DO SOMETHING ELSE FOR A LIVING.**

And that's where verisimilitude has to yield. As important as the appearance of truth is, the actuality of truth is more so.

$1,000,000 Sales Closer's Bible

This exciting new 300 page book can put you among the highest paid people in the world — Professional Sales Closers

My name is Bob Pettet. I'm the President of a West Coast advertising agency . . . and this is the most unusual ad I've prepared in thirty years in the advertising business. You see, it's about "The Closers", which is, beyond a shadow of a doubt, the best book on professional, hard-hitting selling and closing ever written . . . but the ad was written for me (almost entirely!) by a satisfied customer . . . a nationally known Sales Pro.*

Here's how it happened: The day I took this assignment, the publishers of "The Closers" gave me a letter one of their customers had sent to his sales organization after he'd read "The Closers". His unsolicited letter said it all. So, rather than try to top a sincere endorsement with my own copy, I decided to simply reprint it.

Here's what he wrote:

"TO: ALL SALES PERSONNEL
SUBJECT: CLOSING SALES

"As most of you know, I've been a professional in sales and marketing for almost twenty years. Not to brag, but to help you understand the importance of what I'm about to tell you, I've earned millions of dollars in the sales field . . . the reason being, I figured out early in the game that selling and closing is the highest paid profession in the world, only if you take the time to learn it as a science — which it is.

"It's not by accident that a few of us have stayed at the top of this profession. It's a result of years of study and practice, dozens of seminars and extensive reading and listening on the subject of professional selling . . .

CLOSING SECRETS

". . . and, through it all, most of us who've done well have wondered why no one of us ever took the time to put the 'essence' of all of those years, books, cassettes and seminars in one condensed form. Speaking for me, I've been too selfish, too busy selling and too busy making money to devote the year or two I figured it would take to put all of it on paper.

"Well, about a month ago, I was reading a newspaper and saw yet another ad for a book on selling . . . one that, as usual, claimed to 'contain all the selling secrets'. Knowing I'd have to wade through another two or three hundred pages just to pick up a fresh idea or two, I almost didn't order it. But then, remembering that 'you've got to pay the price', I sent off my check and prepared myself for another day of dull reading.

"Ten days later the book arrived. It was called "The Closers". I tossed it in my briefcase for spare-time reading and forgot about it. The next week I was on a plane heading for the East Coast, found the book and started reading just to kill the hours that lay ahead of me.

MASTER CLOSER

"On the first page I found myself pleasantly surprised. By the tenth page I was excited! By the three-hundredth page I knew it had finally been done! Someone, a true sales-pro a Master Closer, had taken the time to put it all in one well-written, easy-to-understand book. And I do mean ALL!

"Everything I'd ever learned from my several mentors. Everything I had learned from a hundred books. Everything I had learned from dozens of seminars. Everything I had learned from countless cassettes. Everything it took me twenty years to pick up in bits and pieces was there! EVERYTHING!

"Upon landing, I went directly from the gate to the nearest phone. I tracked down the author and congratulated him. I also ordered 500 additional copies.

"Folks, if you haven't gotten the message yet, this book is SUPER! It is THE definitive book on selling. I urge you to get a copy now and to read it — again and again!

"As you probably know, I don't usually write bulletins to the field and I don't push books. But I believe so strongly in this one that I'm personally asking you — for your own benefit — to get a copy of "The Closers" . . . and I've asked the company to enclose an order form for your convenience. Please fill it out and mail it today. You'll never regret it . . .

". . . in fact, if you don't agree with my strong endorsement after you've read it, mail it back to me. I'll buy it back at full price and give it to a school in our area. How's that for belief?

"If you're really serious about learning how to sell and close like the best, here's your chance. Order your copy of "The Closers" right now by filling out the attached form or, for even quicker action, by calling immediately.

"With the "The Closers" working for you, I'll soon be seeing you AT THE TOP!"

See what I mean? And, as his letter says, he has since bought hundreds of copies! Well, that's it. No hard sell. No jumping up and down. "The Closers" is the best book on selling and closing ever written. I give you my personal, solemn commitment on that. Everything you and/or your sales organization needs to know about selling and closing is now in one easy to read book . . . 300 pages of sales and closing dynamite!

NO QUESTIONS ASKED MONEY BACK GUARANTEE

. . . AND TO SHOW YOU HOW MUCH WE BELIEVE IN "The Closers", we offer the same money back guarantee our customer makes to his sales force. Order it. Read it. Then, if you don't agree that it's the finest sales and closing book ever written, return it. We'll give you a complete, no questions asked refund and donate the used book to a school in our area. The cost is $19.95 per copy plus $1.50 for postage and handling.

Here's how you order:
For credit card customers,

CALL NOW TOLL FREE (800) 824-7888

Ask for Operator 339J
(If in California, call 800-852-7777, Operator 339J. If in Alaska or Hawaii, 800-824-7919, Operator 339J.)

Or send your check or money order (Sorry, no C.O.D.'s) to "The Closers", 3075 Alhambra Drive — Suite 104, Dept. 339J, Cameron Park, California 95682-9005.

1981 NTFM

*Name upon written request

Figure 5.5 Aside from the patronizing tone, we don't believe the numbers. $1 million is just too big an amount to expect from a "sales closer's Bible." If the ad promised an "Extra $75,000 a Year Income," we'd be more likely to go along.

6

A BENEFIT Performance for the Reader

I keep hearing from learned commentators on our society that the "Me Generation" (sometimes called the "Me Decade"—does a generation last only a decade these days?) has matured into the "We Generation," with greater social conscience.

Much as I want to believe we've reversed the decivilizing process, I conclude that these commentators never have tried to sell anything by direct response. With their philosophy, they'd be clobbered by vendors whose recognition of why people buy what they aren't looking for is closer to hard reality.

In my opinion, the Me Generation has taken over, and when we remind them that they're supposed to take the psychological bars off their windows and care about others, they tell us—by not buying what we're selling—"I don't see any others. What others?"

What People Care About

As the result of heaven-knows-what indoctrination by the insidious forces of evil in our society (maybe heaven doesn't know, after all), these people care only about these three major components of the cosmos:

1. Me
2. Myself
3. I

The Me Generation has been the cement holding the Age of Skepticism firmly in place. Their own skepticism isn't based on the more reasoned question, "Will it work or not?" Rather, it's founded on the totally subjective, "What will it do for me?"

This latter question isn't all that objectionable. Some mail order marketers object to the question, not on the logical ground that it represents a selfish, unstatesmanlike approach to civilized life, but on the more personal ground that they can't answer it.

What a beautiful O. Henry plotline: We have seller and buyer, each wrapped in his personal cocoon of self-interest. Are they both wrong?

Nope. Maybe in some doomsday judgment they're both wrong, but in a situation where *A* wants to sell something to *B* and *B* neither knows nor cares who *A* is, *A* is the one who must crack. A Mexican standoff makes the seller the loser, not the buyer.

How to Sell Buyer Benefit

When mail order copy degenerates to pompous, megalomaniacal chest thumping and doesn't say to the reader, "Here's what's in it for you," the cure is as simple as the diagnosis:

The vendor has said "I"—instead of "You."

Sticking that word *you* into a headline, then again into the first paragraph of body copy, means benefit has to follow. "Now You Can . . . " is a can't-miss headline, because whatever tag-end you use will appeal to the Me-Myself-&-I assemblage.

On occasions when I've discussed the advantages of a "You" approach with other writers, occasionally I'll get an aggressive reply: "Aw, that's old-fashioned. It's a cliché." Invariably the person who rejects "you" as a cliché reverts to "I"—a communications disaster. I once suggested to an unexpectedly angry respondent who said, "Everyone is using *you* copy. We want to do something else," that the venerable *At Last!* by its very nature demanded benefit copy as the next line. This brought what students of rhetoric might send to Guinness as the ultimate squelch: "What's so new about 'At Last'?"

Thus we have this headline and subhead in a space ad for, believe it or not, a group of publication lists:

"Our brightest

star

is a dog."

—It's got a decidedly unfancy name: 'Sirius A'. Its
excellence is without equal. (For other tales of
PROFITABLE excellence, read on.)—

Aside from the cryptographic challenge of this message,
what reason do I have to read on? What's in it for me? Incidentally, I don't agree with a basic premise: *Sirius A* certainly is a
fancy name. How many people do you know named Sirius A?

The formula for benefit is better read by sellers of
personal-improvement products. It has to be, because *benefit* is
the entire sales story.

These marketers have learned that in the Age of Skepticism, mere announcement of benefit isn't enough. The formula
is a little more complex:

**FIRST ANNOUNCE THE BENEFIT. THEN TELL THE
READER HOW THE BENEFIT BENEFITS HIM.**

Odd formula, isn't it? To clarify, think of stating a general benefit, then splashing the center of that benefit with a
sunshine-bright statement of specific benefit.

Here's an example, from a weight-reducing plan:

YOU'LL BE THE

ENVY OF OTHERS

106 Pounds in 5 Months

The Benefit/Benefit Rule came clear to me the day two
separate mailers from travel agencies came in the mail. The first
opened with a benefit—

We Deliver Your Ticket To You

—and continued with a specific of how the benefit works for
me—

You'll Never Stand in Line at a Ticket Counter Again.

I'd have written it a little differently, perhaps something
such as, "We think you're too busy to spend time standing in

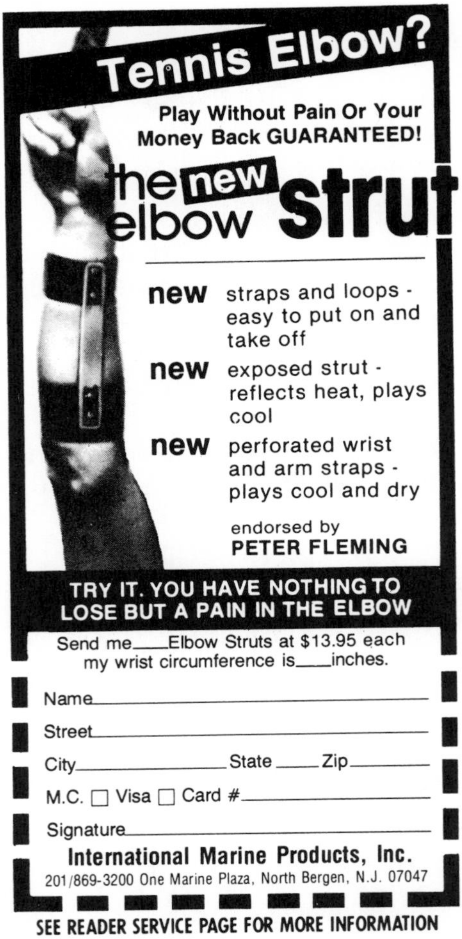

Figure 6.1 Here's proof! An ad needn't be huge and full of copy to make a point. The *benefit* is clear and credible in this 1/6-page ad.

line at the airport" (no, not " . . . too important," because that makes both the agency and me pompous), but the clarity of benefit is the point, especially compared with this standard piece of dull puffery from a competing travel agency:

FULL SERVICE

We are a full service Agency dedicated to doing much, much more than simply making your airline reservation.

We take care of your complete planning, including airline, hotel, and car rental arrangements, quickly and efficiently. This is our number one goal.

(A parenthetical note: Someday someone will program into every word processor a code that will kick out the word "goal" in a non-sports usage. Until then, we all had better watch it. It suggests inability to complete an action.)

The Benefit/Benefit Rule seems automatic for the writers of many of the ads in the weekly tabloids. Some are funny:

Date Your Dream Girl Within 5 Minutes
and PAY NOTHING NOW!

Some pile benefit on benefit. I like this one:

Amazing 20/20 'CLEAR-VUE 20/20 Glasses Let You
BEAT HEADLIGHT GLARE
Help You See In The Dark!
YES! ACTUALLY DRIVE THROUGH BLINDING RAIN,
HEAVY SNOW,
THICK MIST OR EVEN FOG WITH INCREASED
VISION AND SAFETY!

A Point of View Helps

One of the puzzling practices in copywriting is ignoring or omitting a corporate point of view. Great heavens, we're not dispassionate commentators, we're salespeople! Whether we command or cajole them, they respond better to words that don't have implicit thorns sticking out of them.

All of us *give* attention more readily than we'll *pay* attention for the same reason we respond better to *postage-free envelope* than to *postage-paid envelope*. When we have a choice of interchangeable words, let's choose the ones suggesting benefit or product superiority. This has nothing to do with clarity, but rather with reader receptivity.

The rule:

MAXIMIZE BENEFITS WITHIN THE LIMITS OF CREDIBILITY.

If we *think benefits* we won't write this sentence, which otherwise might infiltrate our space ad—

Rand McNally & Company
Russell L. Voisin, Vice-President
Business Products

Get the vital marketing data you need for 1984 business planning... without paying thousands of dollars for expensive information services. Here's how... Russ Voisin

Dear Executive:

Now that you're doing your 1984 business planning, you'll need facts and figures to determine market shares, buying trends, population centers, manufacturing centers and much, much more.

But there's no need to pay thousands of dollars in fees to high-priced information services.

Rand McNally has a data service that's just as comprehensive as the others, much easier to use...and a lot less expensive!

That's right, for just a fraction of the fees charged by other information services, you can lease the Rand McNally COMMERCIAL ATLAS & MARKETING GUIDE data service -- 580 pages of the most up-to-date marketing and commercial data anyone could supply you with, easily accessible in a book format.

Each year over 11,000 major corporations, government agencies, and libraries use the COMMERCIAL ATLAS data service.

Today's society is changing rapidly, so today's businesses demand accurate, timely information immediately. Well-informed, well-managed companies use the COMMERCIAL ATLAS & MARKETING GUIDE data service to plan new territories, evaluate weak sales areas, and look for places to increase their market share. Once you've looked over the COMMERCIAL ATLAS & MARKETING GUIDE, you'll know why so many companies lease it... and why they use it to out-think the competition and move ahead in the marketplace.

(over, please)

Figure 6.2 The handwritten overline promises me a benefit, but what is it? What "vital marketing data" is he talking about? Benefit comes from specificity, not generalized promises.

You'll have the chance to try this new "crash" weight-loss program.

The writer is innocent in the classic sense (artlessness) but guilty in the contemporary sense (thoughtless word choice). *Opportunity* removes the conditional, might-not-work Las Vegas gamble implicit in the word *chance*.

Aw, you might say, is that really important? It depends on your point of view. Words are the only tools we have, and using a less "chance-y" word is what separates us from those limited to basic English.

Key Words for Benefits

I never have understood why some investment houses and some dealers in silver and gold bullion use the word *chance* interchangeably with the word *opportunity*. They aren't parallel. "This is your chance to . . . " suggests only a 50-50 possibility of success; "This is your opportunity to . . . " is sure-fire.

An example of the proper use is this standard opening of a letter from The Bradford Exchange, which treats collectibles as investments:

An exciting short-term opportunity now exists on the booming limited edition collector's plate market . . . .

Some of the conservative investment houses, the recipients of whose letters may not know whether they're getting a recommendation or a dispassionate description, could lift some of the terminology from aggressive peripheral marketers. The Bradford letter in my hand has the word *exceptional* three times on its first page, a tactical mistake, but the phrase, "I'm writing to let you know about it while there's still time to act," has worked in direct mail for many companies for half a century. Other ageless imperations, such as "If you act promptly," "This is the only way I can assure you a . . . ", and "I'd hate to see you miss out," transmit and reinforce the two key selling arguments of *benefit*—

1. Only you
2. Only from us

Promptly, by the way, isn't a word I'd use. It's a cold word, and coolness opens a gap between writer and reader.

Other words that trigger the benefit reaction? Here are a few.

free
easy
for you
you pay only . . .
you'll be able to . . .
Be a . . .
Two weeks from now you'll . . .
Private invitation to . . .

"We make it possible for you to . . . " is better than "We enable you to . . . " I wouldn't have written the letter that begins, "This letter concerns a unique opportunity you have now as a Diners Club Member," because the word *concerns* derails the straight-on exposition of benefit and turns it to an oblique angle.

The Good, the Bad, and the Ugly

In our peculiar 1980s society, the word *benefit* alone can sometimes carry the day. We're so anxious to be special we accept the declaration of benefit even though the follow-up adds nothing to the mix.

For example, this letter wastes no time declaring benefit but makes a self-important assumption that *telling* me it's a benefit parallels *convincing* me it's a benefit. The letter opens cold:

The first benefit of your Associate Membership in the American Museum of Natural History is a year-round subscription to *Natural History* magazine—newly-expanded to 12 colorful, fascinating issues a year. This exceptional publication is *now read and enjoyed by over a million people each month.*

I know, I know, "Associate Membership" isn't the greatest motivator in the world. That isn't the point of this article. Reread this opening looking for benefit. Tough, isn't it?

Later in the same letter, we read:

Perhaps the finest benefit of all is the knowledge that through your membership support, you are helping carry on the incomparable research and education programs of one of the world's leading natural science centers.

Even if the Me Generation weren't firmly in place, I'd question the arrogant assumption that my support of this unquestionably worthy institution benefits *me* and not the institution itself. Some letters can generate a singular attitude of benevolence among readers who otherwise are as benevolent as a slug. This one is too cold and distant to do it for me.

Suppose someone said to you, "I have a personal registration number for you. It's 29,492,885." Would you feel singled out for benefit, or would you think you'd been transported in a nightmare to a Siberian work camp?

Here's the envelope benefit copy from a magazine/organization to which we already belong/subscribe:

> Join Smithsonian
> and see the world unfold!
> Receive, at no extra cost, the new
> Smithsonian Magazine Engagement
> Calendar being held for you under this
> Personal Registration Number.
> 29492885

My uncomfortable feeling of the NKVD being at my door is heightened, not dispelled, by the words "being held for you." Couldn't they have made me feel a little less captured?

The letter inside this envelope begins oddly, I think:

> Whenever you feel hemmed in by the routines and
> responsibilities of everyday life, join SMITHSONIAN
> and see the world unfold its wonders for you.

I understand the Peter Ibbetson Syndrome, but this seems farfetched. Compare it with this letter, which has printed across the top in big letters, "A special invitation to the hero of American business." The letter begins:

> Dear Entrepreneur:
> You're it!
> You're the kind of person . . . .

National Geographic Society

WASHINGTON, D.C.   20036

OFFICE OF THE EXECUTIVE VICE PRESIDENT

June 15, 1983

Each year at this time your Society
asks its members to renew their
memberships for the coming year.

Dear New Member,

The above request —— coming six months ahead of your membership expiration date —— may seem somewhat premature. But there's
a very good reason for it...one that benefits you.

By spreading out, over a number of months, the paperwork it
takes to process annual dues for nearly ten million members each
year, we can substantially lower our costs. And we pass the
savings on to you.

We call this annual inflation fighter
the Summer Renewal Plan. And for more
than four decades it has helped keep
your Society's dues at a minimum.

In 1984, for example, there will be
no increase in Society membership dues.

Compare the price of NATIONAL GEOGRAPHIC with that of other
magazines —— even those that do not feature such lavish use of full-
color photography. And, remember, only NATIONAL GEOGRAPHIC brings
at least four map supplements a year, which sell separately for
$3 each. That's a $12 value in maps alone!

Summer Renewal (along with sound management and healthy growth*)
is responsible for this remarkable value.

The enclosed folder explains more fully how the Summer Renewal
Plan helps keep dues low —— while actually providing more funds for
improving the magazine and for valuable worldwide research and explo-
ration. (Since 1973 the Society has sponsored more than 1,300 expe-
ditions and research projects.)

Please mail your membership dues for 1984 now, so we can continue to offer you the most value for your money.

*In the past ten years,   Sincerely,
 the Society has grown
 by nearly 3,000,000   *Quen R. Anderson*
 members.
                                 Executive Vice President

ORA/jd

Figure 6.3 Although the words *benefits you* are underlined, we can't find much benefit here except for the writer. Declaring "there will be no increase in Society membership dues" is as weak a benefit as I can think of—a benefit by default. It parallels the bank robber's statement of benefit: "Today I saved a bank from being robbed. I changed my mind."

Cologne Trade Fairs.
Your Guiding Lights to Success

Figure 6.4 The ad makes a claim but arrogantly makes no move to substantiate the claim. In an expensive magazine, the advertiser delivers a nonmessage.

This bright approach flatters me without becoming mawkish, incredible, or annoying. It's from *Inc.* magazine, and when it tells me, after a letter full of specific benefits, "This is the kind of information you'll find in every issue of *Inc.* And you won't find it anywhere else," I believe them.

This is in spite of an accompanying brochure with this stuffy copy on its cover:

Introducing

Inc.

The new magazine

that celebrates the courage,

dedication and spirit of

adventure that makes a

business succeed and

a nation stronger.

Maybe two different writers tackled the two components.

While we're on the point of magazines, *Vanity Fair's* revival has been the subject of heavy editorial comment, which made me more than casually interested in the original subscription mailer. The outer envelope was colorful and benefit-filled:

For the first time in nearly 50 years, there will be a
marvelous magazine called VANITY FAIR. Now you can
enjoy the premiere issue FREE without obligation.
Complete details inside.

Except for *there will be*, it's power loaded, which makes the opening of the letter even more puzzling:

"And the name of that town is Vanity; and at the town
there is a fair kept called Vanity Fair."
                    (John Bunyan, *The Pilgrim's Progress*)
"Yes, this is Vanity Fair . . . There are scenes of all sorts:
some dreadful combats, some grand and lofty horse-
riding, some scenes of high life, and some of very
middling indeed; some love-making for the sentimental,
and some light comic business; the whole accompanied
by appropriate scenery and brilliantly illuminated . . . "
                    (William Makepeace Thackeray, *Vanity Fair*)

**GORDON
LIST RENTALS**

Gordon Publications, Inc. ● (201) 361-9060
P.O. Box 1952, Dover, N.J. 07801-0952

August 26, 1983

Mr. Herschell Lewis
Communicomp
9748 Cedar Villas Blvd
Plantation FL. 33318

Dear Mr. Herschell Lewis:

Productivity. In the eyes of your clients, all other
criteria for measuring advertising effectiveness pale by
comparison to productivity. What response do they get for
what they spend?

Productivity is the raison d'etre for Gordon List Rentals.
We rent names and addresses of professionals who are proven
responders. Pure and simple.

We put you in touch with the highly-qualified subscribers to
our high tech, industrial, medical and scientific magazines.
Over 600,000 in all, that can be selected by almost any
method you wish: title, industry, geography, size, nth name,
etc.

And we extend to you, as a recognized advertising agency
representing a user/client, a 15% commission on the base
rental price on all orders placed with us.

Keep thinking productivity, and keep Gordon List Rentals in
mind when you do. If you would like more information or our
free 1983 catalog, please call 201-822-0710 or return the
enclosed business reply card.

Thank you,

Nila Sodano
Account Executive
518 Green Village Road
Green Village NJ 07935
201-822-0710

Figure 6.5 The writer didn't sign the letter, but I don't feel offended; I
do feel the computer-personalized message might have grabbed my
interest if it substituted a benefit for the meaningless word
"productivity."

What an antique overtone this splashes onto the glossy publication that calls itself "a magazine of excellence and innovation." On the other hand, the magazine says it's "as complex and contradictory as the times we live in," and maybe that's the point they're making here.

The Rule of Negative Subtlety

I'm being wry with that last observation, but we can't impart benefit unless we state it, which means we should dig in the rhetorical mines for a rule to govern our use of this powerful sales weapon.

I call this the Rule of Negative Subtlety:

DON'T MASK BENEFIT WITH SUBTLETY. BENEFIT IS WHY THE RECIPIENT IS READING WHAT YOU'VE WRITTEN, SO STATE IT CLEARLY AND DIRECTLY.

We sometimes ignore this rule because we can't shift our cleverness into overdrive when we use it, but how could the benefit of what Standard & Poor is selling be put any more clearly than this:

> Are you making any of these 7 common mistakes in investing?
>
> Some of the most successful investors in America have pocketed thousands of dollars in profits simply by following seven time-proven principles. This is your opportunity to be guided by those principles . . . and to claim a remarkable $29.95 bonus for yourself.
>
> Dear Investor:
>
> By avoiding the mistakes outlined below, you could put yourself in a position to turn a handsome profit over the years regardless of temporary market "reactions . . . . "

The Rule of Negative Subtlety applies to individual words as much as it does to sentences, paragraphs, and whole letters, brochures, and ads.

An example is this overline in yet another magazine subscription mailing:

You are invited to explore an exciting new world of expressive living as a Charter Subscriber to

METROPOLITAN

HOME™

magazine

What's that word *expressive* doing in there? Suppose someone asked you to define *expressive living*. Could you do it?

Benefit is one of the cornerstones of direct marketing. If you still think you needn't watch your words when you transmit benefit, you've missed the chance this book presented concerning this exceptional chapter, now read and enjoyed by over twelve Sirius people each edition . . . each of whom has been awarded Personal Registration Number 29492885.

7

Easy-to-Use, Can't-Fail Writing Tools and Crutches

The First Easy Tool—
Testimonials: A New Golden Age

When Pat Boone stubbed his white buckskinned toes on an endorsement for Acne-Statin skin treatment and was ordered by the FTC to make a personal refund of 25 cents to each purchaser, endorsements and testimonials lost their golden glow for direct marketers.

Few selling weapons have the potency of testimonials, and now this form of descriptive enhancement is back with such strength and frequency that it's surely worthy of dissection.

Is the venerable Art Linkletter type of endorsement/ testimonial being replaced by more credible, less cynical product praise? Only in part. Direct marketers can choose from a broader group of testimonial types, but, no, good old Art for Art's sake is certainly not in eclipse.

Students of this facet of selling by mail should recognize four distinct types of testimonials (I'm combining endorsements and testimonials, which I wouldn't do in a full-day seminar on this subject):

1. The *Straight* Testimonial, which has two subdivisions—
    (a) the *Celebrity* Testimonial, and
    (b) the *Authority-Expert* Testimonial
2. The *Unidentified* Testimonial
3. The *Self* Testimonial
4. The *Bulk* or *User* Testimonial

Each has specific use and value, and making the right decision about which one to use and when to use it can have a profound effect on the credibility and pulling power of your mailing, ad, or commercial.

Figure 7.1 If you read the advertising trade publications, you'll see lots of ads like these. As cynical as the whole concept is, none of the ads gives us a clue as to why McDonald's, in mid-1983, used stern-visaged John Houseman as hired spokesman. Imagine the terror he must have struck in the hearts of children used to gentle Ronald McDonald! It's not as though we have a shortage of celebrities-for-hire.

The Straight Testimonial

The Straight Testimonial has advantages unmatched by any other type of testimonial: it's easy to write, it's credible to the message recipient, and it's usually easy to understand. It's also by far the most common type of testimonial, especially since it comes in two flavors, the Celebrity Testimonial and the Authority-Expert Testimonial.

All of us in this business know that celebrities often are for sale. They usually don't much care what the product is—witness the Joe Namath appearances for panty hose—and they usually are willing to regurgitate the words put into their mouths, or, better yet, sign a statement. While it helps to have sports celebrities endorse a sports product, such thoughtfulness isn't mandatory, especially since other types of celebrities, usually from other fields of entertainment, don't have a specialized talent that might match your product or service.

A recent ad "From America's Top Sports Celebrity Service" offers Lou Piniella, Vince Ferragamo, and John Havlicek (whose names I recognize), along with Jack "Hacksaw" Reynolds, Dwight Clark, Phil Simms, and Rob Carpenter (whose names, I admit with non-jock chagrin, I don't recognize).

I also recently saw a photograph of the marketing development manager of a company called Ilsco Corp., which sells electrical connectors, and their newly signed celebrity, Jimmy the Greek, who has been hired to say, "Odds are Ilsco has the product." Pure hucksterism! To the exasperated copywriter who has fished in the unfriendly and icy waters of logic, looking for a selling argument based on reason, this campaign would make just as much sense as hiring Xaviera Hollander to say, "I'll lay you eight to five Ilsco has the product."

In that particular campaign is the question any copywriter should ask himself, herself, or itself about celebrities. Daniel J. Boorstin once said, sagely, "A celebrity is someone who is well-known for his well-knownness." Are we using a celebrity because we have *no* product advantage?

A warning to all of us, including me: Let's not allow our own cynicism to blindfold us, preventing us from seeing reality. Were they contemporaries, Marilyn Monroe surely would outdraw James Monroe at a fund-raising event, and if the writ-

Figure 7.2 The problem with some celebrity testimonials is that their dependence on the celebrity, instead of specifics, neutralizes the impact. We don't believe celebrities as much as we did before the Age of Skepticism tainted our credibility, and this testimonial gives us nothing on which to chew except a star name—not enough.

ing were at all sane and sensible, her name would pull more direct response leads than an "I like it" from our fifth president.

Celebrity or Authority?

The reluctant conclusion: a Celebrity Testimonial, on the consumer level, probably will outpull an Authority-Expert Testimonial. If I had to reduce this to a rule, it would be—

THE VALUE OF AN AUTHORITY-EXPERT TESTIMONIAL, COMPARED WITH THE CELEBRITY TESTIMONIAL, IS IN DIRECT RATIO TO THE MESSAGE RECIPIENT'S KNOWLEDGE OF THE PRODUCT BEING SOLD.

So it's correct for a mail order ad for the *New Grove Dictionary of Music and Musicians* to quote octogenarian composer Virgil Thomson, " . . . let us all be grateful to Grove"; Thomson would mean nothing as endorser of the *Encyclopedia of Country Music*. Gourmet James Beard logically gives a mild endorsement to Omaha Steaks in premium/incentive publications ("Omaha Steaks are everything I expect a good steak to be"), but in mass-oriented publications an athlete or entertainer, with greater recognition value, would have greater impact—*unless* within the mailing or ad itself is an educating biography telling the reader, "Look who said this!"

In a mailing, the *cross-reference technique* can cause your authority-expert's credentials to be accepted and swallowed whole by the reader. This is as simple as referring to the individual in the letter with the suggestion that the reader look for the quotation by that individual elsewhere in the mailing: "Art critic Joseph Glutz, for one, was impressed by this work. Some of his comments are reprinted in the brochure I've enclosed."

If Joseph Glutz has credentials beyond being the paste-up artist for this mailing, his title might be expanded to "The well-known art critic, Joseph Glutz." If he really *is* well known, he's worth, "You undoubtedly know the reputation of Art Critic Joseph Glutz, editor of *Southwestern Art Monthly*. His comments about this are worth reading."

Some quotable people qualify both as celebrities and as authority-experts. *Washingtonian* uses Congressman Jack Kemp,

"...the greatest musical dictionary ever published."
Charles Rosen, *N.Y. Review of Books*

The gift of a lifetime for anyone who loves music.

"...20 vast volumes excellently produced, crammed with scholarship, magnificently illustrated, a profound pleasure to handle."
Anthony Burgess, *Quest*

"...let us all be grateful to *Grove.*"
Virgil Thomson, *Notes*

"...a constant joy"
"....again and again, looking up one entry, I have been caught by others, which have kept me engrossed until long past midnight." Desmond Shawe-Taylor, *The New Yorker*

Figure 7.3 Although words such as "greatest" and "a constant joy" are nondescriptive weakeners, names such as Charles Rosen, Anthony Burgess, and Virgil Thomson are implicitly authoritative, especially to those who might be interested in *The New Grove Dictionary of Music and Musicians.*

CONGRESSMAN JACK KEMP READS THE WASHINGTONIAN

"Joanne and I never miss an issue of *The Washingtonian.* It is consistently very informative, entertaining, and provocative."

Representative Jack Kemp of New York, chairman of the House Republican Conference, member of the appropriations and budget committees, and rising figure on the national political scene.

The Washingtonian is increasingly must-reading among White House officials, members of Congress, and business leaders. A 1981 survey of 22 city magazines by Don Bowdren Associates ranked *Washingtonian* readers first in median income, first in education, and first in time spent reading the magazine. And it's a very active audience: 38 percent communicated with a public official last year, 25 percent addressed a public meeting, 23 percent took an active role in a civic or social issue, 32 percent are active in civic or charity work.

The Washingtonian is one of the nation's fastest-growing magazines, with advertising last year up 229 pages. *The Washingtonian's* paid circulation (ABC audited) of over 110,000 has an average household net worth of $233,290 and a median household income of $50,470, surpassing the *New Yorker* ($41,548), the *New York Times* magazine ($31,378), and *Smithsonian* magazine ($30,079). With a metropolitan area household penetration of over ten percent, *The Washingtonian* leads all city and regional magazines in market penetration.

THE WASHINGTONIAN
reaches the people who count

Figure 7.4 One of the few who qualify as both celebrities and authorities, Congressman Jack Kemp is a coup as the testimonial giver for the *Washingtonian.* As the flag behind him says so aptly, "Excelsior!"

who says, "Joanne and I never miss an issue of the *Washingtonian*. It is consistently very informative, entertaining, and provocative."

The *Washingtonian* quote brings to mind one of the two caution flags that should attend the choice of spokesperson: First, match the testimonial to the intended message recipient. Jack Kemp is a perfect match for this magazine; regardless of availability, he wouldn't be logical for the *New Republic* (philosophical mismatch) or *Grit* (lack of recognition plus implicit distrust).

Second, without identification, the testimonial giver may weaken the sales argument rather than enhance it. Publishing house Harcourt Brace Jovanovich uses this copy:

> John Irving calls Gunter Grass "Simply the most original
> and versatile writer alive . . . You can't be called well-
> read today if you haven't read him."

John Irving isn't as well known as Gunter Grass; in my opinion his comment helps the sale of the advertised book *(Headbirths)* less than a single line of copy—"The most original and versatile writer alive."

The Unidentified Testimonial

The Unidentified Testimonial has this major advantage over other types: it's the easiest, least troublesome to create.

A space ad for a company offering free products by mail has this boxed quote:

> "If I hadn't received every one of these great gifts I
> wouldn't believe it myself."

Who said that? No one and anyone. It's an unidentified testimonial which, as product puffery, really doesn't need identification.

"Las Vegas Has It All!"

This headline, used by the Las Vegas Convention and Visitors Authority, becomes an unidentified testimonial because it's within quotation marks. As copy it's nondescript, but it gains power by *appearing to be* a testimonial.

The unidentified testimonial seems to be common to

meeting sites. The Philadelphia Centre Hotel uses this:

"Never has a Philadelphia hotel given so much to so
many for so little."

The province of Manitoba:

"Manitoba country . . . a great place to explore."

Harrah's, which has hotels in Las Vegas and Reno:

"Harrah's gives you Star Treatment."

Without the quotation marks, these are simply dull
headlines. With the quotation marks, they're unidentified
testimonials—still dull, by the way.

Since the source of the quotation isn't disclosed, anyone
could have said it. I'm consistently puzzled by unidentified testimonials whose endorsement factor is room temperature. As
long as we're using the device, why not use it effectively? It's
like breaking into a bank vault and taking one bag of pennies.

The advantage of the Unidentified Testimonial is that
it's always available; you never again need lapse into obvious
puffery.

The Self Testimonial

The Self Testimonial is even more available than the
Unidentified Testimonial. The source is—yourself.

An example of this type of testimonial:

"Never In Our History Have We Offered Such Values In
Vitamins!"

—Leonard Clifton, President

Marriott Hotels and Helmsley Hotels regularly use the
Self Testimonial as key headline copy in their space advertising. Here's one example by Marriott:

"When you want to reward them with sunny pleasures,
we do it right."

—Bill Marriott, President,

Marriott Corporation

The message isn't particularly powerful nor clear, but
the concept couldn't be clearer. The testimonial endorsing the

"When you want to reward them with sunny pleasures, we do it right."

—Bill Marriott, President, Marriott Corporation

Some meetings are designed to reward special achievements. Marriott has vibrant resort hotels just made for those special meetings. They may be a little more exclusive, a little more exotic. But for the right people, they're worth it.

Every Marriott Resort has flexible meeting space and facilities. Your meeting will rate the personalized attention of a Convention Manager, first-class catering, and faultless audiovisual equipment.

Marriott's world-class restaurants have chefs who've built menus around regional specialties. And, of course, they have swimming, tennis, golf, night life and the kind of Marriott service that's won Marriott Hotels more 4-star awards from the prestigious Mobil Travel Guide than any other hotel company in the world.

Coordinate your meeting with a resort in its off-season, and your group gets that indulgent do-it-right service at a significantly lower rate —a great value!

For an armchair tour of any of the resorts seen here, or in Hilton Head, S.C., Lincolnshire, Ill., Maui, Hawaii, Lexington, Ky., Ft. Lauderdale, Fla., Vail, Colorado, Mt. Shadows-Scottsdale, Ariz., or Newport Beach, Cal., simply call toll-free (800) 228-9290.

Marriott Hotels

Figure 7.5 As hoteliers become celebrities—a frantic trend we can trace all the way back to Conrad Hilton—the self testimonial becomes more and more commonplace. The relationship between Bill Marriott's quotation and the body copy isn't clear: Did he say that, too, or is someone else gilding his lily?

hotel comes from Bill Marriott or Leona Helmsley or a corporate executive who can use the Self Testimonial to heighten his or her profile and add validity to the selling argument at the same time. Were Gunter Grass to be quoted in a Harcourt Brace Jovanovich ad, "I think *Headbirths* is even better than *The Tin Drum*," my opinion is this testimonial would be stronger than the outside quotation the company used.

Is the Self Testimonial self-synergising? I'd say yes. The effect of a single sentence of self-pollination is more than double the effect of two separate sentences of puffery. The reader accepts the posture of the company spokesman as someone whose testimony is authoritative; in turn, the authoritative testimonial helps sell merchandise, which makes the individual actually more authoritative. Confusing, but probably true.

The Bulk or User Testimonial

I admire those whose copy uses this type of testimonial, because they've done some homework. Either they've sorted through correspondence, sifting out laudatory messages, or they've sent questionnaires to buyers, soliciting comments.

Whatever the technique for acquiring testimonials, the copy platform these sturdy planks build is unassailable. These aren't outside endorsers, paid for their platitudes; they're real, live users.

In bulk, such testimonials resemble ads for political candidates, loaded with names. The intention is to transmit a bandwagon effect—*everyone* who ever tried this is ecstatic.

How many names do you need to qualify for creative bulk rate? Six or eight will do it. The bulk effect comes from the power of the copy overline above the group of testimonials, plus layout suggesting there would be a greater number if only space were available.

The differences between the Bulk Testimonial and the User Testimonial are two:

1. The Bulk Testimonial should quote a maximum of one sentence from each individual and should list name and city.
2. The User Testimonial should underscore the main selling arguments and should list initials and city or state.

End the Pain and Misery of Tired Aching Feet

No matter how long you've suffered — be it three months, or 30 years. No matter what your problems are—corns, calluses, pain in the balls of your feet, burning nerve endings, painful ankles, old injuries, backaches, or just plain sore aching feet.

When you slip a pair of Feathersprings® into your shoes your pain will vanish almost instantly. You'll be able to stand, walk, dance, even run in miraculous total comfort!

What are Feathersprings?
Well, they're a revolutionary foot support unlike anything you've ever seen before. Each pair is custom hand-formed and made for your feet alone.

How do Feathersprings work?
Unlike conventional, mass-produced devices, they actually imitate the youthful, elastic support Nature intends your feet to have.

What do Feathersprings look like?
They're all but invisible. Men and women can even wear them with open-backed sandals. And because you can change them from one pair of shoes to another, one pair is all you'll ever need.

How many people have Feathersprings actually helped?
As of today, over 2,250,000 people of all ages with all types of foot, leg and back problems, are enjoying blessed relief they never thought possible.

How do I know Feathersprings will help me?
We are so certain that Feathersprings Foot Supports will bring you relief

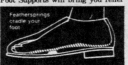

with every step you take, that if they don't work for you . . . we'll refund your money in full with no questions asked.
Don't needlessly suffer pain and discomfort for another day. If your feet are killing you, Feathersprings will bring you relief. Write us for more detailed information. There is no obligation. No salesman will call. Just fill out and mail this coupon. Remember, you have nothing to lose but your pain.

What people have to say about Feathersprings . . .

"Received my wife's Feathersprings two days ago. They are super-neither of us can believe the results. She has had terrible feet for years; already no pain. Incidentally, her sore knee is better . . . As a retired physician, this result is amazing."
Dr. C.O.C., Tucson, Arizona

"I was extremely skeptical when I placed my order, and was expecting to be disappointed. Much to my surprise, I found almost immediate relief from knee and leg pains and corns on my right foot which were a source of continuing pain and irritation have ceased to trouble me."
J.C.J. Meridian, Miss.

. . . "At the present time I still wear the Feathersprings and indeed they perform well after seven years of use."
G.M.G., Dallas, Texas

*Posed by professional models
© 1982 Featherspring International Corp. 13100 Stone Avenue, North, Seattle, Washington 98133

FEATHERSPRING INTERNATIONAL CORPORATION
13100 Stone Avenue North, Dept. P162
Seattle, Washington 98133
YES! I want to learn more about Flexible Featherspring Foot Supports. Please send me your free brochure. I will watch for the large PINK envelope. I understand that there is no obligation and that no salesman will call.

Print Name
Address
City   State   Zip
When in Seattle visit the Featherspring Building.

Figure 7.6 To achieve verisimilitude, this advertiser added stock photos to the testimonials. The line "Posed by professional models" is hidden under the text; the technique, designed solely to make the testimonials more believable, is a good one.

Why not street address? Because of the harassment factor. It isn't just crackpots who write or phone your endorsers; if my name appears in your ad and I live in Walnut Grove, I can expect calls from people whose telephones can reach Walnut Grove without a toll charge. My opinion is that city is more valid than state and is reasonably trouble free for trade and professional ads, but if I'm rolling out nationally or placing a campaign in a thousand newspapers, everyone will rest easier if I use state instead of city.

Since the difference between Bulk and User is quantity, users have a higher profile. Effective user testimonial copy can lean on a single quotation; more than four or five, and you shift into the bulk mode. The specificity that makes a user's comments valuable also makes that user a target for questions or objections, and depending on the media or mailing schedule, initials may be safer than names.

Verisimilitude used to demand an asterisk next to the initials, with the legend "Names and addresses on request"; I've come to think in the Age of Skepticism, that when you suggest the reader doesn't trust you, the reader concludes you wouldn't suggest this unless you'd laced your offer with half-truths, and instead of generating verisimilitude your asterisk is the euthanasia injection helping to kill it.

Vigor, Truth, and Muscle

Testimonials add vigor, truth, and muscle to a selling argument. But if you're using them, using them properly is no more difficult than misusing the technique. Here are two examples, both User Testimonials for a magazine called *Moneysworth*:

Your advice on Social Security resulted in a $3,135 lump-sum cash payment to my wife and $171 monthly pension. The best investment I ever made was my subscription to *Moneysworth*.

(Dr. Herman Hortop; La Grange, IL.)

Moneysworth is aptly named. To paraphrase Churchill, never have so many paid so little for so much.

(Dave Alpern; Pittsburgh, PA.)

Which of these has greater impact? The first. Even the dollar amounts are good. $3,135 is more believable than $5,000. $171 monthly pension is two leagues up from "an increased monthly pension." The second testimonial can't compete with the specifics of the first.

Two quick rules about testimonials, to join the Relative Value Rule:

1. IF YOU USE SOMEONE'S NAME IN PRINT, EVEN THAT OF SOMEONE IN YOUR OFFICE, GET WRITTEN PERMISSION.

2. IN TESTIMONIALS, AS IN ALL DIRECT RESPONSE COPY, SPECIFICS OUTPULL PUFFERY.

Testimonials help the undecided to decide. They weaken sales resistance. They help make an offer appear to be true. For example—

> Copy Pro Herschell Gordon Lewis says, "This book surely qualifies as one of the 100 best I ever wrote!"

The Second Easy Tool— ## Ask a Question

A client who came to me because he specifically wanted ads with more reader involvement inspected my copy, shook his head, and said, "What would you say if I told you I don't like to start a selling argument with a question?"

My answer was automatic: "I'd say you just started a selling argument with a question."

In my opinion, not only are questions valid weapons for adding power and personalization, they're the oldest form of selling argument.

The best-known and longest-running ad of all time began with a question—"Do You Make These Mistakes in English?" For the Sherwin Cody School, the ad ran for 45 years.

Way back behind Sherwin Cody was a man named Socrates, who perfected the technique of winning arguments by asking questions. The Judeo-Christian Bible swarms with questions, as often asked to make a point as to gather information ("What is truth?").

Using questions in headlines will generate vicious opinions, pro and con. Defenders point out the benefit of reader involvement—"Questions literally force the reader into the ad." Detractors point out the antagonism that can result from disturbing passive tranquillity—"Casual readers hate to be challenged."

When to Challenge

I lean toward the pros, not the cons, because what we're supposed to be doing in direct response is disturbing passive tranquillity; if we don't disturb it, our message is unread. The obvious qualifier for this viewpoint is: It depends on the question.

"Are You Impotent?" isn't as salesworthy a headline as "90 percent of All Impotency Is Temporary." Another type of question, "Mocatta Options—What Are Those?" is superior to the expositional "The Benefits of Mocatta Options."

There's a rule here, and it's a simple one:

PEOPLE RESPOND TO CHALLENGES THAT DON'T SUGGEST INCAPABILITY.

That's the brilliance of the venerable John Caples ad, "They Laughed When I Sat Down at the Piano." Had he written, "Do They Laugh When You Sit Down at the Piano?" his challenge would have suggested a deficiency in the reader rather than the writer, who must be scapegoat/surrogate in such circumstances.

"There Are 101 Ways to Own Silver. Do You Know the Best?" skips easily across the delicate tightwire bridging the never-never land between put-down questions that insult and unusual information that piques interest. This particular question appeals to a basic human desire—to test knowledge. How many of us turn down the volume when the radio announcer is about to tell us the title of the next symphonic recording?* How many of us kibitz crossword puzzles and join in "trivia" quizzes enthusiastically?*

---

*Gotcha! You're reading this footnote because I asked a question.

As a guess, 100 percent.

Challenging without insulting can appeal to two of the four great Motivators of the 1980s.

Do you remember the four great Motivators?

They're *Fear, Greed, Guilt,* and *Exclusivity*. A challenge can hit the emotional solar plexus, smack between Guilt and Exclusivity, and the result can be far greater reader involvement than one can generate through straightforward exhortation. Which headline would cause you to look closer?

There Are 11 Presidents' Pictures in This Drawing.

or,

Can You Find 11 Presidents' Pictures in This Drawing?

We've issued the challenge without throwing in the clunker of an insult. I've seen a lot of ads lately that begin, "I Dare You . . . " and somehow these seem a little desperate, a little sweaty, a little disquieting. The reader might take your dare, but he won't like you very much.

If you write, "I Dare You to Find 11 Presidents' Pictures in This Drawing," he might look and look and then smirk, "I found 'em, smart guy." You've made contact, but you haven't made a friend. It's like the bully kicking sand in the face of a 97-pound weakling and then selling him a Charles Atlas course.

The headline for an ad selling a security system hidden in an attaché case is:

Bugged?

I dislike a play on words. It's contrived, and, worse, it's unclear. That isn't the point here. The question makes the rest of the headline readable:

The Secret Connection Briefcase

What if that second line were the entire headline? Who'd pay any attention to it?

Questions Involve the Reader

A question is more logical and more effective in a letter or a space ad than in a brochure or a television commercial. Why? Because a letter has as part of its *raison d'etre* reader involvement, and a space ad must stop the reader as his eyes scurry over the page. Within a brochure, with the mighty exception of a question-and-answer section, questions can damage the strength of a sales argument.

This isn't an absolute, since a great many brochures begin with provocative questions. Within the brochure, a question-and-answer section is a tested, proved defanger of skepticism, especially if one of the early questions seems artlessly candid.

Starting a television mail order commercial with a question can be a mistake, for two reasons: The viewer isn't expecting to be challenged, and before his brain goes into gear the point has flown past him. One way a question technique *is* effective on television is using the *Surrogate Rule* which began with "They Laughed When I Sat Down at the Piano."

A third person, representing the viewer, asks questions which are answered either on camera or voice-over. The viewer can follow the dialogue without losing the thread and can identify with the questioner without embarrassment. A split screen, with questioner on the left and the illustrated answer on the right, is a 21st century version of the Socratic dialogue.

How about envelopes?

My opinion is that hurling down the gauntlet on the outer envelope is iffy. Socrates himself would have trouble with interrogative envelope copy. (Come to think of it, Socrates probably *would* provoke antagonism, because his specialty, exposing others' ignorance through pointed questions, wouldn't land him a creative director's job in a direct mail company.) If you want to test the waters, don't (at least on the outer envelope) ask a question that can be answered (a) "No," or (b) "Who cares?" The envelope should grab interest, not pick a fight, and that's why the wrong type of question can trigger a "round file" reaction.

Which Questions Are Best?

What type of question is best?

Since no one has ever formulated rules before, all this is opinion. They become rules only when you've tried them and you agree with them.

First, I'd avoid the subjunctive. "What if . . . " is weak and can hurt your selling argument because it denies actuality.

"What if I told you that . . . " is hypothetical, and it's a transparently phony question as well. This type of question has less power than a direct statement.

"Have you ever . . . " is a dangerous way to start a question. Unless the reader knows you, he's likely to reply either "No, I've never . . . " or "None of your business."

The best type of question is a direct but nonthreatening challenge, such as this:

What's the name of the one man who can ruin both of us with one phone call?

or,

Interest rates are out of sight. Can you still make money by investing in land?

Remember the "Five W's and an H" from journalism school—*who, what, when, where, why,* and *how*? They're usually safe question openers, provided you don't lapse into the subjunctive—"What if . . . " or "When might you . . . " or "Where could . . . "

If you're selling a product, "who" or "what" is better than "why," because "why" suggests thought/work. For services, "why" comes into its own; the implied benefit of services is more emotionally presented, and "why" is an emotion-spawning word.

"Where" is a universal trouble-shooter. It heads easily into product-sell, and it's a good "starter" word for those who haven't used questions before:

"Where can you go to . . . :" "Where can you find . . . "

Psychologists have told us for years that if we want someone to think we're interested in him, or her, ask a question, especially one relating to that person's field of interest. Why can't we direct response writers learn and use what so many others already know?

The Third Easy Tool—
Parallel Logic

A benchmark of the Age of Skepticism is implicit rejection of any advertising claim.

"Prove it," says the target buyer, his Doubting Thomas response predetermined. "How?" asks the frustrated advertiser. "With parallels," says the logician.

I embrace the professional application of parallel logic, because this is a howitzer in the ongoing battle against skepticism.

What, you ask, is parallel logic?

PARALLEL LOGIC IS THE RHETORICAL KNOT TYING AN UNPROVED CLAIM TO A KNOWN FACT.

We've all seen examples of parallel logic. We've all used it in arguments. We may have seen the kid who sits in the back row, whose command of language is nominal, win a school debating contest because he knew how to create a parallel argument.

What we haven't done is codify some rules of parallel logic, to enable us to achieve deliberately what up to now we've accomplished intuitively.

I'll disclaim in advance: Someone poring through quaint and curious volumes of forgotten lore for two or three months might well uncover a dozen types of parallel logic other than the eight I'll mention. I justify incompleteness on the grounds of origination: Just as no runner would have bettered the four-minute-mile unless someone had started keeping records, so is it impossible to add to a list unless someone starts that list.

. . . Which I've just done. Reread the last sentence and you'll find the most common, easiest-to-create-and-use form of parallel logic.

Parallel No. 1: "Just as . . . So does . . . "

Examples? Since this is the most common parallel, you can find many:

> Just as Norman Rockwell mirrored the America of the 1930s and 1940s, so does Albertine Cordwainer's graphic wit reflect our own time.

or,

> Just as you were startled by the ingenuity of the first electronic calculator, which immediately and silently could divide 73,789 by 653, so will you be stunned by this "second generation" calculator which prints as it thinks any of its eighteen separate functions—and never loses your check balance while it's attending to another chore.

The *Just as . . . So does . . .* parallel needn't use those exact words. Implicit is just as strong as explicit. An example of the *Implicit "Just as . . . So does . . . "*:

> Once upon a time . . .
> Bing & Grondahl introduced a lovely collector plate featuring one of Hans Christian Andersen's fairy tales, "The Little Match Girl." It was their 1907 Christmas plate, and it sold for $1. (Today, its market value is $135.00!) . . .
> Today . . .
> *new* heights of beauty and enchantment have been reached in a momentous new series of fairy tale plates . . .

This example isn't a powerful one because the word parallel itself is incomplete: "new heights of beauty and enchantment" aren't word matches to the first paragraph. (The word "new," too, is overused.) But the implicit parallel is the point, not a particular piece of copy.

The second most common parallel is a kissin' cousin to the first.

Parallel No. 2: "If you . . . Then you'll . . . "

Lots of examples here too—

If you like wild, wacky, way-out comedy, then you'll
love the videotape society which will have you laughing
even as you realize how much you save on each
movie-tape . . . .

Omitting the "you" wording doesn't affect the parallel:

If baseball *cards* can be worth thousands of dollars,
imagine what *these* magnificent baseball memorabilia will
be worth in years to come . . . .

Even as we first recognize the power of parallels, we begin to see the abuse potential they share with all powerful
weapons: because parallels are credible arguments in the Age
of Skepticism, they can be corrupted to make sales points of
borderline validity. The *If . . . then . . . .* parallel is especially
vulnerable to this abuse, because it's custom-made for what I
call the *proofless comparison*:

Created with up to 20 different ceramic colors, Boehm
rose art appears so real that "only the fragrance is
missing."

So you can imagine that competition for their issues has
been very strong among collectors, resulting in *several
quick sellouts*. And whenever a first-issue plate sells out
rapidly, the competition transfers to the secondary
market . . . leading to active trading which can drive up
prices substantially in a short period of time.

Here are some examples of this, from a major plate
exchange's recent price quotes:

First Issue Plate	Issue Price	Quoted Price	Percent Increase
1965 Lalique Annual	$25.00	$1,700.00	6,700%
1968 Rorstrand Christmas	$12.00	$ 550.00	4,483% . . .

The claimed parallel just isn't there, but even in the Age
of Skepticism undoubtedly some readers will accept the *claim* of
parallel as (get this!) parallel to the *fact* of parallel. I don't criticize the practice; it's so widespread it's epidemic. I mourn, not
criticize, the overuse which within the next couple of years will
kill this golden-egged goose.

Meanwhile, let's enjoy such easy-to-write and always effective variations of the *If you . . . Then you'll . . . " parallel such as:*

You loved it at $12.95.

You'll *flip* now, because we've lowered the price to $9.95.

The word *if* isn't itself present; it's implicit in the thought. Put *If* before the first sentence and *then* before the second, and the meaning changes only to become conditional. An interesting variation! Unconditional is stronger than conditional, which means you might write your copy with *if*, then see whether eliminating it makes your prose even stronger.

Here's an *If . . . Then . . .* I find arresting, the opening of a letter selling dolls:

If you were to travel in a time capsule back through the centuries, no matter where you stopped, you would probably find a doll. In an Egyptian tomb . . . on a Greek altar . . . in a French couture salon . . . in an English drawing room . . . and, of course, in any nursery.

Throughout history, dolls have been revered . . . collected . . . and cherished. And today, doll collecting has emerged as one of the most important and best-loved of all hobbies . . . .

Some word problems here, especially *emerged*; still, you can see how *If . . . Then . . .* forces you to mount a coherent, logical, and compelling sales argument. It's one of those pleasant "can't miss" copy approaches.

One last example, from a label-machine manufacturer. The outer flap of the self-mailer has a photograph of a hand, peeling a label off a printout, plus this copy:

If the last stage of your computerized addressing system looks like this . . .

THIS IS THE MACHINE YOU'VE BEEN WAITING FOR . . . .

Parallel No. 3: The Touchstone Parallel.

A category rather than a single word use.

The *touchstone* uses a known person, place, product, or event to legitimize an unknown in the same field:

> In the 1920s you could buy Miami Beach land for a song. Well, maybe a song plus fifty to a hundred bucks.
>
> Within 25 years a whole opera couldn't buy one front foot.
>
> Start singing again! The legacy of "ground floor" land investment lives . . . .

Here's another *touchstone parallel.* I can't decide whether it's charming or crude:

> Bavaria first became famous for fine porcelain during the time of Wilhelm I (1797-1888), King of Prussia and the first sovereign of a united Germany. Under him, this state—the stepchild of the original German china centers of Saxonia, Thuringia, and Silesia—began its rise to pre-eminence among the porcelain-making regions of the German states. And today, the likeness of Wilhelm I is part of the emblem of Konigszelt Bayern and an assurance that the traditional standards of excellence which originally made Bavarian porcelain world-renowned have not been sacrificed to today's market needs.

Whew!

Parallel No. 4: "If they did . . . So can you."

This mighty argument probably is the strongest of all parallels, because it combines the great motivator Greed with what seems to be logical encouragement. A sweepstakes without an *If they did . . . So can you . . .* parallel is like a day without sunshine:

> These people won new cars . . . SO CAN YOU!
> WON A NEW OLDS—Brian Jones . . . .

Parallel No. 5: Quid pro quo.

I like "tit for tat" parallels because they're a challenge—hard to construct. Most *quid pro quo* parallels of the mid-1980s suggest a logical swap: "If you'll do this for me, I'll do that for you." Effective *quid pro quo* parallels don't insult your sense of proportion by suggesting a ridiculously easy quid for you and an impossibly generous quo for the vendor. They suggest equality:

> Give me one day and I'll save you thousands of dollars.
>> J. Franklyn Dickson
>> President
>> Ray Bloch Productions, Inc. . . . .

Or,

> Give me your meetings, your
> conventions and I'll give you my city.
>
> (An inquiry ad for New York City.)

Parallel No. 6: "What if . . . ?"

In my opinion this is the height of the parallel writer's art. A *what if . . . ?* parallel demands communicative skill beyond the ordinary, and we seldom see good examples like this one:

> Suppose you were given some brushes and tubes of oil, then told to paint a great picture. You probably wouldn't know how to begin.
>
> Yet some people assume that all you need to take a great photograph is a great camera. The plain truth is that *your equipment is only as good as your understanding of it!*

This copy, for a set of books on photography, exemplifies the difference between less dynamic standard "What if . . . " copy and the *"What if . . . ?" parallel*, which ties the provocative question to a pre-accepted base.

Parallel No. 7: "You'd expect . . . but it's really . . . "

I like this parallel because it approaches *comparative ad-*

vertising, one of the most effective techniques of force-communications in that other world where people buy from stores and dealers.

The *"You'd expect . . . But it's really . . . "* parallel is not only clear and precise; it has a two-legged foundation, one pillar set firmly in communication and the other in salesmanship. A space ad uses it this way:

Sturdy, Stackable Natural Beechwood Bookshelves
At a price you would expect to pay for plastic!

The parallel is reinforced in the body copy:

Do not confuse this item with "wood tone" or plastic imitations. Our low price is made possible by volume purchases, not by inferior material.

We can attack individual words—*item* and *purchases* seem lazily chosen, the first being nonspecific and the second an opening of the Pandora's box of distribution channels. But you can see how impact mounts. Another:

Your Friends Will Think You Paid $100 For Each Book!
And why not? They're genuine leather. They have exquisite moire end-sheets. They're printed on the finest acid-free paper. Each one has 32 pages of glorious color illustrations . . . .

Since I didn't write this I can attack the hyperbole of the copy, a mismatch for the product; Yet, even as I attack it I can see buyers who otherwise never would consider a book responding to this offer.

The same parallel inspired the writer of this two-page ad for—yup, books:

How did we do it?
We asked these three experts to
put a price on this edition of
Dickens' DAVID COPPERFIELD . . . .

The layout confuses the impact by yelling "$12.50" in 72-point type before we read the guesses of the three experts—$30, $35, and $35. The ad is still potent, and blame for diluted impact goes (of course) to the layout artist, not the copywriter.

Parallel No. 8: "The same (WHATEVER) as (WHOEVER) uses."

This parallel is an ersatz endorsement. It's on a par with our fourth parallel, *If they did . . . So can you.* Catalogs and small space ads can use it as a more-than-effective replacement for a hundred words of puffery. A space ad example:

The Mark of a True Book Lover

This is the same heavy duty embosser used by professional librarians to mark and identify books . . . .

Another (brochure copy):

EXACT REPLICAS

In size . . . in the very alloy of the fine steel . . . in the incredibly detailed inscriptions on the scabbard and the hilt . . . this is so perfect a replica Lord Wellington himself could never know which was his—and which was yours . . . .

Parallels are an excellent crutch for those days when the muse isn't with you but your word processor still must disgorge selling copy. I suggest you write the word "Parallel" in big black marker letters on a sheet of paper and hang that sheet on your mirror, against such an eventuality.

As for this quick primer on testimonials, questions, and parallel logic, I'd like to think it self-qualifies: *Just as* Samuel Johnson, Noah Webster, and Peter Mark Roget listed all the words you can use, *so does* this chapter give you some guideposts for stringing them together.

8

"Say It Again, Sam!"

Schlock Goes the Weasel

Weasel words are healthier than ever.

Let me make this absolutely clear, as a well-known user of weasel words used to say: I admire the writer who can use weasel words effectively. He operates from a bastion of imagination, and imagination is increasingly hard to find these days.

For those who just arrived from the planet Mars, I should explain what weasel words are:

WEASEL WORDS APPEAR TO BE A STRAIGHTFOR-WARD STATEMENT OF POSITION—BUT AREN'T. TO QUALIFY AS A WEASELED STATEMENT, A CLAIM MUST BE AT LEAST ONE-THIRD "HEDGE."

I grew up with one of the great, unchallenged weasel statements of advertising history: "99-44/100% Pure." This marvelous weasel claim is still in use today. How many straightforward expositions of fact have lasted that long?

But much as I admire a skillful user of weasel words, I'm itchy about a development of the mid-1980s: We seem to be spawning a generation of writers who use weaseling to *mislead*—and that isn't playing the game. Perhaps it's time to lay down some Rules for Effective Weaseling.

Before reading on, reread the last sentence of the last paragraph. It's a trap: the word *perhaps* is a weasel word, and if you slid over it, accepting the sentence as though the word weren't there, I've done a good job of weaseling.

On the very day you read this, *perhaps* a television spot is scheduled; it's the current commercial as of the deadline date for this book:

Peugeot—perhaps the smoothest-riding car in the world today.

I said I admire writers who have mastered the craft of writing weasel words. Sorry, I *don't* admire this, because it's primitive copywriter puffery, not inventive weaseling.

Even Weasels Have Their Rules

Want an example of inventive weaseling? Here's one that ran in *Parade*. In the middle of a powerful piece of copy selling inexpensive telephones is this gem:

> These new UDS Computer Telephones will not be sold
> at this price by the company in any store . . .

Did you miss it? The weasel in this sentence is the phrase *by the company*. In my opinion it's a brilliant job! What it says *isn't* what you think it says, but it's 100% (ar at least 99-44/100%) true. The company won't sell this in stores, because the company sells these phones only by mail. (The price was $9.95.) Nothing prevents *another* source from selling the phones in stores (in fact, another ad in the same paper, by a local retailer, offered pushbutton phones for $9.95).

From this beautiful example we can formulate the First Rule of Weaseling:

AN EFFECTIVE WEASELED CLAIM IS WRITTEN SO THE READER SLIDES PAST THE WEASEL WITHOUT REALIZING IT.

See why it's so difficult to do? Like hand-woodcrafting and home-baked bread, weaseling is a vanishing art. The club-footed stompers are trying to dance *Giselle,* and the lack of polish in their weaseling betrays them.

A trade bulletin shows the ponderousness of the worst kind of weaseling, the kind a government clerk might create if that clerk suddenly were appointed GS-13 Mail Order Copywriter:

> This might be considered the nearest approach to our
> new concept.

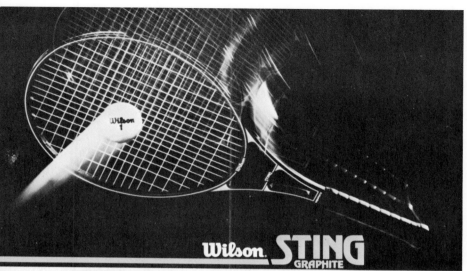

- 100% Graphite
- Fully oversized (no leading racket has a bigger sweetspot)
- Light weight and balanced light in the head for exceptional mobility
- Molded-on Urethane handle pallet reduces unwanted vibration

- Increased density string pattern. More string in the primary hitting area for a more solid response and a better feel
- Top quality high-tack leather grip for superior feel and maximum control

Figure 8.1 Look at the second bullet:"...no leading racket has a bigger sweetspot." Wilson has given us a *double* weasel by using the weasel word "leading" as an impenetrable qualifier and by using parity advertising instead of superiority: The claim *isn't* that this racket (racquet?) has the biggest sweetspot, but that's how we read it.

Nope. Too many qualifiers. The weasel is nakedly apparent. *Zero* in the ability to convince.

Words such as *rather, not really, well may be, just may be*—these are versions of *perhaps*. They aren't cause for rejection, but they aren't cause for applause.

On a purely critical level, I prefer the weaseling of a master politician. The best one I've heard came from the head of an airline machinists' union, who said, "We want to be flexible, but we aren't going to compromise." This type of statement is regarded as a perfect example of weaseling.

Did you catch that? Another trap! *Regarded as* is a good, gray, workmanlike weasel. Imaginative? No. Believable? Yes.

"He is regarded as the Audubon of the 1980s" isn't the work of a writer I'd ever hire, but it's credible.

That brings us to the Second Rule of Weaseling:

CREDIBILITY SHOULD BE THE MAIN PURPOSE OF WRITING WEASEL WORDS.

Some writers weasel for the sake of weaseling, and that's a sign of insecurity, fear of being nailed for flat statements that are true but that they can't prove, or—and please, friends, don't any of you hire a writer who commits this sin— arrogant playing with words because "those people" who read the ad or mailer are only marks in some carny game.

You can see how easy it is to lapse into sermonizing about weaseling. Few aspects of copywriting can excite such violent reactions, pro and con.

Some weasel words have been so overused they're better off unused. "Practically" is one of those. Readers have been trained, through generations of being misled by *practically*, to assume (unfortunately with justification) that the word is a dishrag thrown over an unprovable or borderline claim. A better word: *virtually*. A television commercial says, "New Joy lets dishes dry virtually spot-free." (The supporting video shows a dish that *is* spot-free, raising an interesting point of audio/video morality: If the claim says *virtually* but the illustration says *absolutely*, are we off the hook? Are we still weaseling or have we crossed the muddy border into flat claim?)

World Class Weaseling

The 37-volume "History of Weaseling" probably will begin in the ramshackle office of a used car dealer. Car dealers breed weasels the way some get-rich-quick ads would have you breed chinchillas.

Starting at . . . , from . . . . , (plus destination charge and dealer prep . . . , (60 months) . . . , pre-owned . . . , and the six-point-type *off* after the 48-point $1,000—these comprise the endearing and enduring legacy to the Weasel World from car dealers.

Car dealers also originated the once-great weasel, "No one sells for less," which, in various corruptions, has spread like Dutch Elm Disease to other facets of marketing. Financial institutions say, "No other bank gives you higher interest"; airlines say, "No one has lower fares." This technique is called *parity advertising*, and in fields where—because of government regulation or product sameness—no one can claim superiority, "We're as good as they are," properly presented, can actually generate a "We're better than they are" response.

It's the automobile manufacturers who carry the damnable responsibility for one of my least-favorite weasels: "If you can find a better (WHATEVER), buy it." Grounds for a boycott, it's that unimaginative!

A weasel hatched only within the past several years is the phrase *world class*. No one quite knows what it means, but *world* is the biggest there is, and *class*, aside from being what we all wish we had, is categorizing. I've seen so many *world class* ads lately that if they're all true a world class tennis player can put on his world class tennis wear, drive his world class car to a world class tournament, and use his world class racquet (or "racket") to lose the match before the entire peon-class world. Only when I heard a pianist described as a "world class accompanist" did I realize how far the herpes-like infestation of World Class Weaseling has progressed; we'll have to wait for it to burn itself out.

Loved These, Hated Those

Catch this weasel:

A booklet from a direct response marketing company, candidly titled "444 Begged, Borrowed, Stolen, and even a few Original! Direct Response Marketing IDEAS!" makes this offer:

> Permission to reproduce anything in this booklet is hereby granted, provided appropriate credit as noted is acknowledged.

See the weasel? These people want quote credit for ideas admittedly not their own. Questionable ethics.

Figure 8.2 A & B Is any product *not* world class? Here we have World Class Bars (precious metals, not liquor-serving) and a World Class 800-room hotel.

Here's a qualifier for the *New Yorker*'s "Awards We Doubt Ever Got Awarded Department":

> Waterbed Outlet has been awarded the highest rating by consumers for outstanding Waterbed values.

Generally, the "unidentified accolade" weasel is one we can do without. The writer isn't showing cleverness nor integrity, grist for the critics of direct response advertising. Here are several more examples of unidentified accolade weasels:

> One art authority has said that she has earned a place among wildlife artists of the first rank—such as the famous John James Audubon—in this most exacting of artistic genres.

Great heavens! This must be National Let's Exhume Audubon Month. Lots of problems with this copy, but the sickly weasel is the weakest. (I know, I know—*most exacting of artistic genres* is a close second.)

An ad in a meeting-planner publication makes this extraordinary claim:

> In Honolulu, everyone's talking about the same thing.
> The new Halekulani.

Are they, now? In that case there's no point having any news reporters in Honolulu—except the one from "That's Incredible."

The self-cancelling weasel is an unprofessional version of the machinist union leader's comment I quoted earlier. The difference is lack of finesse, which rips the camouflage off the weasel, stripping it of its ability to sell by deception:

> An unprecedented opportunity for the discriminating collector:

> You are cordially invited to become one of the select 20,000 people worldwide who will have the privilege of acquiring the first-ever collection of stamps officially issued simultaneously across the Commonwealth.

I know you see the first self-cancellation—*select* and *20,000* (there *is* a rhetorical way to make this huge a group seem select, but it isn't used here); but do you see the second? It's

"In Honolulu, everyone's talking about the same thing. The new Halekulani."

From October '83, meetings in Honolulu will never be the same again. Because now you can plan your meetings in a truly unique resort. The new Halekulani.

With consideration to the needs of the most exacting meeting planner, the Halekulani's 4,300 sq. ft. ballroom is divisible into two parts for simultaneous meetings, plus four break-out rooms. Overlooking the gardens and with a large balcony, the ballroom can entertain up to 500 people.

But rest assured, there will never be more than one selective meeting or conference in progress at the new Halekulani. For those discerning enough to choose this unique resort as a meeting venue, its exclusivity will be carefully preserved. If Honolulu's on your agenda from October '83, come and see what everyone's talking about.

To find out more, call Steve Maroney at 808-922-1651.

A REGENT® INTERNATIONAL RESORT

HONG KONG BANGKOK KUALA LUMPUR MANILA COLOMBO FIJI SYDNEY MELBOURNE ALBUQUERQUE NEW YORK CHICAGO PUERTO RICO HONOLULU MAUI MONTREAL

Figure 8.3 If you believe the headline in this ad, I have a nice bridge I'd like to sell you.

select and *worldwide*. The vastness of *worldwide* cancels any remaining seminal value of *select*.

I have this same feeling about this one:

Taro is pure protein. It also has a lot of carbohydrate.

The "hara-kiri" weasel intends to show benefit but inverts itself. Here's one in which the writer meant to emphasize exclusivity of source; instead, the copy opens a hornet's nest by suggesting you go comparison shopping:

Stores may have other, more expensive bird miniatures,
but they will not have these.

Why suggest what other vendors *do* have? The statement invites comparison shopping, and you raise an otherwise-quiescent question.

On the other hand, I enjoyed the ⅔-page magazine ad whose well-done weaseling began in the headline:

UNITED STATES TREASURY
MINTING ERROR*
Creates Rare Collecting Opportunity

The asterisk leads us to a boxed block of copy pointing out the "error"—the Susan B. Anthony $1 coin is about the same size as a quarter. An error in judgment, yes; an error in *minting*? Great weaseling, especially since millions of these coins have been minted. Why is it good? Okay, wise guys, decide what *you'd* have done if you, as writer, had the assignment of scrabbling around to find a selling proposition for these coins.

Can, May, and a Fit Conclusion

The words *can* and *may* are preludes to weaseling, and all of us use them. Sometimes it's because the lawyer tells us, "You can't say it works for everyone. You can only say it *can* work for everyone." Or, "You can't say, 'You'll be trim and fit.' You can only say, 'You can be trim and fit.' "

Can has force because in the minds of many readers it's interchangeable with *will*:

. . . This means that you—and any covered member of
your family—can have the best in medical care.

It means that *you may never need to worry again* about the
sky-high costs of serious illness or injury.

The reader interprets both *can* and *may* as *will*. The very
next paragraph is a masterpiece of weaseling:

This $500,000 Gold Card Protection pays
100% OF YOUR ELIGIBLE CUSTOMARY EXPENSES—
both in and out of the hospital!

The writer uses a diamond-tipped technique: *eligible*
and *customary* are masked by emphasis. Here's professional
weaseling, not a job for beginners.

You see how effective use of weasel words can build a
sales argument where none exists. But if you decide to dip a
pen into these frothy waters, watch out for the undertow. It's
strong, and it can pull you under. It's the core of the Third Rule
of Weaseling:

> **THE TEST OF THE DIFFERENCE BETWEEN EFFECTIVE
> WEASELING AND A DASTARDLY LIE SHOULD BE—IS
> ANYONE HURT BY BELIEVING YOU? IF YOUR AN-
> SWER IS A RELUCTANT YES, TRY ANOTHER TACK.**

Knowledge of what may be good or bad, what may be
effective or ineffective, and what may damage the reader as it
also may damage your reputation—this background in the use
of weasel words can make a difference in what well may be a
professional crossroads. For a wordsmith, this knowledge is regarded as 99-44/100% of world class writing.

How many weasels did you count in that last paragraph? If you're the winner you may get a trip to Hawaii—if
you can afford the fare.

Redundancies: Not Quite Weasels,
They're Just—Redundant

When I went to school, we learned that redundancies
are—well, redundant. A phrase such as "Free Gift" would get

you a "D" in a creative writing course. "Ever hear of getting a gift you paid for?" the instructor might snort.

The doubts set in about 20 years ago when I met a man who claimed to have written the screenplay for a movie titled, "The Giant Behemoth." In the classic snobbery of academia, I chided him: "Ever hear of a tiny behemoth? How about, 'The Giant Pygmy'? How about, 'The Great Big Giant Behemoth'?"

I still recall his anticipation of my objection. "The public wants the doubling and trebling of descriptions," he explained, with the quiet, edge-of-exasperation patience one grants to a not-quite-bright seven-year-old. "You tell them once, they doubt you. You tell them twice, they believe you."

This homily fell into limbo after I went to see the movie and failed to see the would-be guru's name among the screen credits. It revived a couple of years later when a more lavishly produced picture was released: "It's a Mad Mad Mad Mad World." Who needs four Mads? Yet, if one tries out the title with fewer Mads, it doesn't quite work.

The same reaction is generated by "Free Gift," the redundancy accepted by many direct response writers and critics who reject out of hand such brilliant double clichés as, "He was immortalized for all time to come." "Free" is, as we all know, the most powerhouse word in our arsenal; "Gift" is pretty strong, too. Put them together and the effect is unmistakable: No one misunderstands. That's the purpose of the intentional redundance: *No one misunderstands.*

Use Redundancy for Clarity

If professional direct response writers limit their redundancies to those that deliberately enhance clarity, the rule of grammar we all learned so long ago can be suspended. Whatever helps us to communicate clearly with our target readers, viewers, or listeners should be cherished, even if in our "white mail" we get an occasional outraged cry from an English teacher.

So we can defend the "Special Preferred Below-Issue Price." The tumbling overdescription isn't fumbling overkill—it is, rather, a *gestalt*, creating a single massive impression as though it were a single word.

The product or individual we describe isn't just "inestimable," it or he is "unbelievably inestimable." The glory that comes from buying whatever you're selling won't just "continue"; in fact, it does more than "continue on and on"; on a cosmic plane, it will "continue on and on, forever."

As a pedagog, I teach this maxim: "Good writing is lean." I blue-pencil words such as "very" because they weaken the description. As a direct response writer, I refer without blushing to "this very offer" and "the very paper you're reading now." I even have stooped to, "I'm very, very pleased to be able to . . . ," without pride but without blushing, because when we work inside the experiential background and logical argot of the recipient of our messages, we can't throw thunderbolts from Mt. Olympus the way we can in a classroom.

Let's apply the Redundancy Factor to "Satisfaction Guaranteed."

The phrase stands as is; it's a common enough overline in copy. But let's remember that we live in the Age of Skepticism. "You tell them once, they doubt you. You tell them twice, they believe you."

Ah! "Satisfaction Guaranteed" becomes "Satisfaction 100% Guaranteed." Want more? "Satisfaction 100% Guaranteed or Money Back." Full orchestration? "Satisfaction 100% Guaranteed or Your Money Will Be Refunded in Full."

Embellishment, Not Absurdity

Carried to absurdity, redundancies are just that: absurd. "He's an unmarried single bachelor without a wife"; "she's a youthful young juvenile." The words don't reinforce each other; they're identical.

The Redundancy Factor doesn't mean you can open *Roget's Thesaurus* and empty out all the parallel words atop each other. Rather, it's *embellishment*. The artist hasn't just created "An Accomplishment;" it's "A Genuine Accomplishment." "Leather" becomes "Real Leather" or (better) "Genuine Leather." But it isn't "Real Genuine Leather." The rules aren't that easy.

If parallels don't qualify as valid direct response redundancies, what types of redundancy do qualify? There are two: *repeats* and *overwrites*.

An example of the *repeat* redundancy: "This is positively the last and final time . . . "

An example of the *overwrite* redundancy: "Not one single solitary soul . . . "

Thus, "You will appreciate yet another advantage you will enjoy . . . " is a repeat redundancy; "This is positively the last time, your final opportunity . . . " is a hybrid; "This preferred priority position . . . " is an overwrite redundancy.

```
 MEM-O-GRAM

COLLINS CHEVRON                    JUNE 1, 1983
8741 W. BROWARD BLVD.
PLANTATION, FL. 33324




   FROM- COLLINS CHEVRON

      LEWIS
      9748 CEADER VILLAS BLVD
      PLANTATION        FL33324



*SAVE 10 PERCENT ON ALL BIG AND SMALL MECHANICAL NEEDS*
JUST BRING IN THIS COUPON-OFFER EXPIRES END OF NEXT MONTH

DEAR CUSTOMER.                                          M
                                                        E
   OUR *COMPUTER CARE* SERVICE SHOWS YOUR 1969 CHEVROLET M
MAY NEED THE FOLLOWING WORK                             I
            1. OIL-LUBE-FILTER                          O
            2. TIRES BALANCED AND/OR ROTATED            I
                                                        G
   AVOID UNNECESSARY REPAIR COST. CALL 472-7911 NOW FOR R
AN APPOINTMENT OR COME IN. WE WILL BE HAPPY TO SERVE    A
YOU. PLEASE BRING THIS LETTER WITH YOU.                 M

                          SINCERELY.
   CALL  472-7911         LEE COLLINS
                          COLLINS CHEVRON
   SAVE 5 CENTS OFF A GAL AT FULL SERVICE ISLAND W/LETTER
```

Figure 8.4 I'm no longer cowed by computers. So the weasel-computer at Collins Chevron, showing my 1969 Chevrolet "may" need work, didn't bother me at all—especially since I never owned a 1969 Chevrolet, and now it's too late to get one.

Of the two forms, repeats are easier for the writer than overwrites. What could be simpler than doubling the words: instead of "No," we have, "No, no." The tradition is, in fact, poetic. Samuel Taylor Coleridge's Ancient Mariner uttered the ultimate wail of solitude with this repeat redundancy: "Alone, alone, all, all alone; Alone on a wide, wide sea!"

With such a literary heritage, why do I attack this current redundancy champion, which in one seven-redundancy paragraph is almost a textbook of the art:

> . . . but only if you return your preferred (1) priority reservation before the final (2) expiration date. (3) After that, I can't guarantee shipment. So be sure to send me (4) to my personal attention, your reservation, immediately—(5) right now, (6) before you forget. (7) Delay can be costly . . .

Like The Brave Little Tailor, this writer hit seven with one blow. The reader who isn't fidgeting or snoring must have this subliminal reaction: "Enough, already! Quit pitching so hard!"

Don't Over—Redund

What's my point? Good redunderheads don't pile it on. They're sensitive to the realization that we can't bore people into buying. The technique isn't quite an art, but it's well beyond the sledgehammer tactic.

As redundancy gains respectability (look at the Mercedes-Benz ads: they use the word to describe the backup systems in brakes and suspension; domestic car dealers lapse into redundancy to describe this "foreign import"), analysis inevitably follows. I myself* view it as a variation of a 1930s concept of human psychology called *behaviorism*. Behaviorism, oversimplified, suggests that the memory cells respond most to the greatest number of sensory impressions.

In the Age of Skepticism this idea can be a gun with a plug at the end of the barrel, ready to explode all over your daily mail count. What does make sense is repeating your

---

*Did you catch it? "I myself" is a redundancy.

message enough times and enough ways to break through the fortified triple barriers of skepticism, apathy, and distraction.

As you repeat and overwrite, the reader ultimately is supposed to synchronize with you. Assault after assault crashes against the fort, gouging through distraction, stomping apathy, and finally melting the final barrier, skepticism. (I say "reader" rather than "listener" or "viewer" because the time factor in broadcast commercials is a merciless phrase tightener.)

Even though it may mean suspending some of the rules of lean-fleshed rhetoric, consider occasional deliberate lapses into redundancy. Some cold list recipients will thaw, if only because they respond to the intensity of repetition.

Test it. The results could be a happy, happy surprise.

9

I'll Huff and I'll Puff and I'll . . .

Too much direct response copy is dull, and not always because the wording is flat.

Copy is dull because it's overwritten. It's dull because it lapses into puffery. It's dull because it's pompous. It's dull because it's megalomaniacal. It's dull because it ignores what the reader wants to read. It's dull because it shows off vocabulary.

All these flaws, distilled in a single pot, reflect the reason most bad copy misses its target: It doesn't communicate.

That's what this chapter is about.

The First Huff-and-Puff:
The Bore/Snore Effect

A dullard can make even the most fascinating story boring. Did you ever pay to attend a speech or seminar, then find the presentation so flat and dull that your mind wandered far afield from the droning words about the subject you'd laid out dollars to hear? Did you ever sit through a lecture or sermon delivered with such deadly tedium that even the most confirmed insomniacs became glaze-eyed?

More to the point, have you ever gotten a piece of mail from a vendor trying to sell you something and within three paragraphs been bored out of your mind by the unrelenting monotony of the approach?

The ability to present a sales, fund raising, religious, or political argument in so stultifying a manner that continued attention is impossible, is called the *Bore/Snore Effect*. Don't be surprised that some direct response writers are masters of it. Our profession is a textbook-perfect breeding ground.

More than 20 years ago, in his book *Confessions of an Advertising Man*, David Ogilvy said, "You cannot bore people into buying." Despite the veneration for this gem over almost a generation, the amount of Bore/Snore mail I myself get suggests that while St. Ogilvy may be revered in our land, his followers are lucky to mount a bare majority.

Consider, for example, the opening of this letter from one of America's biggest financial institutions.

Dear Mr. Lewis:

As an interested investment savings customer, we want you to know about all the outstanding savings opportunities available from the Citibank Investment Savings Center.

CitiCertificate. Our unique 9% day-to-day savings account earns you far more interest—63% more—than day-to-day savings. With daily compounding, you earn an effective annual yield of 9.55% . . .

Snore!

Sure Cure for Insomnia

Here's a negative challenge for you: Of a hundred ways the writer might have begun this communication, he or she chose number 101:

Dear Friend:

Norman Rockwell has emerged as the most beloved artist in America. Ever since his masterpieces first appeared on *The Saturday Evening Post* covers more than 60 years ago, he has captured the respect and pride of this nation.

This ever-increasing love is easy to understand. Rockwell's combined works present a "group portrait" of America that has never been equalled by any other artist! . . .

Snore!

Look at the catalepsy-inducing words: *emerged, respect, pride, ever-increasing love, combined works* (whatever that means)—slow-moving, colorless terms that throw sand into

SMITHSONIAN INSTITUTION
Washington, D.C. 20560
U.S.A.

*   *   *   *   *   *   *   *   *   *

*   <u>A very special invitation to our members</u>:   *

*   Examine without risk <u>Smithsonian</u> magazine's   *
        new Tenth Anniversary Anthology . . . The
*   best seller hailed by <u>Publishers Weekly</u> as   *
        a "splendid volume" that "has something
*   for everybody" . . .   *

*   *   *   *   *   *   *   *   *   *   *

Dear Associate:

    If you enjoy the monthly visits of <u>Smithsonian</u> -- your magazine from the
Mall -- this letter will bring you some very agreeable news indeed.

    <u>Smithsonian</u> has just celebrated its tenth birthday, a great occasion, worthy
of marking in an extraordinary way. Worthy, our editors believed, of a handsome
book, superlatively printed, containing the most delightful and memorable of the
1,200 articles and thousands of striking pictures published since <u>Smithsonian</u>
began. Though the task of selecting the best from so many pleasures has been
formidable, the editors believe they have succeeded; and with great pride we offer
you a magnificent, 320-page anthology of a momentous decade. It is called:

                THE BEST OF SMITHSONIAN

    An Anthology of the first decade of <u>Smithsonian</u> magazine

    More than 50 thousand Smithsonian Associates have already purchased copies.
But, according to our records, you have not yet received this landmark book. I
want to invite you now to examine it (without obligation, of course) and to own
it if you wish, at a most attractive saving. But first, please let me tell you
why we are so enthusiastic, and why I hope you will want to see it for yourself.

    Like the magazine, this wonderful book ranges a world of reading interest:
articles and columns that made history; arresting and lucid contributions to
human knowledge; pieces that tickled a million funny bones; hundreds of lavish
color photographs. Here you will discover the pictures, the important writing,
the unforgettable humor you may have missed, and meet old favorites again --
all gathered in a handsomely printed and bound volume for lifetime enjoyment.
Consider these delights:

        * Richard O'Donnell engagingly re-creates the April night of
        Paul Revere's ride -- and gently shatters some of our fondest

Figures 9.1, 9.2, 9.3 These three letters have a common characteristic: They're dull. Try reading through even the first pages; your attention wanders because nothing in the writing grabs that attention. The shortest letter, headed "Dear Collector/Investor," found a way to make itself even harder to read: It's set in all capital letters. What a cure for insomnia this trio is!

FEDERAL MONETARY CENTER

...**"AN OPPORTUNITY TO PURCHASE
A VERY UNIQUE PROPERTY.**

DEAR COLLECTOR/INVESTOR

HERE IS A SILVER OPPORTUNITY TO MAKE A TRULY UNIQUE ACQUISITION.
FEDERAL MONETARY CENTER IS NOW OFFERING TO THE GENERAL PUBLIC A
LIMITED SUPPLY OF U.S. GOVERNMENT BRILLIANT UNCIRCULATED NEW
ORLEANS SILVER DOLLARS.

ALL KNOWLEDGEABLE COLLECTORS ARE AWARE OF THE OVERWHELMING
RESPONSE TO THE U.S. GOVERNMENT'S SALE OF CARSON CITY DOLLARS
AND THE CONTINUING STRONG DEMAND FOR SILVER DOLLARS. THIS
HAS PROMPTED THE FEDERAL MONETARY CENTER IN NEW ORLEANS TO
MAKE AVAILABLE A VERY LIMITED NUMBER OF U.S. GOVERNMENT
BRILLIANT UNCIRCULATED SILVER DOLLARS THAT WERE MINTED ALMOST
100 YEARS AGO.

WE EXPECT A STRONGER REACTION TO THESE "NEW ORLEANS" SILVER
DOLLARS THAN WAS EVIDENCED BY THE UNITED STATES GOVERNMENT'S
CARSON CITY SILVER DOLLAR SALE. THIS MEANS THAT OUR **LIMITED**
QUANTITY SHOULD MOVE EXTREMELY FAST.

THEREFORE, TO TAKE ADVANTAGE OF THIS UNIQUE OFFER TO PURCHASE
THESE VALUABLE AND HISTORIC COLLECTIBLE COINS, CAREFULLY READ THE
ENCLOSED MATERIAL AND RETURN YOUR SIGNED ORDER FORM IN THE
POSTAGE PAID ENVELOPE.

YOU'LL BE GLAD YOU DID.

CORDIALLY,

HUGO ANDERSON
PRESIDENT

P.S. BECAUSE OF A VERY LIMITED SUPPLY OF THESE RARE COINS, YOUR
DELIVERY CAN ONLY BE ASSURED IF YOU ACT QUICKLY, ESPECIALLY IF
YOU PLAN ON ORDERING A NUMBER OF COINS FOR FAMILY AND FRIENDS.

Figure 9.2

The Easton Press
47 RICHARDS AVENUE
NORWALK, CONN. 06857 ● 203-853-2000

You are invited to acquire
the world's greatest works of literature --
beautifully illustrated ... bound in <u>genuine leather</u>
and accented with 22 karat <u>gold</u>.

RSVP

within the next 21 days, please.

Dear Recommended Subscriber:

The Easton Press is planning to print and bind a limited number of collections of "The 100 Greatest Books Ever Written". Your name has been proposed as a person who might like to own one of these collections.

If you accept this invitation, you will be joining the select company of connoisseurs who appreciate the finest in literature and recognize the ultimate in book craftsmanship.

Yet -- and this is surprising -- the expense is quite modest in relation to the rewards gained.

Just having these beautiful books in your home will establish a special atmosphere and a distinctive tone. The books will symbolize your respect for culture and tradition. And, of course, they will immeasurably enhance the decor of your home.

You and your family will be surrounded by the world's great literary masterpieces:

100 great books by the world's best-known authors. Books which have endured the test of time and survived changes in fashion. Books which have something to say and much to give to every generation.

You will recognize the writers instantly. Shakespeare. Chaucer. Dante. Darwin. Milton. Hardy. Dostoevski. Plato. Aristotle. Tolstoy. Poe. The giants of literature. The basis of culture as we know it. If a person were to read these 100 books and nothing more, he would have the foundation of a fine education.

These are books you will be proud to have in your home -- that you will encourage your children, and their children, to read. And now, at last, you can enjoy these books as they <u>should</u> be enjoyed -- in truly luxurious <u>leather-bound</u> collector volumes.

And, importantly, these are books <u>fully bound in genuine leather</u>. They must not be confused with part-cloth bindings. There is no comparison ... for the richness and quality of full leather is unsurpassed in the bookbinder's art. And, every volume is accented with precious 22 karat gold.

Figure 9.3

145

the reader's imagination. And the writer tips his hand as surely as if he's writing, "Mene, mene, tekel, upharsin," when he puts that thoughtless exclamation point at the end of one of the least-exclamatory sentences we've seen this week.

Some uninspired writers, who feel inspiration is necessary to prevent the Bore/Snore Effect, use mechanical devices such as overlines as a replacement for an original idea. Sorry, Bunky: you're wrong on both counts. 1) Inspiration *isn't* necessary; a primitive knowledge of how to motivate people is. 2) Overlines work when they're more than a collection of lethargic words.

An example of a Bore/Snore overline, plus somnolent letter opening:

. . . "AN OPPORTUNITY TO PURCHASE A VERY UNIQUE PROPERTY"

DEAR COLLECTOR/INVESTOR:

HERE IS A SILVER OPPORTUNITY TO MAKE A TRULY UNIQUE ACQUISITION. FEDERAL MONETARY CENTER IS NOW OFFERING TO THE GENERAL PUBLIC A *LIMITED* SUPPLY OF U.S. GOVERNMENT BRILLIANT UNCIRCULATED NEW ORLEANS SILVER DOLLARS.

ALL KNOWLEDGEABLE COLLECTORS ARE AWARE OF THE OVERWHELMING RESPONSE TO THE U.S. GOVERNMENT'S SALE OF CARSON CITY DOLLARS AND THE CONTINUING STRONG DEMAND FOR SILVER DOLLARS. THIS HAS PROMPTED THE FEDERAL MONETARY CENTER IN NEW ORLEANS TO MAKE AVAILABLE A VERY LIMITED NUMBER OF U.S. GOVERNMENT BRILLIANT UNCIRCULATED SILVER DOLLARS THAT WERE MINTED ALMOST 100 YEARS AGO.

WE EXPECT A STRONGER REACTION TO THESE "NEW ORLEANS" SILVER DOLLARS THAN WAS EVIDENCED BY THE UNITED STATES GOVERNMENT'S CARSON CITY SILVER DOLLAR SALE. THIS MEANS THAT OUR *LIMITED* QUANTITY SHOULD MOVE EXTREMELY FAST . . .

Snore!

You doze off peacefully, but your sleep is troubled by a dream that becomes a nightmare: You're at a dinner party, and you're stuck throughout a lengthy dinner making conversation with the person who wrote that copy.

Lots, and lots of problems here. Reread the overline and you'll see a grammatical problem: *unique* is an absolute word. Something either is unique or it isn't; there's no construction such as "very unique." But skip that. What does the overline accomplish in its dulled attempt to pull you into the letter?

As the letter drones on, after the unpunctuated greeting, we wonder why it was set in all caps. To suggest a telegram effect? Then why the slow pace? Why say, "U.S. Government" in one paragraph and "United States Government" in the next? Why use nondescript phrases such as "The General Public" to describe us, the recipients? Why emphasize the word "limited" twice, without naming the specific limit? (The brochure, also all caps, specified 14,165 units.)

Speaking of overlines . . .

The august Smithsonian Institution sacrificed power for dignity with this one:

A very special invitation to our members:

Examine without risk *Smithsonian* magazine's new Tenth Anniversary Anthology . . . .The best seller hailed by *Publishers Weekly* as a "splendid volume" that has something for everybody" . . . .

Snore!

Visualize a visit to a bookstore. An owlish clerk sees you pick up a book. He rushes over, and with barely suppressed excitement, says, "That book was hailed by *Publishers Weekly* as a splendid volume that has something for everybody." Would you buy that book? Would you, in fact, buy *any* book from him?

Here are the first two paragraphs of the letter that follows the overline. As you read the words, you can feel the languor drifting over your reaction.

Dear Associate:

If you enjoy the monthly visits of *Smithsonian*—your magazine from the Mall—this letter will bring you some very agreeable news indeed.

Smithsonian has just celebrated its tenth birthday, a great occasion, worthy of marking in an extraordinary way. Worthy, our editors believed, of a handsome book, superlatively printed, containing the most delightful and memorable of the 1,200 articles and thousands of striking pictures published since *Smithsonian* began. Though the task of selecting the best from so many pleasures has been formidable, the editors believe they have succeeded; and with great pride we offer you a magnificent, 320-page anthology of a momentous decade. It is called:

THE BEST OF SMITHSONIAN . . .

Snore!

Smithsonian seems bent on creating respect, not orders. It's as though the copy were wearing a monocle and removes itself from the pace of us ordinary folk. A parenthetical comment: This is the first Smithsonian mailing I recall that has an obvious grammatical error (the partial sentence, beginning with "Worthy, our editors believed").

Other Borer/Snorers

Taking too long to get around to answering a question you yourself ask is another component of the *Bore/Snore Effect.* A publication called the *Collector Investor* starts its message with:

Coming in the September issue:

Okay, let's see what's in the September issue:

Whether they're private collectors, dealers, museum directors, corporate art officials, involved in trusts, estates or other forms of asset management, reading the *Collector Investor* every month keeps them factually informed on changes in your marketplace.

For September, *Collector* Investor's editors are developing the type of issue which has rapidly given *Collector Investor* a reputation for honest and authoritative information—the type of coverage *Collector Investor's* audience demands and has come to expect . . .

Snore!

Imagine writing the first two paragraphs of a communication design for action—in this case, placement of ads in a specific issue—without including one specific within those paragraphs. One reader can account for a roomful of yawns.

Why does the Bore/Snore Effect infest direct response copy with such great virulence compared with conventional retail print or broadcast copy?

One reason is that so much direct response copy, fighting to kindle the powerful "Only you . . ." response, instead degenerates into a Eustace Tilley snobbishness that even the most boorish status seeker finds tedious. Words get longer, thought becomes muzzier, the need for specific selling arguments disappears. An example, excerpted from a letter accompanying a "Greatest Books" mailing:

> Just having these beautiful books in your home will
> establish a special atmosphere and a distinctive tone.
> The books will symbolize your respect for culture and
> tradition. And, of course, they will immeasurably
> enhance the decor of your home . . .

Snore!

What's a "special atmosphere"? How about a "distinctive tone"? Can you think of any task more difficult than finding an exciting motivator in books that "symbolize your respect for culture and tradition"? Can you visualize them immeasurably enhancing the decor of your home?

The Causes and Cures of Bore/Snore

What are the causes of the Bore/Snore Effect? Is there a cure? In my opinion five major causes breed the Effect:

1. The writer wants to impress the reader with his vocabulary.
2. The writer disregards the experiential background of the reader because his own is so much more worldly.
3. The writer has a "What's good for General Motors is good for the country" arrogance, stemming from lack of touch with human society in general.

4. The writer is afraid to spill out his logical selling argument because he has so little confidence that the lengthy buildup becomes his huggy-blanket.
5. The writer completely misreads his target-prospect and that individual's motivations, and, sensing this, uses blunderbuss terms instead of rifle-shot specifics.

How do we cure it?

A can't-fail exercise is asking one of these writers to create a package for a vacuum cleaner and then force that writer to compare the weary rhetoric with the words of a good vacuum cleaner salesman at the local Sears store.

The big problem is persuading those who write this brand of copy to visit Sears. Invariably (see causes 2 and 3 above) mingling with natural communicators and absorbing their approach isn't a recognizable trait. I'd opine that few Bore/Snorers watch Bugs Bunny on Saturday morning.

If you're in the office with a Bore/Snore writer and are asked to read a piece of copy, shock treatment is a far better contribution to professional development than kindness. Settle back, read a few paragraphs, and then project a response mirroring that of the ultimate recipient:

Snore!

The Second Huff-And-Puff:
The Braggadocio Syndrome

Almost every youngster learned this ditty before the age of six (sung to "Little Brown Jug").

I love myself, I think I'm grand!

I go to the show and I hold my hand.

I put my arm around my waist—

I get too fresh and I slap my face.

For too many direct marketers, "I love myself, I think I'm grand!" is neither joke nor parody; it's an operating philosophy that, chased down, caught, anesthetized, and dissected on the table of advertising effectiveness during the Age of Skepticism, doesn't have much going for it.

I call this the *Braggadocio Syndrome.*

Self-stroking advertising doesn't build image these

days, let alone sell merchandise; in fact, "I'm great!" is a challenge the message recipient loves to meet: "Prove it, Buster!"

Most of us lapse into the Braggadocio Syndrome for one of two reasons:

1. We have more space for product description than we know how to fill.
2. We genuinely think that what we're selling is the best, but we don't know how to convince the reader.

On the positive side, yelling, "I am the greatest!" does attract attention. Muhammad Ali proved that. But visualize the public reaction had he fought in a lackluster fashion after making that claim; sports fans would have shoved that phrase down his throat, because in the Age of Skepticism, chest thumping generates antagonism.

There's a simple cure for the Braggadocio Syndrome. Before I share this with you and the Nobel Prize Committee, let's be sure that what I call Braggadocio is what you call Braggadocio.

To me, the archetype of Braggadocio advertising is a headline I've seen for every type of product from automobiles to zircons—"If You Can Find a Better (whatever), Buy It."

Did you ever analyze the pomposity of that headline? Aside from the completely noncommunicative message, which isn't the point of this section, how do you like being told what to do by someone who talks down to you with no benevolence whatever and who doesn't even bother to mount a selling argument?

More Samples of Braggadocio

A weekly publication that was a mail order tradition before I was born has this line on page one, right under its name: "America's Greatest Family Newspaper." I know they mean well, but isn't there a descriptive word to replace "Greatest"?

A headline for a space ad in an expensive publication,* for a collectible: "No Wonder Everybody Wants (name of item)!"

---

*I mention this because about 10 percent of the space was used for this bit of bragging trivia. That's about $3,000 for braggadocio.

For garden equipment:

"This is the Lawnmower That Has It All!"

Did ever a headline make the product it touts seem less important than this one? "A (whatever) of Importance."

An ad that asks us to write for a price list for art production equipment has this headline—about 20 percent of the ad: "Quality—demand it! *We* do." In the same publication, an ad for an air brush has this headline: "Any Way You Slice It . . . (company name) Measures Up!"

A selling letter from a manufacturer of customized plastic bags opens:

Creative Merchandise That Sells!

Dear Retailer,

(Company) is pleased to present our new products catalog for your use and convenience.

We're especially excited with our many new products . . . "

(*And it drones on.*)

For a direct response service company:

You have nothing to lose and much to gain . . .

Among David Ogilvy's treasured rules for creative writing are six words of pure gold: *Puffery is no substitute for fact.*

We read this once again, nod our heads sagely, and then write headline copy with words such as "Quality" or "Service." We start our selling argument with "We." Ah, Mr. Ogilvy, come out of retirement and walk the land once again! Here's the entire selling copy from a postcard mailing by a list management company:

(Name) Will Increase Your List Rental Income.

If you are looking for more income from your mailing list . . . or package insert program, come to the pros— (name). We're a young firm; ready and eager to maximize your profits by marketing your list professionally.

Suppose I were unhappy with my list manager. Yes,

I'm interested in increasing my income. But this is the Age of Skepticism. In a competitive selling atmosphere, each contestant had better turn on his most powerful comparative sell. This copy proves only that the company is sold on itself, for no apparent comparative reason. (It also proves that someone has a problem with punctuation.)

Lots of "we" and unproved claims of superiority—these are the most visible signs of *braggadocio*. Now that we're all trained braggadocio spotters, how about that simple cure?

The Simple Cure for Braggadocio

It's so easy that you—as I do—will feel at first there must be more to it; it can't be this simple:

> WRITE EVERY SPACE AD HEADLINE AND EVERY FIRST PARAGRAPH OF A LETTER AS THOUGH YOU HAD ONLY TWO INCHES OF SPACE FOR YOUR ENTIRE SELLING ARGUMENT.

That's the advantage direct response writers have over people who write ads for automobiles, beer, and detergents: we know the reader is keeping score, and even if we've wasted the headline we settle down to specifics before our ad is done.

That's why in this analysis I've (1) eliminated brochures from the mix, since some of the elaborate 8, 12, and 16 pagers are crawling with braggadocio but also, simply because of their enormous capacity for copy, with lots of specifics; and (2) limited the premise to headlines and letter openings.

The writer who buries his selling argument, his hard and convincing claim/proof of superiority, his reason why you should buy—*and buy now*—deep in the body copy, this writer who defends his copy with, "What the heck, it's all there, isn't it?" doesn't know what's important to the recipient, who has been trained by television and politicians to sift unproved claims from verified evidence.

Direct response writers are blessed with too much discipline to abandon fact for puffery as their complete selling argument; but if they compress their selling arguments into two-inch ads they have to think lean thoughts.

My Son, The Fulfillment House.

Figure 9.4 A candidate for Strangest Ad of the Year, this one makes the ghastly assumption that we're interested in the family, and the ghastlier assumption that we'll believe the obviously octogenarian mother concocted the sophomoric and witless copy. Warmth might have saved the ad; without warmth, it's nonselling braggadocio.

IF YOU DON'T HAVE ROOM FOR VERBOSITY, YOU
HAVE NO CHOICE: YOU CUT THROUGH RHETOR-
ICAL FAT AND LEAVE ONLY THE LEAN, SLIGHTLY
MARBLED SELLING ARGUMENT—THE EYE OF THE
STEAK. NO BONES ABOUT IT!

Smallpox and polio have been eliminated. Since the
cure is at hand, let's all, as word doctors, agree to wipe out the
Braggadocio Syndrome.

The Third Huff-and-Puff:
The Government Bureau Notification

Proof that 1984 is here is the degeneration of some mail
order copy into communications that might have come from a
government bureau.

Big Brother has an annoying mannerism that is creeping
into direct response: the "I'm Not Responsible" stipulation.

Here are two examples of the I'm Not Responsible
stipulation:

You have been selected to receive this information.

This elegant bracelet was determined to be the
surpassing symbol of opulence.

My question is: by whom?

Who selected me? Who determined that this bracelet is
the surpassing symbol of opulence? Who takes the responsibility for these cosmic pronouncements?

A Message from Franz Kafka

You can see the implicit gutlessness of the I'm Not Responsible stipulations. The writer doesn't say, "I chose you."
He doesn't say, "I think this bracelet is the surpassing symbol
of opulence." The voice of authority is unidentified, and it's my
opinion that the reader is bothered by this Kafkalike bureauc-
racy, on two levels:

1. It's a depersonalized sales argument;
2. It leaves logically asked questions unanswered.

An otherwise highly personalized mailing falters and
needlessly loses personalization on its order form: "Payment at

this time is not required." Why not, "Send no money now"?

The phrase "There is . . ." is one we all use. It's common speech pattern, since (here's a metaphor for you) it helps us fly over the craggy peaks of fact we can't climb because we don't have the informational alpenstocks. In print, we have more time for research or invention, and "There is . . ." should be watched as an indicator of I'm Not Responsible the way we watch a thermometer between the lips of a slightly fevered child.

Figure 9.5 This ad appeared in *Art Product News*, a trade publication. Although a photograph of the product line appears in the ad, not one word of solid descriptive copy gives us a reason to write "for a dealer near (us)." Meaningless puffery is exasperating when we want to know sizes, cost, materials, and dimension markings.

Examples:

There is every reason for you to consider this unique offer. (*No supporting reasons given.*)

There isn't much time left.

There is no longer any reason for anyone to suffer from annoying flies and mosquitoes.

"There is . . . " is a depersonalizer, and even though it's a mild one I wish we all had the time to go back over every piece of copy to get rid of the "There is . . . " sentences and replace them with stronger, personalized references.

A letter from an investment analysis service says:

Your portfolio and your tax advantages will be analyzed, digested, and distilled . . . carefully, expertly, advantageously.

Digested and distilled? They're making a serum out of my investments. But who are they? Had the copy read, "We'll study your portfolio, then make recommendations, just as we've done for thousands of investors who want expert opinion," *they* become *we*. Impersonal becomes personal.

Certainly you're right if you say, "Hey, wait a minute. You know perfectly well who 'they' are. It's implicit in the letter."

Is implicit as powerful as explicit?

The Attitude Gap

The argument isn't that no information is being transmitted; it's that in a society in which we're regarded as units by the post office, the phone company, the credit card issuers, and every business computer, we react favorably to an approach that doesn't regard us as a faceless, nameless number within a zip code or area code. We want the headwaiter to say, "I'll have a table for you in a few minutes," not, "You'll be seated in a few minutes." We want the sales clerk to say, "I'll have this suit ready for you Tuesday," not, "Your suit will be ready Tuesday." We want someone to care; we want someone to take responsibility; we want to suspend reality and believe that a message says, "Only you . . . . "

The gap, then, isn't one of information; it's one of apparent attitude. Personalizing a piece of "resident"-addressed mail often requires little more than a grammatical shift from the third person to the first or second person.

My suggestion is a simple one to apply: Eliminate the suggestion of mysterious forces, unknown beings, hidden puppeteers. If you make a promise, make that promise a personal one. If you set a deadline, you're the one setting the deadline.

Is there any exception to the rule of personalized responsibility? Sure. In that last exhortation are the seeds of the one logical exception: By being at the mercy of powers larger than ourselves, we can evoke sympathy:

> Much as I'd like to, I can't extend the deadline.
>
> It isn't up to me. So I urge you . . .

Yes, you and I both suffer. We're allies, victims of "them." Even though this approach is a simple reversal of the same I'm Not Responsible stipulation, it has strength provided it isn't played to the point of crying-towel collapse.

If you're editing a sales letter for your next mailing, consider an alternative version in which every promised action is personalized. It's worth testing, at least; and I, for one, would be interested in learning the result of that test.

The Fourth Huff-and-Puff: The Pompous Pitch

What do words such as *indeed, therefore, utilize, culminating, perusing,* and *destined* have in common?

If you recognize these as symptoms of the galloping pomposity symbolic of overwriting, proceed to the scholarly apex—or, as communicators who feel less endangered by the language would put it, go to the head of the class.

Sir Walter Scott still lives in the quill-penned daisy-wheels of some direct response writers. He's larded with King James, Blackstone, and the fellow who writes the small print in insurance policies.

The result is copy that turns attention to dishwater as it struts, preens, and shows off.

The First Rule of Overwriting Avoidance

One of the basic rules of copywriting, a maxim you might paste onto your typewriter, is this First Rule of Overwriting Avoidance:

WRITING THAT DRAWS ATTENTION TO ITSELF IN-
STEAD OF THE PRODUCT OR SERVICE IT'S SUP-
POSED TO SELL IS UNPROFESSIONAL REGARDLESS
OF THE AVERAGE NUMBER OF SYLLABLES PER
WORD.

Collectibles often are art related, and the rhetoric used by their vendors sometimes gets pretty wild. I wonder what motivation the writer expected to generate in the reader's mind when he or she began a four-page letter with this:

> For, lo, the winter is past, the rain is over and gone; the
> flowers appear on the earth; the time of the singing of
> birds is come, and the voice of the turtle is heard in our
> land.

It isn't exactly starting off the pitch (for a collector's plate) in high gear, is it? But the writer is dogged if uninspired, moving from the *Song of Solomon* to old reliable Anonymous for another treacly quotation as the first copy line of the brochure that accompanied that letter:

> When winter, slumbering in the open air, bears on his
> softened look a dream of spring, a little flower awakes, a
> happy flower that, smiling up from the hard, chill sod,
> bids us be of good cheer, for lo! the winter is past, and
> the time of blossoms and the singing of birds is at hand.

The plate had to have as its theme either a turtle or flowers; flowers it was, but slogging through the quoted verbiage is a triumph only for *Bartlett's Familiar Quotations,* at the expense of the power a cold mailing should bring to bear on its reader target.

A letter for a competing collectibles company begins:

> Some time ago while perusing a museum publication,
> I . . .

That word "perusing" is deadly. Gee, whiz, Mister, don't you mean you were *reading* it? I suppose a museum publication might cancel your subscription unless you perused it instead of reading it, but I don't think I'd take my kids to that museum.

The Second Rule of Overwriting Avoidance

This, early on, brings us to the Second Rule of Overwriting Avoidance:

FORBIDDING WORDS LOCK THE READER OUT. FAMILIAR WORDS AND VERBALISMS, SHORT OF LOSING YOUR DIGNITY, INVITE HIM IN.

This brochure copy for, yes, another collector's plate, locks us out with this phrase:

. . . transmitted to fine Pickard china . . .

Why *transmitted*? *Transferred,* perhaps, or *brought;* they're clear. But *transmitted* suggests an urgency that denies art instead of enhancing it. Pomposity has replaced the writer's commission—to communicate.

One more collectible example: A mailing for a Christmas plate has this turn-off on the envelope:

Prompt action is well-advised.

The snide threat isn't lost on me, especially since I campaign for mailings in which someone says, "I," or "You," or "We," or "He," or even the mysterious "They." "Prompt action is well-advised"? The second sentence to that might be, "Windows and legs can be broken, you know."

It turned out I wasn't wrong to conclude from the envelope copy that pomposity also lay within. After referring to the art style as *object d' art illumine,* but never illuminating this phrase with an explanation, the writer's description of the plate turned out to be *nondescriptive,* in as many words as possible:

(The artist) has made possible a collector's plate for Christmas which is as exquisite as it is extraordinary. An artistic achievement of worldwide note . . . so perfect in its intricate detailing . . . so rich in its colors . . . that words are simply inadequate.

Might be. Certainly *these* words are inadequate. The series of " . . . " are the writer's, by the way, not mine.

The Third Rule of Overwriting Avoidance

In the middle of this package is the seed of the Third Rule of Overwriting Avoidance:

IF YOU USE A FOREIGN PHRASE, EXPLAIN IT, AND EXPLAIN WHY YOU'VE HAD TO USE IT IN THE FIRST PLACE.

That rule would kill off the company that had on its envelope:

"Raros Thesauros Tempus Efficit"

That same Latin phrase is on the letterhead; no translation, which means to the reader, "We know something you don't." It isn't surprising to find in the letter such phrases as "Notwithstanding all of these factors" and the word "purchase" used as a verb. The brochure keeps the same tone, pointing out that the product "will bear the hallmark of Phoenix Fine China." Who, I wonder, started this use of the word "bear?" It has a tinny ring of phony elegance, like a rented tuxedo with too-wide lapels.

The Foreign Phrase Rule also would eliminate this one:

"*Ex pede Herculem*," as they say.

If they say that, Lord knows what else they'll say. And anyway, you already know who *they* are—the faceless wraiths on whose backs we lay responsibility for quotations we shouldn't be quoting in the first place.

To all of "them" I offer this suggestion:

Scanderi arborem ("Go climb a tree").

The Fourth Rule of Overwriting Avoidance

Overwriting has serious as well as comic consequences. It's serious to have no idea what this writer was trying to tell us:

> We Francophiles have looked forward to the
> denouement of a resplendent visual drama.

We have? Golly.

So we naturally come to the Fourth Law of Overwriting Avoidance:

WRITE ON A LEVEL OF MUTUAL INTEREST, RATHER THAN AS INSTRUCTOR-TO-STUDENT. IF YOU CAN'T HELP YOURSELF, AT LEAST OFFER THE READER THAT MARVELOUS ESCAPE PHRASE, 'AS YOU KNOW.' . . .

Pomposity is an attitude, but it can be controlled by medication so the people out there will never know we have it. What's the medication? Word changes, that's all.

We see the word *for* instead of *because*; we see *cinema* instead of *movies*; we see *indeed* for no reason whatever; we see the word *of* inserted with a manicured but butterfingered hand, after a form of the verb "to be"—"He was of gentle bent," instead of, "He was gentle.'"

An attempt to be Olympian creates a chasm between writer and reader. When we remind ourselves of what we're supposed to be doing—bridging the natural distrust that makes every cold list mailing suspect—we see what a dangerous pilot pomposity can be for our fragile paper dart.

In my opinion a paradox exists in some overwritten pomposities: they're the result of a writer trying to impress the reader with information the writer doesn't have. Result? Bluster.

The Fifth Rule of Overwriting Avoidance

Perhaps transmitting (not to fine Pickard china) the Fifth Rule of Overwriting Avoidance will clarify:

THE SUGGESTION, "YOU MUST . . . ," UNBACKED BY A LOGICAL REASON, IS BLUSTER RATHER THAN LOGICAL SALES ARGUMENT BECAUSE IT HAS NO FACTUAL CORE.

While I was puzzling out the proper way to phrase this rule, my mail brought me a textbook example. A brochure describing art prints had this telling nonsell:

> It is important to remember that each work of art is
> entirely handpainted to order . . .

Of course the writer gives no explanation as to why it's important to remember that. "It's important because I say it is." (Is the English translation of this, "I used the word 'important' because I had no facts to present"?)

We fault the writer, but perhaps that scribe is a victim, as we are, of the person who commissioned the job, who handed over some pictures and thin descriptions with the instructions, "You point out how important this is, get me?"

As a selling argument, we might mount a powerful emotional pitch around the idea of the last bastion of hand craftsmanship in an impersonal, hostile world of machines and depersonalized code numbers. To some, annoyed with the industrialization of art, that might well be "important"; an unexplained imperative is important to none.

The "we dance at springtime" approach to copy puts horn-rimmed spectacles on the typewriter, which seems to clear its beribboned throat with every half-dozen words:

> The (NAME OF COMPANY) proudly and joyfully
> announces an event of great importance to serious
> collectors—and to all who delight in the wonders of
> nature!

> The event—bringing with it the hopeful spirit and the
> delicate beauty of springtime—is the issuance of an all-
> new collection of original songbird sculptures.

Songbird sculptures are neither original nor important—*unless* someone justifies the claim. Without that explanation, it's nothing more than another example of diarrhea of the typewriter. "Hopeful spirit?" A bewildering tie of two words. "A fresh spirit of hope," perhaps, but who can rewrite poetry begun by someone else?

The Sixth Rule of Overwriting Avoidance

The strained attempt to impart importance is one of the cornerstones of pompous overwriting. The cure is in the Sixth Rule, the most difficult to implement but the *sure* cure for copy such as this, a headline for an acrylic spa:

The finest non-pharmaceutical way to relax, relieve the stress and strain of our daily lives.

Non-pharmaceutical? That suggests a kinky doctor, with grimy fingernails, sending you to a seedy drugstore for a capsule (red, naturally) to relax you. Ah! It's far superior to a spa, but since the police arrested the doctor . . . .

The Sixth Rule of Overwriting Avoidance is an ultimate remedy, but since it's amputation, not restoration, the doctor should beware of slashing overuse:

> **BEFORE SENDING TYPED COPY TO THE TYPESETTER, CIRCLE ALL ADJECTIVES FOR EXAMINATION. DO THEY ADD TO THE READER'S UNDERSTANDING?**

Fighting the Dark Prince, Pomposity

Pompous overwriting is like original sin; it lurks darkly in all of us, and, aided by increasingly skeptical message recipients, we flail away at this insidious enemy wherever we spot it. Unfortunately, we have less trouble spotting it in another writer's copy than we do in our own.

Tying the Six Rules of Overwriting Avoidance to positive action can help us in our fight:

Rule 1: Writing that draws attention to itself instead of the product or service it's supposed to sell is unprofessional. In positive terms this rule means *Show off what you're selling, not your vocabulary.*

Rule 2: Forbidding words lock the reader out. Familiar words and verbalisms, short of losing your dignity, invite him or her in. In positive terms this rule means *Write convivially, as though you're a relative of the person reading the message.*

Rule 3: If you use a foreign phrase, explain it, and explain why you've had to use it in the first place. In positive terms this rule means *Since we have so many thousands of English words, use them first, saving foreign terms for circumstances you specifically don't want the reader to understand.*

Rule 4: Write on a level of mutual interest, rather than as instructor-to-student. In positive terms this rule restates my personal philosophy of force-communication: *Write within the experiential background of the reader, not yourself.*

Rule 5: The suggestion, "You must . . . ," unbacked by a logical reason, is bluster rather than logical sales argument because it has no factual core. In positive terms this rule means *Adding the words "This is why" before the words "you must" forces the writer to add at least a quasi-factual core.*

Rule 6: Before sending typed copy to the typesetter, circle all the adjectives for examination. In positive terms, this rule is yet another reprise of the venerable but still apt copy rule, "Puff is no substitute for fact": *Eliminate adjectives that do nothing to further reader understanding.*

You'll notice I didn't use the word "important" to describe any of these rules. You'll never know what withdrawal symptoms my own typewriter is suffering.

The Fifth Huff-and-Puff: The Nonargument

Is an insidious movement starting?

Are more direct response writers trying to be tricky instead of force-communicative? Are more writers afraid of going nose-to-nose with the reader?

I ask these questions because there seems to be a rash of *Nonarguments* in ads and mailers these days.

A hasty definition:

A NONARGUMENT IS A STATEMENT THAT MAY BE TRUE OR PERCEIVED AS TRUE BUT DOESN'T HAVE ANY MOTIVATORS.

On the same day I pasted together this definition, I puzzled over two cases of writer's cramp that came to me in the mail.

One made this claim:

Destined to become a family heirloom.

The other had as the lead copy in the brochure:

This Collection Will Accent Your Home with Elegant
Distinction.

How, I wondered, will the typical recipient of these
nonarguments react? The eye slides over this rhetoric without
pause. Might it be because there's nothing to absorb?

While I ruminated, I picked up an attractive brochure
from a company that competes head to head with the "Elegant
Distinction" mailer. The brochure's cover had a single picture:
a carefully photographed color shot of an old-fashioned alarm
clock, the type with the two ringer-bells on top. The alarm was
set for 6:45 a.m.; the clock showed 8:18. The copy made no
sense whatever in that pictorial ambiance: *An artist's loving tribute to the magic of little girls.*

Is it wrong to mount such a mismatch? I think so.

The Cryptic Challenge

It's unfair to ask the reader to unscramble the selling
argument as though he or she were an archaeologist struggling with the cryptography of the Rosetta stone. More than
unfair—it's unprofessional. The Nonargument inevitably has
this communications problem: it starts in the middle, with an
assumption that the reader's information/want base pre-exists.
Since it exists, the vendor reasons, I have no need to establish
it. The result parallels starting a conversation with, "In other
words . . . "

A logical (or illogical) example is this space ad:

GRAVITY GUIDING INVERSION BOOTS.™ You can
safely hang upside down from any sturdy horizontal
bar. Hospitals, universities, and professional sports
teams have been using the Gravity Guiding Inversion
Boots™ with success for the past 20 years. $84.

The illustration showed a creature of indeterminate sex,
hanging upside down. I suppose one can conclude that hanging upside down, in what appear to be enormous ski-type
hooked boots, is somehow good for the health. But why put
the reader to this test? Why not tell him so—and how?

If you examine space ads and mailing packages whose copy mounts a nonargument, you'll formulate this rule:

**COPY DEPENDING ON A NONARGUMENT INVARI-
ABLY OMITS READER BENEFIT (See Chapter 6).**

The rule can be a warning to us all: Have I told the reader what's in it for him or her?

In a highly professional mailing for "Original, U.S. Gov't. Gold Coins" was this curious enclosure, which turned the sales pitch into a nonargument:

> SPECIAL NOTICE DEADLINE EXTENSION 740, MORE
> ORIGINAL U.S. GOV'T GOLD COINS MINTED AS
> FAR BACK AS BEFORE THE CIVIL WAR FOUND IN
> GUARDED VAULTS will be released to the public. If
> you initial—and Include this Deadline Extension Notice
> with your order for U.S. Gov't. Minted Gold Coins We
> will extend our original offer for *an additional 30-days* (or
> sooner if limited supply runs out). But, this original
> Deadline Extension Notice must accompany your order.
> Duplicates or photostatic copies will not be accepted!
> Valid only for U.S. Gov't Minted Gold Coins Offer.

It wasn't the comma after the 740 that threw me. It was the neutralizing effect this enclosure had on the rest of the mailing. I had noticed that the offer reached me sixteen days after the expiration date printed in the main brochure; this extra nonargument, whose intention seemed to be to make me the villain for what was either a postal service delay or an inability to get the mailing out on time, added a dimension of incoherence as well. A sales argument became nonargument.

Does Raw Description Sell?
Does Spoiled Impact Sell?

Nonarguments seem to be proliferating. Raw description is being used as the selling point, whether that description indicates benefit or not:

> This is the first Rockwell figurine collection ever to
> honor American patriotism.

It reads like an obscure baseball statistic—the batter who hit the most triples against left-handed pitchers with two outs in the third inning. Struggling to invent a "first" can pull the sales argument out of the message recipient's orbit.

We also struggle with extra *obfuscating* words:

> He's coming. From the shores of sunny Spain.

Once again, we've turned the target on end. The intrusion of "From the shores of sunny Spain" is a nonargument draining power from the logical sales appeal. The description is damaged by two words, *shores* and *sunny,* neither of which are germane to the sales argument.

A parallel nonargument in which a few words spoil the impact is this opening paragraph of a four-page letter:

> Driving home from the supermarket the other afternoon,
> I suddenly burst out laughing at something I saw on the
> car ahead of me. It was a bumper-sticker, whose
> message carried me back more years than I'd care to
> admit. It said, "Have You Hugged Your Kids Today?"

What kind of deranged lunatic bursts out laughing at that bumper sticker? The scene is right out of an old Vincent Price movie—the maniac bursts out laughing because the pieces of a squeezed-to-death child are in his car trunk. How much warmer and mood preserving it would have been to change "burst out laughing" to "smiled and felt just the trace of a tear at the corner of my eye." The words work for you, not against you.

Sometimes a nonargument can be funny. A mailing piece for a $9500 sculpture quotes the sculptor of a realistic bronze of a cowboy roping a cow:

> On the big spreads, where pens are few and far between
> and squeeze chutes almost non-existent, it falls to the
> working cowboy to do what needs to be done. A couple
> of men who can run up on a wild range cow twenty
> miles out in the mountains and who can rope and
> stretch her out to doctor her are some kind of hands.
> Branding, vaccinating, castrating, herding, and gathering
> cattle are one thing, but roping a wild cow on her own
> ground is another.

With one word, reality goes beyond salesmanship; even the hardiest of us wince.

You can see the rule forming:

DETAIL UNRELATED TO THE BUYER'S APPETITES BECOMES A NONARGUMENT, WHICH BECAUSE OF ITS IRRELEVANCE SKEWS THE REACTION.

If we reverse this to create a positive rule, it would be:

APPARENT TRUTH IS INSIGNIFICANT IN A DIRECT RESPONSE SELLING ARGUMENT UNLESS THAT TRUTH IS BUILT AROUND TARGET-BUYER MOTIVATORS.

Okay, this problem is wrapped up. Now, let me tell you a story that will cause you to burst out laughing, just as I did. There was this cowboy roping a steer, and after branding and vaccinating it, he . . .

10

Confusion, Contradiction, Complication, and "So What?"

My candidate for most confusing ad of the decade is one you've probably seen: it's the four-color, heavily produced ad for Renault cars, with this headline and first paragraph:

WHEN THERE IS A CAR
FROM A COUNTRY THAT
DESIGNED THE CONCORDE . . .
. . . a car designed by the first people
to fly so far into the future . . .
why drive an ordinary car?

To which the reader, *if he's trying to draw a logical conclusion from the sales argument,* must answer:
"Huh?"

The Confusion Factor

It isn't just that *any* car from both France and England qualifies under that peculiar eligibility; the ad also is a king among kings of nonsequiturs.

Why, you may ask, was I so kind? Why did I give the writer (or more probably, writers, since this undoubtedly was a creative team effort) that out—"if he's trying to draw a logical conclusion from the sales argument?"

It's because a logical conclusion may not have been any part of the intent.

And that, dear friends, is my point of attack: The infection has reached us, the last outpost of logical selling argument, the practitioners of direct response communication.

An alarming discovery: Here we are, thigh deep in the Age of Skepticism, and the Confusion Factor is spraying the gray paint of obscurity over countless selling messages. Worse, we've begun to *accept* the Confusion Factor as one of the tolerable types of advertising message results.

Our exposure to television commercials and over-art-directed print ads numbs us to accept ads such as this Renault page, which have no intention of mounting a logical selling argument. These ads deal in the watery success gauges of terms such as "associated" and "noted," not in that ugly, hard-boiled word duo, "motivated" and "sold."

But we're not supposed to be in that watery world. Our copy must kill with the first and only shot. How could this infection spread to our ranks? How could one of us write this, as the entire full-page ad (other than coupon copy)?

> TELESIS™
>
> Three Essential Ingredients for Self Miracles are (a) Imagination (b) Awareness and (c) Confidence. Unite these Positive Mental Energies and YOU will develop the Higher Consciousness necessary to attain the Pinnacle of self, Power and Love at $14.95.
>
> MAIL COUPON TODAY!

Pictured in the ad is a book titled *Change Is the Answer*. This title isn't mentioned in the sparse copy. Have you reached the same two conclusions I did?

1. The copywriter knew nothing of product or target prospects and was regurgitating words from a puff-sheet someone put on his desk.
2. Huh?

The Infection Spreads

Proof of the infection is that it's even showing up in direct response ads on the trade level. Suppose you're reading *Incentive Marketing* and see this headline:

delicious

Whatever conclusion you might draw would be gray-spray painted by the illustration, a grocer holding a soccer ball in a display that combines fresh apples, oranges, and pears, and bushel baskets of soccer balls, footballs, and basketballs. Here's *every word* in the ad other than address and coupon:

> delicious
>
> Delicious is an appropriate statement for Spalding Sports Incentive Programs. Call the Pros for any assistance in planning your next program. Ask for Bill Barry.

Again, inevitably and sadly, we draw two conclusions:

1. A mad art director seized control of this ad. It's the Invasion of the Message Snatchers.
2. Huh?

Some direct response writers offer semiserious apologies for space ads: "They're only lead generators," or, "We're only testing the *idea*, not the copy."

This is the same spirit a puppy's owner exemplifies when he shrugs and smiles after his mutt has messed on your rug: "We're still training him." Sorry, friend. You're a professional communicator or you aren't.

Is it professional, then, for a magazine to mail a renewal plea for itself, with an American Express application card as an unexplained additional enclosure? The explanation might be, "It's extra income for us," which, because the recipient gets that mailing and asks, "Huh?", parallels, "We're still training him."

The Confusion Breeding Ground

The Confusion Factor can breed in the quagmire of pseudofolksiness. I warn the writer of this next example, a direct response letter, that when one becomes enamored of the *technique* of writing, form supersedes substance, the medium becomes the message, and we get the gray paint of obfuscation all over our communication. Here's the opening of his letter:

> I'd be richer today if my granddaddy hadn't had one fault. He was a high stakes poker player, but that wasn't the problem. He was just so absent-minded, he'd

Christian Dior: Men's Clothing
Dress Shirts, Neckwear and Accessories for Men.
Sportswear and Jewelry for Women.

The day the Diors gave up smoking, they went out in search of a better bad habit.

Figure 10.1 Whenever I think the infestation of confusion into mail order ads is out of hand, I look at some of the megalomaniacal ads in conventional consumer magazines—and I feel better about the copy I write. West of the Hudson River, this ad might as well have been written in Sanskrit.

wander off somewhere right in the middle of a winning streak, and leave his money on the table.

A lot of companies the size of yours are leaving money on the table. They have a winning hand in the form of a unique product or service, yet they're leaving the pot on the table for other players to walk away with.

Huh?

The Order Killer: Confusion in the Coupon and on the Envelope

The point of magic clarity should be the coupon. I think I know what you'd say if this display copy abutted the coupon of a mailer whose own confusion is rampant since two separate offers are combined—Ringling Brothers displaying Siamese twins, one's head joined to the other's rump:

> Attach or enclose Extra Discount Coupon at left . . . then complete Extension and/or Book Order forms below to earn Extra Discounts up to 30%
>
> Mail completed form to arrive *before* the deadline date printed on your Extra Discount Coupon.

Even if I understood the message, I'd assume they have an Extra Discount Coupon at the left. Nope. Instead, there's another message (maybe this is a cryptography game!) in that space: "Attach or enclose your Extra Discount Coupon here!" Clarity isn't helped, by the way, when they omit punctuation after "30%," especially since capitalized words seem to be chosen at random. So we react:

"Huh?"

The Confusion Factor has attacked envelope copy:

> If you refuse to believe
> that any one person
> publication, or nation
> holds a monopoly on
> THE TRUTH
> this extraordinary
> news monthly is

for you
GUARANTEED

Huh?

Sloppiness + Carelessness = Confusion

We find confusion in sloppy copy:

Think back to Christmas Eve, like when we were young,
filled with the sounds and smells of Christmas magic.

Huh?
If I were ever full of the sounds and smells of Christmas
magic, I might be full but my house would be emptied of other
people.
We find it in acknowledgments, such as this "Order Ac-
knowledgment" which came to me about a week after the merchandise arrived:

Items not in stock will be shipped separately as soon as
they become available from the manufacturer.

Huh? (*Double* Huh: these people told me in the sales literature that *they're* the manufacturer.)
We find it in careless merge/purge of a mailing whose
copy I've said, in this very book, I admire:

Quite frankly, the American Express card is not for
everyone . . .

Huh? The recipient now has counted four of these
messages. She's already a card holder, under the exact name to
which this communication was mailed. Well written though it
is, we reluctantly conclude that perhaps the American Express
card *is* for everyone.
We find it in too-clever, undecodable formats. We find
it in loose-sheet letters that don't all come out of the envelope
together. We find it in descriptions that don't match the same
items' descriptions in the coupon. The possibility of our saying,
"Huh?" is almost at an epidemic stage.

OFFICIAL
STAR TREK ™

200TH ANNIVERSARY BUCKLE

Plated With **SOLID SILVER**
Hand Decorated With
PURE 24 KARAT GOLD

History was made in 1783 near Paris, France, when two men climbed into a hot air balloon for the very first time and rose above the earth. It was man's First Flight.

200TH ANNIVERSARY

To celebrate the 200th Anniversary of this First Flight, Gene Roddenberry, the creator of Star Trek, has authorized a special *one year only* commemorative Star Trek Belt Buckle - to be produced in a limited edition - plated with pure silver, hand decorated with *pure 24 Karat Gold*. Each buckle will be hand engraved with its own serial number. And to protect the integrity of this anniversary edition, it will be issued for *this year only* and then never again.

PERSONALLY REGISTERED

Each buckle is personally registered and individually numbered on the reverse and comes to you in a handsome gift box. Every buckle is accompanied by a certificate attesting to the authenticity of this 200th Anniversary issue. And you are protected by our Money Back Guarantee.

IMPORTANT NOTE: Registration numbers are assigned on a first come, first served basis as orders are received. In order to receive the lowest numbers, we urge you to act promptly. (Limit 5 buckles per order)

Figure 10.2 Hold it! Has it really been 200 years since we first saw Mr. Spock? What confusion this writer has generated by calling this the "200th Anniversary Buckle" without telling us what it's the 200th anniversary of. As it turns out, after we're thoroughly bewildered, we learn it's the 200th anniversary of the first hot air balloon. Now we have another hot air milestone to commemorate in another 200 years.

Antidotes for Confusion

So what do we do?

I'll risk having my suggestions called simplistic: I hereby propose three primitive rules that in combination are absolute antitoxin for the Confusion Factor:

1. Don't let any piece of copy off your desk until you can say without crossed fingers, "My mother would understand it."
2. Never again try to impress the people in the office with your cleverness at the typewriter.
3. Match your message to your recipient.

It's too late to wipe the gray spray from ads already run and sales literature already mailed. But let's throw away those spray cans today, before we get that mess all over us.

Overcomplication—an Ongoing Problem

Overcomplication is an ongoing problem of direct response writing, but it's one of the most controllable. That it's so rampant suggests carelessness and sloth, not lack of education or talent.

If you think overcomplicated writing is a wholly owned subsidiary of the federal government, you're thinking of only one technique of overcomplication—the use of heavy, ponderous words. The bureaucrats have leased some of their obfuscatory* language to the stodgier insurance companies, credit bureaus, and textbook-catalog writers.

The First Rule of Overcomplication is one I hope you recognize:

WHEN THE READER MUST GO BACKWARD TO RE-EVALUATE WHAT HE HAS READ, THE WRITER HAS OVERCOMPLICATED THE COMMUNICATION.

Telltale Signs of Overcomplication

An easy tip: Four phrases inevitably leading to complications are *that which* ("The recording, that which is the subject of this letter . . . "), *in that* ("The superiority lies in that its construction . . . "), *as it were* (" . . . an orange off-red, as it were . . . "), and *notwithstanding the fact that* (no example needed for this useless phrase).

Two *reverse* indicators of complicated verbiage are *in short* . . . and *in other words*, phrases that mean whatever has gone before is admittedly unclear. What a repulsive professional admission! But there are at least three other ways for the direct marketer to overcomplicate:

1. By trying to write poetry instead of communication.
2. By using words that make little sense in the contextual structure.*
3. By injecting irrelevant and self-contradicting descriptions.

I started a file on the first of these ancillary* overcomplications when I saw a mail order space ad for an ivory sculpture of two horses rampant, called "The Challengers." Here's the entire copy block from the ad:

The Steed is an Emblem of Grace,
Courage, Speed and Perseverance,
classes under the element of Fire,
ready to meet the Challenges of Life.
These powerful elephant tusk ivory
beauties are skillfully carved
by hand, indicated by the
definition of muscles and deep
bean-shaped pupils. They look
remarkably realistic, pulsating the
Courage to Triumph.
These unique Steeds are sure to be
prized, as a masterful work of art,
and encourage their owners to meet
the challenge.

---

*Deliberate examples of overcomplicated writing. See how they impede our comprehendatory concrescence?

Ezra Pound is alive and writing mail order copy!

Tempted as I was to classify this piece of copy under "Confusion" instead of "Complication," I stuck to my guns because I realized the writer's intent: to create a mood. For me, phrases such as "powerful elephant tusk ivory beauties" and "deep bean-shaped pupils" are about as poetic as the Irish washerwoman, and that they help complicate the description leads me to the Second Rule of Overcomplicated Writing:

DELIBERATE NONDESCRIPTIONS REFLECTING THE WRITER'S ATTEMPT TO BE POETIC OR CLEVER BECOME COMPLICATORS RATHER THAN EXPLAINERS.

A writer from the same scholastic ambiance ("school" to the rest of us) wrote this first paragraph of a brochure for a pendant:

> For the Victorians, romance was a matter of intrigue. A
> simple look . . . or smile . . . had a message all its own.
> And a well-chosen gift of love truly spoke from the
> heart.

Verbiage isn't the cause; except for *Victorians*, no word has more than two syllables. No, what complicates the thought is the word *intrigue*, which makes the word *simple* incomprehensible. The concept of romance being a matter of intrigue is itself complicated, and the failure of the writer to prove his claim complicates the whole description. So we have the Third Rule of Overcomplication:

UNEXPLAINED MISMATCHED WORDS COMPLICATE THE DESCRIPTION AND REDUCE READER CONFIDENCE.

Deliberate mismatchings were called "conceits" by poets of the Romantic period. I doubt the Romantic poet origin of this copy:

> Last year Parade readers bought 1.9 million microwave
> ovens. Lined up, those ovens would be 300 miles longer
> than the Alaskan Pipeline!

The Russians wouldn't dare sabotage that pipeline, with 1.9 million microwave ovens radiating away, destroying

Figure 10.3 A logical question: What is it? The muddy picture doesn't help, and the words "No warm up time required" rules out computers. The ad appeared in the *Antique Trader.* Fortunately, it gives an address for "additional sales information"; somehow, we aren't surprised by the copy at the bottom left, advertising napkin holders. Huh?

their capillaries. Yes, yes, but is that the message the writer wants to communicate? Obviously the message is aimed at prospective advertisers. Obviously 1.9 million microwave ovens is a big number. But what's it all about, Alfie? *Parade* doesn't say those microwaves were sold through ads in its pages. The statistic complicates *Parade's* space-ad sales story when we move to the next paragraph, a classic conceit because it's a non sequitur:

Why do People read Parade? Parade provides timely
journalism from some of America's best writers! Pulitzer
Prize winning writers like Alex Haley, Norman Mailer,
Herman Wouk and others.

(That fellow "others" is one prolific writer. I see his
work everywhere. And why the capital P on People?)

The interrelationship of selling components is vital for
coherence in a sales argument. The hit-and-run microwave reference is grist for the Fourth Rule of Overcomplication:

**IRRELEVANT, SELF-CONTRADICTING, AND NON
SEQUITUR DESCRIPTIONS INTERFERE WITH THE
READER'S ABILITY TO PENETRATE A SALES
ARGUMENT.**

How, you ask, can copy be self-contradicting? Easy.
Here's a paragraph from a brochure selling a collector's plate
(curiously called "collector" plate by this writer):

A collector plate by Thornton Utz is a work of
consummate artistry from the earliest stages. Utz may
create as many as 20 rough sketches before determining
the best position and attitude for each character. Then
he refines his chosen sketch, experimenting with
expressions, coloration and details of personality before
beginning to paint.

Remove the phrase "from the earliest stages" and the
selling argument comes clear. With that phrase in there, we ask
how a rough sketch can represent consummate artistry. The
writer overwrote, and we the readers can't make the pieces fit.

Beyond the four major rules, minirules abound. The
credit card company mailing for a foreign language course,
whose letter begins, "Today the world is getting smaller all the
time," suffers from a *nonreinforcing redundancy* (see chapter 8), a
complicator not only because it starts the sales argument in low
gear but also because we can't jam the square peg *today* into the
round hole *all the time* without coming to a comprehension
stop.

Another minirule: Impersonal communication is more
likely to appear complicated than personal communication. Try
this copy from a savings and loan institution letter:

Dear Customer:

We are very pleased to offer you the opportunity to
effect substantial savings in future interest on your
mortgage loan by increasing your monthly payment
which also will pay off your mortgage early. This
increased savings to you is the result of your additional
prepayment combined with a possible "reduction" in
your present interest rate. The specific required amounts
have been calculated and are enclosed for your
consideration . . . .

This one paragraph is half the letter. A second paragraph, equally long, equally cold, completes it. The message—a genuine benefit for the homeowner—seems more complicated than it is because it's so impersonal. The rewrite breaks
the message into chewable components:

Dear Customer:

   Your best investment just got better.

   We're delighted to be the financial institution
you've chosen to carry your mortgage. And because
you're one of our preferred customers, we now make it
possible—*for a limited time only*—for you to take advantage
of our Loan Discount Offer.

   Here's the offer: . . .

The rewritten letter has nine paragraphs and a p.s. It's
still a one-page letter, as was the two-paragraph prototype. But
it's in chewable bites, each bite flavored to be palatable to the
reader.

   We as direct marketers should be able to simplify a sales
argument. If we add mortar to the walls of complication we're
supposed to tear down, we should apply for jobs as brick-
layers—at the Tower of Babel.

. . . Which Leads Us to "So What?"

   If a you want to tell a reader *everything* about a subject,
subscribe to the *Encyclopedia Brittanica* reference service and ask
for bulk fact. When it comes in, retype it, and you have a piece
of copy.

Selling copy? Isn't *selling* what we're supposed to be doing?

I see fund-raising copy that insists on telling me exactly how each electronic brain scanner works in the hospital. The facts probably are right, but factual accuracy won't get me to open my checkbook. *Selected* facts might.

In the vintage year 1983 I delivered a piece of copy to sell a collectible being issued for the 100th anniversary of the Brooklyn Bridge.

My client raised an issue that exemplifies perfectly the difference between bulk fact and selected fact:

"Hey, nowhere in this piece do you mention either John Roebling or his son Washington Roebling, who designed that bridge."

My answer was automatic: "So what?"

That John Roebling designed the Brooklyn Bridge and that he died before it was built, leaving the staggering responsibility of supervising its construction to his son Washington, is an inescapable fact of history. But those two names combined and squared wouldn't sell one additional bit of Brooklyn Bridge memorabilia, compared with the interrelationship of what we're selling and the bridge's centennial. It's an inescapable fact of salesmanship.

Visualize, if you will, the classic sales situation. A salesman at Sears is trying to sell you a vacuum cleaner.

"This was made in Waltham, Massachusetts," he boasts. "The special brush assembly was invented by a man named Grover C. Whiteside. It uses eight amps of electricity."

Would you buy a vacuum cleaner from that man?

Select Your Facts

When one sells—in person, over the phone, or by mail—the ability to select selling facts out of the huge grab bag of available information pays off in a higher percentage of sold merchandise.

This exemplifies the First Rule of So-What Turn-off Control:

SELECT AS YOUR KEY SELLING ARGUMENTS THOSE
FACTS AND SUGGESTED BENEFITS THAT SATISFY THE
INTENDED BUYER'S PROBABLE PSYCHOLOGICAL
MOTIVATORS.

A mailing for a photo laboratory opens its letter with
this first paragraph:

Dear Photographer,

The art of photography is growing in popularity more
now than ever before. Today's 35mm cameras give the
serious picture taker many new options and the ability
to capture sharp, detailed photographs with brilliant
colors. Working with different lenses and filters, and
experimenting with flash will help you perfect your
picture taking abilities.

So what?

Two paragraphs before the end of the letter, carefully
hidden, I'm told I'll get a discount coupon on Kodak film and a
free 112-page booklet called *Better 35mm Pictures*.

What if this letter had opened with a question or two:
"Why does a $2.00 sky filter add contrast to the clouds and not
affect the rest of your picture? What happens if you shoot 'out-
door' film indoors? If you aren't sure of the answers, we
have . . . " The letter not only avoids the So-What trap; it sets
me up to buy something, which a So-What approach never
does.

The "So What?" Turn-Off

A letter selling subscriptions to a magazine opens:

Dear Fellow American:

If you love your family, your home, God and your
country—you're not alone.

You're in the mainstream of life in America today.
Yes, unless I'm very wrong about you, you enjoy all the
qualities I've just described. You're committed,
unashamedly, to your faith in God, your country, your
family—and yourself.

So what?

Another magazine tests our vocabularies, along with our patience, with this overline printed in boldface above the "Dear Reader" salutation:

> "A home is not a mere transient shelter: its essence lies
> in its permanence, in its capacity for accretion and
> solidification, in its quality of representing, in all its
> details, the personalities of the people who live in
> it . . . . "

> (H. L. Mencken)

So what? The stunningly difficult syntax is nearly impenetrable. From Edgar Guest's "It takes a heap o'livin' in a house t' make it home," to Polly Adler's "A house is not a home," we have a great many more memorable quotations. But shouldn't we ask ourselves, whether the quotation is easy or tough, familiar or obscure: "Will the reader ask, 'So what?'— and quit reading?"

With considerable anticipation I opened a mailing that had this legend on the envelope: "Finally—a practical analysis of government, media, and industry policies affecting advertising." A bit ponderous, I thought, but straightforward, and certainly pertinent. But apparently a different writer handled the sales message inside that envelope. Here's the opening:

> Dear Professional:
>
> Your company's or client's advertising efforts are
> influenced by a variety of factors, ranging from a sound
> analysis of the competitive marketing situation to a
> thorough understanding of the products or services
> being advertised.

So what?

Deep in the letter is a usable opening paragraph:

> Everyone who's spent time in the advertising business
> knows the horror stories of campaigns scuttled at the last
> minute, despite healthy investments of time and money,
> because of potential legal problems . . . .

The difference between the opening paragraph and the ultimate sales argument (mounted too late to salvage prospective buyers who don't have the patience to hunt for the quarry) is the core of the Second Rule of So-What Turn-off Control:

> USING A "SO WHAT" STATEMENT AS A MAJOR SELL-ING POINT ADDS CONFUSION IN DIRECT RATIO TO THE READER'S OWN PRODUCT/SERVICE INTEREST/KNOWLEDGE.

The third rule is more sophisticated. Before I lay it on the table, an example of one of its two facets:

A group of wild-eyed demonstrators parades in the middle of Main Street, chanting mindlessly, "Save the whales!" The average citizen recognizes only that Kansas has few whales. He doesn't recognize that a larger issue— *unexplained*—is at hand. He asks, logically, "From what?"

Ah!

How $E^2 = 0 =$ So What

Relevance comes clear only from an explanation that surmounts the major equation of the Age of Skepticism—$E^2=0$: *When you emphasize everything you emphasize nothing.*

The problem, clinically put, is: Every point of emphasis has the implicit negative power to detract from every other point of emphasis.

So—

If you stand on a street corner yelling, "Save the whales!" expect either, "From what?" or, "Why me?" How *can* you get that same person to contribute to a save-the-whales campaign? It's part of the Third Rule, of which this explanation is the first half. Here's the second half:

Cause the reader to feel stupid or left out and that reader will give you "So what?" as a knee-jerk response. You say, selling storage tanks for liquid fertilizer, "Ultraviolet Stabilizers Added," and you've shown off at the expense of the reader's rapport. Is it that much more difficult to write, "Ultraviolet Stabilizers Added for Sunlight Resistance," giving a clue why those stabilizers are there?

"Sponsored by the Royal Society for the Preservation of Birds," unexplained, says to the reader, "I know something you don't"; that we see such $E^2=0$ references so frequently doesn't mean it's good selling. Oh, no, it means the writer either is under instructions to be snobbish (I admit—once out of two dozen times, this does work) or the writer has insufficient product/service knowledge to mount a sales argument coherent to the reader.

"Picasso painted this during his famous 'Blue Period.'" Period. We don't explain the Blue Period or tell why it's famous. We don't identify the other periods as points of reference. The statement is flat and unadorned, and the reader concludes that everyone but he knows what it is. What could be a more natural defense than "So what?"

I say, if the statement qualifies for a trivia quiz, either box it—identifying it as trivia—or forget it. To make it work for you, identify it, in terms comprehensible to the reader, as a *benefit*, or, in fund raising, as a *threat* to safety or happiness.

At last, then, the Third Rule of So-What Turn-off Control:

"SO WHAT?" BECOMES "HERE'S WHY I WANT IT" IF BENEFIT IS ADDED TO THE RHETORICAL MIX.

Any questions? Yes, you there, puzzling over what all this means. Uh-huh. A good question. I'll repeat it:
"So what?"

11

"Hello. God Speaking."

God is alive and living in your word processor.

Ever since Smokenders began running a series of "God Speaking" behavior-predicting ads—"You Will Stop Smoking October 11"—the Deity seems to have been busy writing ads. Or at least, some of the ad writers have been sitting in His chair.

Now, as often happens with trendy copy, Godlike pronouncements are filtering down to direct response copy.

Patriarchs, Prophets, and He

We've had "Patriarch Copy" for a long time: the "Frankly, I'm puzzled . . . " insert has been around so long it's become a cliché. This approach is the kindly old head of the clan, speaking through the hoarfrost on his beard, with years of wisdom coating his "Now, come on, Little Man" lessons to us. "I want to share this with you while there's still time," says the Patriarch from his ancient rocking chair.

But God is more dynamic. He isn't puzzled by your stupidity in not ordering; he's mildly annoyed. "I didn't give you free will to ignore my offer," his surrogate fumes at us in print.

But at least God isn't a prophet of doom. His competitor, the prophet Jeremiah, is. Jeremiah just sent me a letter that proclaims, "The end is near!" Read the opening:

Several weeks ago the Internal Revenue Code was amended.

ANYONE SELLING A GOLD KRUGERRAND OR SILVER BULLION BAR OR RELATED ITEMS WILL IMMEDIATELY BE REPORTED TO THE INTERNAL REVENUE SERVICE.

CALHOUN'S COLLECTORS SOCIETY
Since 1928
A tradition of integrity

RARE U.S. GOLD COIN UPDATE

Several weeks ago the Internal Revenue Code was amended.
ANYONE SELLING A GOLD KRUGERRAND OR SILVER BULLION BAR
OR RELATED ITEMS WILL IMMEDIATELY BE REPORTED
TO THE INTERNAL REVENUE SERVICE.

My Dear Friend:

Has George Orwell's "1984" arrived early? The terror that Orwell expressed at having our Government interfere in the intimate affairs of our life has come to pass - one year earlier than that author reckoned. Without fanfare ALL U.S. citizens will have their Krugerrands, Silver Bars, other gold and silver items registered AND REPORTED by the person or firm who buys them. THE ONLY EXEMPT ITEMS ARE THE "COLLECTIBLES"; the rare and artistic gold and silver items not considered mere bullion!

Section 6045 of the code was totally changed by Subsection (a) which reads (in part): Every person doing business as a broker shall ... make a return ... showing the name and address of each customer...showing gross proceeds.

Continued interest in hard-assets even in these "disinflationary" times has kept the price of gold above $400 per ounce - the price of silver above $11.00 per ounce. The Government knows, just as you do, as ANY thinking person must know, that $200 billion of Federal debt can only lead to massive inflation and enormous rises in the values of hard-assets - once again. The all-out war against hard-assets acquired in the "underground economy" through unrecorded cash payments is on. But, as in the early 30's, all numismatic (collectors) coins of our country are exempt from this edict.

"We expect the new round of inflation at its peak to reach 25% by the end of 1985, or the first half of '86."
Pamela and Mary Anne Aden
(Aden Research, highly respected gold analysts)

We have taken an important step to help you in the very serious game of trying to protect your assets. We stepped up our search for American Gold Coins. THIS IS ONE OF THE MOST IMPORTANT ACTIONS TAKEN BY THIS COMPANY IN ITS HISTORY. Let me explain why ...

Rare Coin Division. 200 I.U. Willets Road. Albertson. New York 11507   (516) 294-0054

Figure 11.1 Jeremiah is the prophet of doom; here, after telling us how bad things are, he becomes our savior. Does the word "terror" really belong in this sales argument? Those who got the mailing were the judges.

My Dear Friend:

Has George Orwell's "1984" arrived early? The terror
that Orwell expressed at having our Government
interfere in the intimate affairs of our life has come to
pass—one year earlier than the author reckoned.
Without fanfare ALL U.S. citizens will have their
Krugerrands, Silver Bars, other gold and silver items
registered AND REPORTED by the person or firm who
buys them. THE ONLY EXEMPT ITEMS ARE THE
"COLLECTIBLES"; the rare and artistic gold and silver
items not considered mere bullion!

You might or might not know it from this copy but Jeremiah was trying to sell me something.

I've often pointed out that Fear is a mighty motivator,
and although the tie between Fear and Salesmanship may
come too late in this letter, I'd sure be interested in knowing
how it pulled.

The Dire Warning has several standard openings, all of
which usually work if they're followed by a statement of condition the reader accepts as pertinent to his condition:

- "If you don't . . . "
- "Unless you . . . "
- "Soon it will be too late to . . . "

The difference between a Godlike pronouncement and
a prophecy of disaster lurking behind the next bush is the authority of tone. Jeremiah assigns responsibility elsewhere; God
accepts it. Both might start a sales argument with "If . . . " or
"Unless . . . "; neither would be conditional; in a split test either might outpull the other.

Would God Say, "Of Course"?

The strongest aspect of "God Speaking" copy, and the
reason it works so well in the Age of Skepticism, is its straightforward, *un*subtle approach. By now we all know one of the
Great Rules of force-communication for the mid-1980s:

**A SALES ARGUMENT DECREASES IN EFFECTIVENESS
IN DIRECT RATIO TO AN INCREASE IN SUBTLETY.**

If "God Speaking" copy degenerates to subtlety, it mutates and can no longer be itself. It's the Voice of Authority that sells us, not the logic of the words.

Even lousy copy has muscle when God writes it:

> You have to do something drastic to keep muggers,
> rapists, and thieves out of your home. I'm here to help
> you do just that.

Think of the other ways the writer might have attacked this sales argument. Is any of them as effective in grabbing the reader's attention?

Speaking from His exalted position as leader of the S.W.A.T. team, whoever wrote this gives us a pure Godlike message:

1. You still have freedom of choice.
2. If you exercise that freedom of choice, you'd better choose what I'm selling or you'll be in trouble.

But God is benevolent, which leads me to feel His netherworld competitor wrote this corruption of the Smokenders ad:

> On November 1, every other source of personal
> computer software might as well close its doors.

The end may be near, but salvation is at hand. No matter how foolish we may have been in the past, the ray of hope shines through our own murky history:

> Dear Friend:
>
> If you had purchased the very first Norman Rockwell
> figurine for $15.00, today you would own a "Rockwell"
> worth about $270 on the secondary market. The
> appreciation in value: 1,700%.
>
> And if you had bought the very first Goebel figurine by
> Sister Maria Innocentia Hummel, "Puppy Love," your
> "Hummel" would be worth $315 today. The figurine has
> appreciated 156 times its original issue price.
>
> But if you missed out on these spectacular acquisition
> opportunities, don't despair. For today I can offer you
> the *first-ever* . . .

Can an Angry God Sell?

God is at his best as a direct response writer when He isn't angry. Do we still love the One who drives us from Eden, who drowns us as we cling vainly to the rudder of Noah's boat, who challenges us to measure up to His expectations? Chances are, we do; but it's an uncomfortable love, and it isn't the Divinity we prefer as our immortal mentor:

> We mean what we say. Do you?
>
> We promised details about the most exciting vacation trip you've ever taken. Those details are exactly what we've sent you.
>
> Now, how about you?

When anger is tempered with benevolence, it's more like the God we like to think never strays from our corner:

> Dear Lynn Gumbel:
>
> Your name as it appears on the enclosed free address labels is not on our list of subscribers to The Dakota Farmer magazine. We are genuinely concerned about that.

God wants only the best for us:

> Now, because you were lucky enough to be singled out to receive this letter . . . (an offer from Playboy Clubs: is He a member?)

Am I really "lucky" to get an offer to enjoy the "modest current Key Fee of $25—actually less than 7¢ a day"? The word bothers me. Not only isn't it a Godlike suggestion, but by making me "lucky" instead of "chosen," this writer insults both my position and my intelligence.

God also works for *Business Week*. He writes me:

> I KNOW SOMETHING VERY IMPORTANT ABOUT YOU.

Dark secrets bubbling out? I thought our relationship was confidential. What a discomforting way to start a subscription letter! Here's the opening of the letter, as complete a demographic mismatch as I've ever seen:

THE DAKOTA FARMER

SAINT PAUL, MINNESOTA 55116

Rt 2
Alcester, SD   57001

Dear

Your name as it appears on the enclosed free address labels is not on our list of
subscribers to The Dakota Farmer magazine. We are genuinely concerned about that.
We believe The Dakota Farmer meets your needs better than any other farm magazine.

Our information indicates that your family is directly involved in farming or
ranching. If so, then The Dakota Farmer is must reading for you. It's packed with
the kind of information and answers agriculture's ever-changing challenges
require. During 1982, we are celebrating our 100th year of providing helpful
service to farmers and ranchers in the Dakotas. However, we have no intention
of resting on our laurels.

In upcoming issues we will feature articles vital to the continued success of
your operation. Articles such as:
  * "Reduced tillage- how to fertilize for it"
  * "Beef contract locks in price, reduces risk"
  * "The most profitable crops you can plant in '83"
  * "Gear baby pig rations to weaning age"
  * "Make your home more energy efficient"
  * "Would a computer fit your farming operation?"

In addition, twenty-three times each year we include reports on ag-related state
and national legislation, the market outlook, financial guidance, and even a two
or three week weather outlook. Plus, a popular Handy Hints column provides readers
with countless do-it-yourself ideas. (Just one practical idea that you use will
more than pay for your subscription.) Our famous Watchdog column has saved our
readers thousands of dollars by alerting them to questionable business practices.

It's not all business, though. Each issue contains articles for the pure
enjoyment of the whole family. The Dakota Farmer is one of the few farm magazines in
America today that still retains the farm family home section.

We look forward to your subscribing to The Dakota Farmer. Our regular one-year rate
is $7 per year for twenty-three issues--a real bargain in itself! However,
as a special introductory offer, if you'll complete the questions relating to
your farming or ranching interests on the enclosed discount certificate, sign
the form, and return it to us, we will enter your two year subscription for
only $10.50. That's less than 25¢ per issue! Put another way, the $10.50
price represents a 25% savings.

Figure 11.2 God may have given us free will, but he reserves the right
to check up on us and straighten us out when we stray—as the recipient of this letter has done.

Dear H. G. Lewis;

Although I've never met you, I know you're on a career path that can lead to limitless rewards.

You have chosen a field that is the new frontier of business. And you are keenly aware of the need to stay on top of it. Whether you have a working knowledge of ADA, SNOBOL, APL, FORTH, LOGO, LISP or all of them, you know the *passwords to the future are to be found* in new languages and on undetermined voyages through uncharted territories.

Talk about undetermined voyages through uncharted territories! Whoever worked out that message, to that list, had better start lighting candles. I'll LISP all over their SNOBOL and melt it.

The Godlike Imperative

Our job is force-communication. So let's force them. "We highly recommend this superior solution for all hot tubs and spas" isn't the way God would sell chemicals by mail. He'd change "We" to "I" and flail the reader with dynamic opinion: "I wouldn't recommend a spa or hot tub solution I didn't use myself. In my opinion, it's the best."

One of the few arguments we respect during the Age of Skepticism is the voice of ultimate authority. That voice thunders from this space ad aimed at senior citizens:

Does Medicare Really Care?

You must attend this FREE lecture to benefit from the Cross-Plus Plan.

Will a senior citizen—or anyone—voluntarily attend a "lecture" (why didn't the writer say "seminar" or "slide-film show" or even "get-together"?)? Except for that, the imperative tone demands compliance.

Deal with Attorney Mary Lou Carson, Esq.

I found that one amusing, since "deal with" can have an eye-for-an-eye meaning the writer didn't intend. Still, the imperative tone may move some potential clients off dead cen-

BusinessWeek

1221 Avenue of the Americas
New York, New York 10020

H. G. Lewis
Communicomp Inc
P. O. Box 15725
Plantation, Fla.   33318

            I KNOW SOMETHING VERY IMPORTANT ABOUT YOU.

Dear H. G. Lewis:

        Although I've never met you, I know you're on a
career path that can lead to limitless rewards.

        You have chosen a field that is the new frontier
of business. And you are keenly aware of the need to
stay on top of it. Whether you have a working knowledge of ADA, SNOBOL, APL, FORTH, LOGO, LISP or all of
them, you know the passwords to the future are to be
found in new languages and on undetermined voyages
through uncharted territories.

        If I'm right about you, I know something else.
Simply running in the fast track isn't enough. You'd
like to be a leader in it.

        One way to do it is to input the right informa-
tion program. A state of the art information system
that speaks the language of success.

        Business Week has always helped business lead-
ers keep their lead by being just that. Business
Week takes you outside the information processing
field to give you the perspective that makes you
more knowledgeable, more confident, more likely to be
promoted than other executives in your company.

        It makes the connection between your business,
government, the stock market, interest rates, other
companies, and international developments. It explains the effects of one area of business on another.
Like the way financial strategies can make or break
a technological advance. How a management reorgan-
ization can sabotage months of research and development. How office automation can revolutionize or
traumatize an outside sales force...and what can
be done to make the transition work!

        Look over the index in the enclosed brochure.
You'll find out not only how much we cover, but
also how easy it is to pick and choose the items
that interest you most.

Figure 11.3 *Business Week* takes a godlike posture, but the wires are down somewhere. Their assumption about the author's career not only is off the track; they'd be ear-burned to know what he thinks of the paragraph that uses "input" as a verb and follows up with an incomplete sentence.

ter, although I wish we could persuade lawyers to follow the lead of enlightened bankers and take off their vests in their advertising. "Esq." is a button-bursting pomposity.

I told you God is benevolent; you may have known it even before my revelation. The mixture of benevolence and imperation is the key to many action-producing ads that otherwise would fall flat:

I WANT YOU—
TO BE SUCCESSFUL!
Discover the Secrets of Those Who Made It Big!
Positive Attitude SEMINAR

The wallop implicit in a piece of copy intensifies when we abandon the old-fashioned, passive "It is recommended that . . . " and "It is felt that . . . " for a more spirited imperative: "Listen!"; "Read this!"; "Take note!"; "Attention!"; "I suggest that you . . . "; "I did it and so can you."

The "I did it and so can you" approach probably isn't God himself speaking; it's the fellow who was accepted in Heaven and appointed gateman. This technique goes all the way back to "They laughed when I sat down at the piano," and it's still heavily in use today:

I made myself a millionaire,
and I can make you one too.

or,

You've earned the right to be wealthy.
Now I'll make it happen for you . . . if you let me.

"Wealthy" isn't as emotion charged as "rich," but nobody except Him is perfect.

"I'm Speaking to YOU"

The I/you relationship, once accepted by the reader, is a fertile meadow in which order forms grow fat. If you can hit stride in the first sentence, you've grabbed the reader; but it's like sprinting at the beginning of a mile run, because you can run out of steam and falter badly. Here's an example:

Dear Client:

I'm writing with significant news. The noted realist
painter, Charles Gehm, has completed his latest
collector's plate—"Hansel and Gretel." And according to
one critic, it could be his finest work in any medium yet.

By degenerating into the subjunctive—"it could
be . . . "—and using an unidentified testimonial with negative
overtones—"one critic"—this tightly inflated opening springs a
leak.

Here's a strong opening, and even though it's almost
poetic, somehow it holds its pace:

I want to make you rich.

Rich—in enriched knowledge and understanding of your
profession. Rich—in information denied the general
public. Rich—yes, perhaps rich in dollars too. You are
after all, master of your own fate.

Am I master of my own fate, hypnotized by this Siren
Song? Is He being generous or just tantalizing me to get my
subscription?

The Lawd Works in Mysterious Ways

We all know people in direct marketing who confuse
themselves with God.

Some are chosen and some are lucky. When the chosen
ones share their secrets, the rest of us are lucky; when the lucky
ones share their secrets, it can cost us if we ourselves are
unlucky.

One reason I like "God Speaking" copy is its directness.
I'm a bleacher-bum fan of the writer who uses power-crammed
words and sentences. Even when the message doesn't work, at
least it's vigorous enough to get attention; and this is the kind
of writing that sometimes works *because* of the technique, even
when what's being sold isn't particularly worthy.

How do we know whether we're chosen or just lucky? I
don't know about myself, but I've been up all night writing this
chapter. What time is it? Seven a.m.? Oh, all right: Let there be
light.

12

Catalog Copy— How Long and How Strong?

In the follow-the-leader game of catalog copywriting, it isn't surprising when the writer finds on his desk another company's catalog with a note: "Write our copy like this."

The catalog with the note is for consumer electronic items; the writer is selling industrial screen-printing equipment. So what? The other guy's catalog is always greener, and probably in the offices of the consumer electronics company someone is saying to another writer, "You took half a page to describe a cordless phone. Why can't our copy be crisp, like this?"—flashing the industrial screen-printing catalog.

We've come a long way, Baby, from the days when catalog writers had a good old Sears catalog as their Writers' Bible. Since the floodgates of Hell opened a few years ago, list swapping and desperate groping for cold-list response brings a laughable superabundance of catalogs to the average household; raw laws of economics and the impossible cost of "live" sales calls have turned business and industrial suppliers toward this economical avenue of marketing.

Two directly conflicting theories of catalog copywriting have matured, side by side, as the catalog flood reaches its high point.

Theory 1: The Age of Skepticism, permeating the mid-1980s, demands long copy. Completeness = Integrity; Integrity = Buyer Confidence; Buyer Confidence = Sales.

Long copy answers every question the reader has, making catalog buying parallel to retail shopping and spelling out every benefit, one of which will motivate the reader to buy.

Theory 2: The mushrooming cost of production, printing, list rental, and postage makes it near-impossible for a catalog to pay for itself when it has only three or four items on a page.

Less flowery word paintings and more disciplined descriptions can double the number of products in the catalog, or cut by half the number of pages.

As philosophies of catalog writing harden around these two theories, attitudes polarize so firmly they become dogmas. If we're formulating rules of catalog writing, I'd make this Rule 1:

> **WHEN YOUR APPROACH TO CATALOG WRITING AND APPEARANCE IS BASED ON YOUR OWN LIKES AND DISLIKES INSTEAD OF THOSE OF YOUR TARGET BUYERS, THE POSSIBILITY OF LOSING MONEY RISES IN DIRECT PROPORTION TO THE PSYCHOGRAPHIC GAP BETWEEN YOU AND THOSE BUYERS.**

The word to overlay all catalog copywriting is *logic*. An example:

Suppose you're leafing through a catalog. As often as not, something with a color choice is on a black-and-white page. The copy reads:

> Available in three colors:
> Midnight Peach, Grackle, and Five.

Descriptive copy becomes nondescriptive. The catalog house would have been better off with *no* color description, giving us Rule 2 of catalog writing:

> **UNDERDESCRIPTION IS WORSE THAN NO DESCRIPTION.**

This isn't the place for copy condensation based on "lack of space." Something else should go, and the color description should be expanded to minimal understandable description:

> Available in three colors:
> Midnight Peach (deep russet brown), Grackle (medium gray), and Five (variegated stripes).

No room at all? Not a line available for copy stretching? Then eliminate the line "Available in three colors:"; this becomes implicit when the next line, listing the colors, becomes explicit.

Substitutes for Long Copy

A catalog has this as one of a number of paragraphs describing a microwave oven, under a retouched photograph of the oven itself:

> You can cook a whole meal at one time in this spacious 1.5 cu. ft. oven. Put the peas and carrots, the beans, the brussels sprouts, the cauliflower, or whatever you can place in a flat container down below. The roast, fowl, or other main course sits on the glassine tray, without crowding.

What's wrong with this copy?

You get an "A" only if you listed both major deficiencies. The first is that the message would have enormously greater impact from the single line, "You can cook a whole meal at one time," with a line drawing of the microwave, door half open to show the components of a whole meal inside.

The second deficiency stems from the writer's lack of either information or communicative talent. Words such as *whatever* or *other* are like *et cetera*—they have no place in descriptive copywriting. The laundry list of possible vegetables and entrees is incomplete, and the copy would have been ludicrous if it were complete. Listing serves no purpose, especially since the writer didn't mention soup or dessert. What if I wanted to defrost a frozen pie? Could I do it? It's part of the meal, and if I squeezed it into the microwave would it be done at the same time? Would the flavors transfer?

As you can see, long copy isn't synonymous with clear copy.

Another example is this superfluous copy for a cassette player:

> This fine electronic machine uses all standard cassette tapes. Just place them in position, close the "window," and record or play to your heart's content.

NYLON —Industrial Grade

With ease of fabrication and many superior properties, Nylon has found wide application for bearings, bushings, washers, seals, gears, guides, rollers, wear plates, fasteners, insulators, forming dies, sleeves, liners, and many other parts.

Properties

- High wear and abrasion resistance
- Low coefficient of friction
- High strength to weight ratio
- Corrosion resistance to alkalies and organic chemicals

- Non-abrasive to other materials
- Noise dampening characteristics
- Good electrical insulator

SHEET	ROD	SQUARE BAR (Annealed)	HEXAGONAL BAR (Annealed)

STANDARD SHEET SIZES 12" x 48" & 24" x 48". SOLD IN SQUARE FOOT INTERVALS ONLY.

STANDARD LENGTHS 8 FT.; SOLD IN FOOT INTERVALS. Advise if lengths over 6 ft. can be cut to ship UPS.

STANDARD LENGTHS 4 FT. SOLD IN FOOT INTERVALS

STANDARD LENGTHS 6-8 FT. NOMINAL; SOLD IN FOOT INTERVALS. Advise if lengths over 6 ft. can be cut to ship UPS.

Stock No.	Thk. in.	Price/ sq. ft.
47421	1/16	$ 4.10
47422	3/32	$ 6.56
47423	1/8	$ 8.58
47424	3/16	$14.94
47425	1/4	$18.00
47426	5/16	$23.60
47427	3/8	$27.20
47428	1/2	$32.40
47429	5/8	$43.80
47430	3/4	$49.80
47431	1	$65.80
47432	1-1/4	$89.60
47433	1-1/2	$104.20
47434	1-3/4	$128.20
47435	2	$139.80

Discount: Less 5 % 8 sq. ft.; less 10 % 24 sq. ft.; less 15 % 48 sq. ft.; less 20 % 96 sq. ft. or more.

Stock No.	Diam. in.	Price/ ft.
47401	3/16	$ .20
47402	1/4	$ .32
47403	3/8	$ .52
47404	1/2	$ .86
47405	5/8	$ 1.52
47406	3/4	$ 2.08
47407	1	$ 3.36
47408	1-1/4	$ 5.46
47409	1-1/2	$ 8.20
47410	1-3/4	$10.32
47411	2	$13.26
47412	2-1/4	$19.40
47413	2-1/2	$23.20
47414	2-3/4	$27.80
47415	3	$36.20

Discount: Less 5 % 24 ft.; less 10 % 72 ft.; less 15 % 144 ft.; less 20 % 288 ft. or more.

Stock No.	Size in.	Price/ ft.
47-47316	1/4	$ .75
47-47328	5/16	$ .91
47-47317	3/8	$ 1.43
47-47318	1/2	$ 2.10
47-47319	5/8	$ 3.32
47-47320	3/4	$ 4.23
47-47329	7/8	$
47-47321	1	$ 7.25
47-47322	1-1/4	$13.28
47-47323	1-1/2	$16.97
47-47324	1-3/4	$23.20
47-47325	2	$29.62
47-47326	2-1/2	$45.80
47-47327	3	$59.63

Tolerances: ± .025".

Discount: Less 5 %, 10 ft.; less 10 %, 20 ft.

Stock No.	Size Across Flats-in.	Price/ Ft.
47-47520	3/16	$ .50
47-47521	1/4	$ .69
47-47522	5/16	$ .89
47-47523	3/8	$ 1.21
47-47524	7/16	$ 1.70
47-47525	1/2	$ 1.87
47-47526	9/16	$ 2.83
47-47527	5/8	$ 3.38
47-47528	3/4	$ 3.92
47-47529	7/8	$ 6.11
47-47530	1	$ 8.13
47-47531	1-1/8	$ 9.56
47-47532	1-1/4	$13.47

Tolerances: ± .000" — .005" Across Flats.

Discount: Less 5 %, 10 ft.; less 10 %, 20 ft.

TEFLON

Chemical—Virtually universal chemical inertness; of commercial chemicals, only molten alkali metals and gaseous fluorine at high temperatures and pressures attack Teflon. Virgin-not glass filled.

Heat Resistance—Continuous service to 500°F; intermittant to 550°F. Nonflammable.

Friction—Lowest coefficient of any solid. No slip-stick characteristics; static and dynamic coefficients are equal. Nothing sticks with any strength to unheated surfaces.

SHEET TFE	ROD TFE	SQUARE BAR TFE	TEFLON BONDING KIT

SIZES 1/32" thru 1" SOLD IN STANDARD SHEET SIZES OF: 1' x 1', 1' x 2', 1' x 3', 1' x 4', 2' x 2', 2' x 3', 2' x 4', 3' x 3', 3' x 4', and 4' x 4'. SOLD IN SQUARE FOOT INTERVALS.

STANDARD LENGTHS 10 FT.; SOLD IN FOOT INTERVALS. Advise if lengths over 6 ft. can be cut to ship UPS.

STANDARD LENGTHS 1'-4'; SOLD IN FT. INTERVALS.

Stock No.	Thk. in.	Price/ sq. ft.
47481	1/32	$ 5.08
47482	1/16	$ 10.44
47483	3/32	$ 15.06
47484	1/8	$ 19.30
47485	3/16	$ 39.10
47486	1/4	$ 51.00
47487	5/16	$ 64.60
47488	3/8	$ 76.50
47489	1/2	$102.00
47490	5/8	$127.50
47491	3/4	$153.00
47492	1	$204.00
47493	1-1/4	$255.00
47494	1-1/2	$306.00
47495	1-3/4	$357.00
47496	2	$408.00

Discount: Less 5 % 8 sq. ft.; less 10 % 16 sq. ft. or more.

Stock No.	Diam. in.	Price/ ft.
47501	3/16	$ .42
47502	1/4	$ .62
47503	3/8	$ 1.28
47504	1/2	$ 2.15
47505	5/8	$ 3.66
47506	3/4	$ 5.06
47507	1	$ 8.25
47508	1-1/4	$ 17.69
47509	1-1/2	$ 22.70
47510	1-3/4	$ 30.50
47511	2	$ 36.97
47512	2-1/4	$ 80.65
47513	2-1/2	$ 94.40
47514	2-3/4	$111.15
47515	3	$128.17

Discount: Less 5 % 10 ft.; less 10 % 50 ft.; less 15 % 100 ft.; less 20 % 200 ft. or more.

Stock No.	Size in.	Price/ ft.
47-47540	1/4	$ 1.75
47-47541	3/8	$ 3.87
47-47542	1/2	$ 7.01
47-47543	5/8	$ 10.49
47-47544	3/4	$ 14.67
47-47545	1	$ 25.18
47-47546	1-1/4	$ 38.44
47-47547	1-1/2	$ 58.71
47-47548	1-3/4	$ 78.27
47-47549	2	$100.67

Tolerance on square: ± 10% of thickness.

Discount: Less 5 % 10 ft.; less 10 % 20 ft.

"CHEMGRIP" Bonding Kit contains everything necessary for the bonding of 2 to 4 square feet of Teflon TFE. Kit is compactly packaged in a durable cylindrical case and contains: one set (2 tubes) of cement, one bottle of treating agent for preparing surfaces of TFE for bonding, non-stick mixing tools and complete instructions.

47094 Kit $20.00
OK to bond to steel up to 250°F.

Figure 12.1 An industrial catalog with a multitude of size and price listings dosen't offer much latitude for the inventive copywriter. Always remember that information is more important than romance—if you have room for only one of them. (In today's marketplace, a little romance goes a long way in catalogs when competitors have near-identical items.)

E

LUXURIOUS
PURE SILK

IN BRILLIANT
JADE, ALSO

F

IN
BLACK,
TOO

G

E. Pure silk: soft and smooth next to your skin,
cool, sensuous, indulgent, with a glow all its
own. The perfect chemise, a study in simplicity,
for unadulterated sophistication. The details: a
timeless, round banded neckline, strikingly right;
an exquisite tucked front; stunning tailored
workmanship. Back zipper. In Resplendent
Creme, Glistening Jade. Hand wash or dry clean.
6-16. B01172. Silk Chemise. $69.00.

F. This sweet & simple dress in fine georgette has
a secret that's not revealed until you turn around.
The glamorous deep back bow creates a stunning look you'll enjoy year-round. Belted stretch
waist. Washable. In two colors: RoseViolet, Black.
4-18. B46920. Back-Bowed Dressy. $42.00.

G. Refined elegance is yours in this Periwinkle
treasure. Richly detailed bodice opens to reveal
an alluring ecru lace panel; lace teams with the
periwinkle to create splendid double collar &
cuffs. Sashed stretch waist; paired pearl buttons
at neck to close or not. Fine polyester double
georgette. Dry clean or hand wash. 8-18. B03558.
Periwinkle & Lace. $53.00.

H. One of nature's most perfect creations—
the seashell—is translated into exquisitely
embroidered lace which adorns the flattering
surplice bodice; elegantly full skirt. Shiny satin
ribbon enhances the stretchy waist. Back tie
closing. In luscious washable Ivory polyester knit.
6-18. B12583. Shell Lace Supreme. $50.00.

Figure 12.2 Here, romance becomes description. The average
home gets so many fashion catalogs the only difference is product
presentation. Powerful copy not only can outsell overproduced photography; it's far cheaper. This excellent copy creates a desire to buy,
through its personalized, emotionalized flavor.

Copy is attackable: I'd have said *electronic instrument,* not *electronic machine,* and I'd suggest to the student writer who mindlessly typed the meaningless cliché "record or play to your heart's content" that he or she look for a more suitable profession.

But suppose I'm wrong about a more important assumption—the entire feature is obvious and unnecessary. The writer still is wrong, because a simple "callout" ("Uses all standard cassette tapes") with a line to the window would have far greater power and information transmission.

Here's the *first* paragraph of descriptive copy in a limited editions catalog:

> Royale® plate stands offer collectors both quality and beauty as well as lasting service. Royale® is a division of House of Rynberk® of Crestwood, IL.

Talk about copy with no redeeming features! The copy gives us neither information nor exhortation, and all those "®" symbols are stultifying. What's the alternative? It's Rule 3 of catalog copywriting, the most important of all rules because it has the biggest potential for increasing response:

YOU CAN'T MAKE A MISTAKE IN COPY THRUST IF YOU BEGIN WITH READER BENEFIT.

Inset pictures and callouts are logical substitutions for long and less effective descriptions. A better solution exists for situations in which display of a number of products with similar characteristics brings a dulling redundancy in descriptions:

If a page is "coherent"—that is, the items are interrelated—a single generic copy block can cover all the items on that page. Specific product-by-product copy emphasizes sizes, colors, and models. The generic copy should be at the top or in a position where its relationship to all the items is clear.

(If the page has diverse products, with *some* products having common characteristics and some not, the writer and layout person might separate a portion of the page; but if this isn't possible, safety lies in redescribing each item, since reader crossover from copy block to copy block can't be predicted.)

Triple Grip Can Clips for Paint Cans

No special tools or equipment needed. A light tap with hammer and screw driver locks clip in position.

Triple Grip Can Clips meet all United States Postal Service and United Parcel Service Regulations.

A universal can clip that prevents accidental opening or spillage during handling or shipping. Manufactured in two sizes to fit all paint cans. The Triple Grip Can Clips are the safest and most easily applied seals for cans and containers on the market today. After extensive tests, they are now used by the largest paint, lacquer, ink, oil, grease, solvent and other specialty manufacturers in the United States. Triple Grip gets the job done quickly, with positive safety at minimum cost.

No. 6100 SMALL CLIPS

For Quart, Pint, ½ Pint & ¼ Pint Cans. Use 4 Clips per Can.
1,000 Minimum Lot.	$29.44 per 1000
5,000 Lots.	22.50 per 1000
25,000 Lots.	19.02 per 1000

Weight per 1,000—1 lb. 12 oz.

QUANTITY
SEE PAGE 3
DISCOUNTS

No. 6110 LARGE CLIPS

For Gallon & ½ Gallon Cans. Use 6 Clips per Can.
1,500 Minimum Lots.	$34.72 per 1000
6,000 Lots.	26.09 per 1000
15,000 Lots.	22.05 per 1000

Weight per 1,000—2 lbs. 12 oz.

NO. 7850 PAINT CAN CLOSER Complete with adaptor. Closes half pint, pint, quart and gallon cans.
$119.64 ea.
Shipping weight—17 lbs.

7850

Figure 12.3 Is meeting U.S. Postal Service and UPS regulations the key selling argument? Lots of space on this catalog page to emphasize some of the other copy points—the clips prevent accidental opening or spillage during handling; they're the safest on the market today. Opinion: The layout artist allowed too much space for a simply described product; the copywriter then overwrote because too much space was available for a basically simple description.

Copy Length Depends on Who Reads It

Readers of your catalog fall into one of three groups:

1. Those who already know a product and immediately recognize product benefit;
2. Those who have a "touchstone" knowledge, giving them a loose, less-than-familiar understanding;
3. Those who have no prior benefit knowledge.

(In a polyglot catalog, readers will switch categories on each successive page. A reader can fall into Group 1 for cordless telephones and sink to Group 3 for talking telephones.)

Required copy length grows as typical readers move from Group 1 to Group 3. For those in Group 1, copy can be comparative rather than descriptive; for those in Group 3, benefit should be followed by some "what is it?" copy.

An example of this is the pocket calculator. When the calculator first appeared in early 1970s catalogs, writers used paragraph after paragraph to prove it actually did long division. Readers of those catalogs, used to office machines that could multiply numbers by multiple pulls of the handle but couldn't under any circumstances perform numerical division, had to overcome implicit product ignorance.

Today we never would buy a calculator that *didn't* perform numerical division, nor is one marketed. We say, "Full-Function Calculator," covering all the basic mathematical capabilities, then use further description to explain what ours does *beyond* those capabilities. Our product knowledge makes primitive description unnecessary.

Rule 4 of catalog copywriting is hidden in that example:

KNOWING THE DEMOGRAPHIC AND PSYCHO-GRAPHIC CHARACTERISTICS OF THE TYPICAL READER HELPS THE WRITER KNOW HOW TO DE-SCRIBE EACH ITEM IN A CATALOG.

Business catalogs needn't explain technical terms obvious to their readers, but consumer readers aren't so homogenized. An industrial plastic buyer might be insulted by the copy-block headed "What Is PVC Pipe?" because he thinks you think he's uneducated within his professional field; but the question—and its answer—would make sense in a consumer catalog of lawn furniture.

A mailed catalog typically is aimed at a mixture of prior buyers, cold-list names, and family members or office associates whose product knowledge can range from intimate to non-existent. Common sense tells us to aim copy at the largest group of potential buyers.

Other Determiners of Copy Length

About half the catalogs mailed today have a "personalizing" letter either on their inside front cover or adjacent to the order form.

Many of these letters are wasted words. The space might be better used to add more products for sale.

Here's the opening of an inside-the-cover letter in a catalog that came to me recently:

> Dear Customer:
>
> We are pleased to bring you this exciting collection from designers and craftspeople around the world.

A suggestion (not a Rule, because it's an opinion): If this is the best you can do, skip the letter. I'm unswerving in my loyalty to Rule 3; this opening is the archetype of thoughtless puffery, an impossibly poor substitute for reader benefit.

In general I like introductory letters, because (properly written) they're personalizers, and personalizers separate your catalog from the others on the coffee table.

Personalizing is the great trend of the mid-1980s and a logical reason for longer copy, because of Rule 5 of catalog copywriting:

PERSONALIZING—CATALOG COPY SUPPOSEDLY WRITTEN BY AN INDIVIDUAL—DEMANDS LONGER COPY THAN IMPERSONAL CATALOG COPY.

Why? Because lead-ins, transitions, and homey touches can't be rushed or given as bulletins. It just requires more words to say, "I never knew where to put all those handwritten recipe cards Aunt Margaret gave me until I saw this solid pine recipe chest," than it does to say, "Solid Pine Recipe Chest."

Giving a catalog a personality builds loyalty in the Age of Skepticism, and we don't have a lot of loyalty builders as easy or dependable as this.

Rule 6 of catalog writing is the reverse of Rule 5:

"HOTLINE" OFFERS—FIRST-COME, FIRST-SERVED, WHILE THEY LAST—DEMAND SHORT DESCRIPTIVE COPY.

Why? Because *verisimilitude* disappears if you first claim you have only a handful or the price is ridiculously super-special, then oversell with too many words of copy. Keep Hotline copy short and you'll have coherent copy.

The next rule is a little more abstruse than the others but valid:

POSSESSIVE COPY SHOULD BE LONGER THAN OB-JECTIVE COPY.

I warned you it's abstruse! This Rule 7 simplifies itself with this explanation: Possessive copy ("Our incomparable navel oranges . . . ") is incomplete without rhapsodizing. The reader expects it and is in fact disappointed if the word "incomparable" doesn't generate reinforcing description.

Objective copy ("Navel oranges . . . ") is self-contained and self-limiting. Hybrid copy ("Juice-laden navel oranges . . . ") doesn't need the ornamentation of personalized copy but to stay in character should have more meat on its bones than objective copy.

Does length = strength? Catalog copywriting is fast becoming a specialty—almost a subculture in direct marketing. Within a few years it could justify a "how to" book of its own.

How to Tie Copy to Illustrations

Every time I read that a catalog producer has sent a bunch of models and a battery of photographic technicians to the Great Wall of China, to shoot the product or fashions for a new catalog, I wonder not only about the sanity of the enterprise but about the way that catalog will relate its copy to the illustrations.

In a well-thought-through catalog, copy and illustration form a one-piece impression. Each is in key with the other.

You and I both have seen catalogs in which the photographs, inexplicably, were shot on shipboard (although nothing about the product was nautical), in an Italian village (although the product had no ethnic overtones), or in a zoo (although the exotic backgrounds and animals had no relationship with the prosaic product).

Some companies do this regularly, having deadly serious meetings: "Should we go to Lesotho?" "I hear they eat Americans in Lesotho." "Then let's use European models." Art direction supersedes marketing, and decisions can be costly.

Rules 8 and 9 of Catalog Writing

From this base, to make those decisions *less* costly, we have the Eighth Rule of catalog writing:

IF YOURS IS A COMPANY WHOSE ILLUSTRATIONS DELIBERATELY SHOW BACKGROUNDS NOT RELATED TO PRODUCT, COPY SHOULD EXPLAIN THE LOCALE *and* ADOPT THE FLAVOR OF THE LOCALE.

I'm not, for heaven's sake, attacking catalogs whose illustrations *do* show backgrounds related to product. Here are garments made of Icelandic wool; what's more natural than shooting them in Iceland? There are coats made of New Zealand suede; the New Zealand background helps sell them.

So we have the Ninth Rule of catalog copywriting, an inverse of Rule 8:

USING BACKGROUNDS THAT PROVE THE VALIDITY OF SOURCE OR CLAIM ADDS TO VERISIMILITUDE. IF BUDGET PERMITS, IT'S A FINE IDEA.

We show product-in-use, *at the site of use,* and our illustration gains descriptive clarity and argumentative strength.

We show product-ready-to-sell, at point of origin, and our claims for that point of origin become true.

Chinese cloisonné at the Great Wall? A borderline case, since we have the country of origin but no selling logic. Chinese fashions? A more logical matchup.

Rule 10 of Catalog Writing

Illogical backgrounds aren't the only inadvertent mistakes catalog planners commit. Propping is an even more common hazard.

"Propping" is the selection of accoutrements to enhance the visual appeal of a photograph. Sometimes those charged with this responsibility aren't sufficiently familiar with corporate philosophy; other times, and even worse, sometimes the company itself doesn't think of its *position* in the marketplace when propping a photo.

The copywriter gets a sheaf of photographs. They're crisp, they're exposed properly, and the colors are on the nose; what they lack is a relationship with the company.

"Hey," says the hapless copywriter, "the model is wearing a $29.95 dress, and she's posed next to a Rolls-Royce. What am I supposed to do with this?"

The writer has two choices: he either (a) cops out, writing a straightforward piece of copy that ignores the majestic automobile; or (b) he remembers the Tenth Rule of catalog writing:

IF THE PROPS OR BACKGROUNDS AND THE PRODUCT BEING SOLD ARE AN OBVIOUS MISMATCH, COPY TO EXPLAIN THAT MISMATCH IS MANDATORY.

That's what copywriters are for! We don't need a high-powered wordsmith to regurgitate a fact sheet; the copywriter shows his or her professionalism the same way a doctor does—not by prescribing two aspirin tablets but by using the golden hands that, on the word processor keys, justify those outrageous creative costs.

Chicken or Egg—or Chicken Soup?

Does copy or illustration come first?

It isn't a chicken-or-egg analogy. Invariably the illustration comes first. The copywriter, if he's a professional, suppresses the urge to moan, groan, complain, and make the job seem tougher than it is. He accepts the photographs (or for that matter the drawings) and plows doggedly ahead. If he's a realist, he'll admit the job is *easier* because the illustrations came first.

Having them on hand, whether they're the way he personally would have shot them or not, is a big advantage. I myself prefer having pictures staring at me when I'm writing catalog copy, because knowing what's in the pictures when you write the copy is a sure way to avoid rewriting—or, worse, having a printed catalog with unclear product descriptions.

The one caution flag is Rule 11 of catalog writing:

WHEN SIZE OR USE IS UNCLEAR, COPY MUST COVER THE PICTORIAL LACK.

Why should this Rule even be necessary? Why are photos shot with limbo backgrounds? Why does a piece of machinery squat in a dead pose on a sheet of seamless paper, with no visible clue indicating its size or use?

That question is easy to answer if you've ever had to fight deadlines, photograph equipment that weighs eight tons and has to be shipped to Pittsburgh tomorrow, or had one day in which to shovel fifty products in and out of a pre-lit area, while the shutter clicking stops only during camera reload periods.

But the overriding determinant of what to do and what to say is *clarity*. If the catalog reader can't understand what you're selling, if the product descriptions are unclear, if the typical reader can't interpret a textual reference because the relationship with the picture needs amplification, additional plastic surgery is in order.

Two Easy Solutions

Look through your own catalog to see whether this problem pertains to any item in the catalog. Chances are, you'll find a dip below the anticipated sales volume because reader confidence is down for those items.

"Hold it," you complain. "I've used every available inch of space. I can't add more description."

One easy band-aid is putting copy *on* the picture.

Callouts can explain nongraphic functions, and those callouts can be either one-point printer's rules extending to the margins or, more simply, type laid over the illustration the way a mapmaker places city names over the topographical illustrations on a map.

Don't load up a picture with callouts or descriptive words; impact decreases as the amount of callout words increases. But with lean picture-related copy you'll find that intensity of readership leaps, and, properly worded, a callout can combine *sell* with description.

Plump, sun-dried apricots from Australia...without a doubt...the finest you'll ever taste.

We traditionally sell out of this fine fruit...order soon to avoid disappointment.

Our naturally sun-dried Australian Apricots are one of the world's finest taste treats. Grown without the use of chemicals, they're hand-selected to ensure you receive only the biggest and juiciest. A special patented process is used to preserve their Australian goodness. Compared to your standard dried apricot, a gourmet gift of our plump, Australian Apricots is sure to be thoroughly appreciated ...right down to the last delicious bite. They've even been packed in a decorative wooden box that can be reused after the apricots are gone.

Order soon to avoid disappointment.

Available in limited supply, this fine fruit is unconditionally guaranteed fresh and backed in full by our "'You be the Judge,ᴍ'" guarantee of satisfaction. We encourage you to order yours soon, because they're very popular and usually sell out. Net wt. 2 lbs.
No. 9293 . . . . $18.50

Do your own comparison test: ordinary dried apricots (near right) aren't nearly as plump or juicy as our Australian Apricots (far right).

Figure 12.4 Here's a perfect partnership: The large photograph shows the product at its best; the inset "comparison" photograph clarifies the competitive benefit. The result: solid sell + clarity.

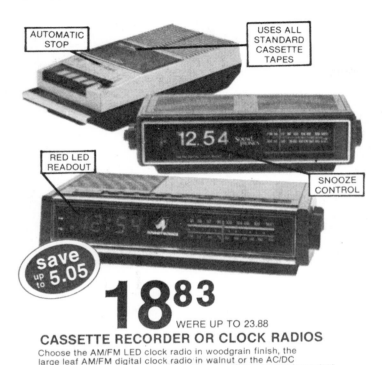

AUTOMATIC STOP

USES ALL STANDARD CASSETTE TAPES

12.54

RED LED READOUT

SNOOZE CONTROL

save up to **5.05**

18⁸³

WERE UP TO 23.88

CASSETTE RECORDER OR CLOCK RADIOS
Choose the AM/FM LED clock radio in woodgrain finish, the
large leaf AM/FM digital clock radio in walnut or the AC/DC
cassette recorder with easy push-button operation. All one low price!

Figure 12.5 "Callouts"—lines pointing to the feature on an illustration—are often easier to understand than many words of copy.

A second solution is ringing the basic glamor photograph with line drawings, each of which shows a particular function or use. An example: the basic photograph shows a folding bicycle, being ridden (by an adult, I hope, since showing a child doesn't indicate that an adult *could* ride it but showing an adult doesn't exclude the child). Inset is a drawing of the bicycle, folded up (held in the air by a woman, I hope, since having a man holding it doesn't indicate how lightweight it is); another inset might show the full-size seat.

Here's a classic problem: You have a photograph of a display unit—a rack of key rings that have the names of various makes of automobiles, or a rack of pantyhose of various degrees of elasticity and sheerness. How can you tell the catalog readers which cars or which types and sizes are represented and which aren't?

The two ways of handling copy are at the mercy of the amount of available space. If you have room to set a complete listing in six-point type, you'll cut down the number of inquiries asking for that list. If you have space only for a generic description, you make that description *appear* to be specific—"Every major U.S. and foreign make"; "All the most popular sizes."

The Obvious Conclusion

Having read this far into *Direct Mail Copy that Sells*, you may have absorbed a premise by now. It's especially pertinent to catalog copywriting:

Coherent force-communication needs three ingredients—*benefit, verisimilitude,* and *clarity*. Any technique used for relating copy to illustration must embrace that premise.

**Instant Aerosol
Urethane Foam In A
Long-Lasting Jumbo Size**

A revolutionary product for the do-it-yourselfer who wants industrial quality rigid urethane foam.

Just spray it where you want it to silence irritating auto rattles, fill or stabilize hollows and thin-walled sections of models. Also insulates pipes, patches leaks, seals holes, fills cracks. A clever way to make flotation chambers in boats. Expands up to 3 times its volume. Dries to the touch in 20 minutes, may be shaped in 2 hours. Dries fully in 24 hours. The entire can makes 1 cu. ft.

Lightweight, non-toxic, won't absorb water, won't rot or dissolve in most chemicals. Easily drilled, sanded or cut. Accepts any paint, lacquer, plaster. Sticks to almost anything except polyethylene. Net wt. 36 oz. minimum.

V-3321 Aerosol foam **$17.50**
Three or more ....**Each $16.50**

Figure 12.6 There's little value in a thoughtless approach such as this—showing an aerosol container when we're selling do-it-yourself urethane foam spray. A first-year student could think of a better way to illustrate *benefit* instead of *package*. The copy suggests some exciting uses; the photograph is static.

So the question, "Have I told them what they're seeing? (clarity) *plus* what it'll do for them? (benefit), *and* done it with words and pictures they regard as credible? (verisimilitude)" must generate a total YES or the sales argument runs the risk of failure. If you have the time, show questionable copy to a child, or to your mother, and ask for a recapitulation, based only on the sum of picture + copy, of why someone should buy.

You'll know quickly enough whether you've succeeded in your catalog salesmanship.

This year, put a 1,000 sq. ft. wildflower meadow under someone's Christmas tree.

Suddenly a "can opener" is the most important gardening tool you can own. Inside Norm Thompson's "Meadow in a Can™" you'll find the makings of a 1,000-square-foot wildflower meadow...a natural carpet of constantly changing color that makes every day like going for a ride in the country...without ever leaving home.

A special mix developed by wildflower experts.

Together with the Clyde Robin Seed Co. (the nation's leading authority on wildflowers), Norm Thompson is proud to offer a product that will make any yard the showplace of the neighborhood. Seventeen different kinds of wildflowers are included in the mix to give you an explosion of color and fragrance that changes constantly throughout the year. Your meadow will welcome spring with bright Shasta Daisies, then gradually change into a sea of Bachelor Buttons and vivid Cosmos. A blend of annuals and perennials ensures a never-ending array of extraordinary color from early spring to late fall...year after year.

Easy to plant...nearly care-free.

"Meadow in a Can™" can be planted any time of the year (easy step-by-step instructions included). Use a little for small gardens, or the whole can for 1,000 square feet. You can water your meadow if you like, or let Mother Nature take care of it. The only thing we suggest you do is mow it once a year.

Satisfaction guaranteed.

"Meadow in a Can™" is a terrific answer to colorful planting around the yard or for beautifying that vacant lot next door. And for people with larger planting problems, we offer a special Acre-Pak...40 cans for $750. A great gift idea, and satisfaction is guaranteed or your money back. **No. 9645; $19.95**

17 kinds of wildflowers:
Bachelor Button • Purple Prairie Cone Flower • Shasta Daisy • Cosmos • California Poppy • Blue Flax • Lupine • Primrose • Baby Blue Eyes • Black-eyed Susan • Shirley Poppy • Indian Blanket • Yarrow • Bright Cone Flower • Chicory • Chinese Houses • Bouncing Bet

Norm Thompson

MEADOW in a CAN.

Figure 12.7 No amount of copy could equal the impact of a photograph showing an endless meadow of wildflowers. Few will analyze the claim: 1,000 sq. ft. is an area 20 × 50 feet, or 40 × 25 feet; the area in the photograph is far larger.

G. **Mike and I are weekend athletes.** We play tennis, ride bikes and take long walks—all *thirsty* activities. Until we discovered this soft thermos pouch, we always carried the old-fashioned heavy jug. No more worry about breakage or excess weight. The insulated pouch holds a gel pack that keeps beverages hot or cold. It has a handy clip that fits on my belt or bike and a convenient front pocket. Holds one quart. Best of all, when empty, it folds away compactly. $5\frac{1}{2}'' \times 12''$.
#C4707 SOFT THERMOS POUCH
$20.00

Figure 12.8 Isn't that a cigarette? The copy doesn't clarify it's the drinking straw, from the pouch offered for sale. If clarity is in question and you don't have time to re-photograph, make a textual reference ("You'll never spill a drop, drinking through the unbreakable plastic straw . . . ").

13

Let 'em Eat Cake: Fund Raising by Mail

That same fund raiser who can squeeze an extra hundred dollars out of a dead body over the phone or in a personal confrontation sometimes wonders, to his or her bewilderment, why the same charisma doesn't work in the mails.

Just as many writers are terrible speakers, so are many spellbinding speakers poor communicators by mail. On analysis, the competitive failure of many fund-raising mailings seems to stem from one of a dozen creative mistakes.

I call them *creative* mistakes because *factual* mistakes don't exist in this sophisticated avenue of direct response. I can write an industrial plastics catalog and be plagued by problems of fact; if the copy misstates a fact, we get complaints, returned merchandise, and maybe even a lawsuit if a piece of machinery breaks down because the reader trusted our words.

But in fund raising if the writer makes a mistake, the mistake probably is one of psychology rather than fact. What happens as a result?

Nothing.

That's the ultimate curse of a fund-raising campaign that leads to one of the twelve rules I'll describe to you: *Nothing happens*. The recipient of the message hits you with the worst weapon imaginable—apathy.

What we're always looking for is a way to keep our mailing out of the wastebasket. In that respect, fund raising differs not at all from any other mail order venture.

The Twelve Rules of Fund Raising

We know these rules but because of haste, because of an overblown notion that everyone in the world thinks our project or institution is as important as we think it is, or because we think our copy has to wear a vest and go, "Harrumph!" every few paragraphs—and all these reasons are our own fault—we ignore the rules and suffer the consequences.

Enough prelude. Just what are these solid-gold rules we shouldn't ignore?

I've compiled a dozen of them. Ignoring any of them is a creative mistake that absolutely, positively will cut response:

Rule 1: Tell the Reader What to Do.

Isn't that easy? Why are you contacting the reader anyway? If you say, "Of course I tell the reader what to do," good for you, but take a look, this afternoon, at some of the samples you've collected of mailings by others. Some of them are pretty silly because they rhapsodize about a better world and they may even say, "You can help"—but they don't tell me what to do. They may reach me, even inspire, but ultimately I'm a reader, not a participant.

You want my check? Tell me so. You want to use my name? Tell me so. You want a hundred of my letterheads and a list of my friends? Tell me so. I may reject your demand, but that's better than my saying, "Protect the grizzlies—a good idea," and filing the piece in the paper shredder.

Rule 2: Make the Reader Feel Specially Chosen.

If you think computer personalization makes me feel chosen, you're right only if that computer personalization actually looks personal. Technology is on our side these days because it's no problem to send out 600,000 letters, each one apparently hand typed, in one mail drop.

In my opinion, opening a letter with, "You are one of 200 million Americans who should be concerned with a problem confronting us all," is more than a mistake. It's a kamikaze approach to fund raising. It's like saying, "You were chosen because you were born," or, "This is a special offer only to those whose names are listed in the phone book."

Cosmic issues don't concern us. We talk about statesmanship, but we don't vote for candidates who are best for the country, we vote for the ones who are best for us. We hate people who smoke in restaurants unless we want to enjoy a good cigar. Most of all we don't want to be part of the mob.

So the person who says to us, "Only you . . . " can get us to turn handsprings. He can persuade us to join a key club in Albuquerque even though we live in Bangor, Maine. He can sell us time sharing in a condominium in Guam. And he can get us to contribute, or even participate, in a fund-raising effort we'd otherwise ignore or sidestep. What power in those two words, "Only you"!

That power bleeds over into the third rule:

Rule 3: Offer Recognition.

What's the recognition? A plaque. A certificate. A trophy. A desk ornament. Unless the donor is chief justice of the Supreme Court, he can always use another certificate to display on his wall. If you really want to nail him down, frame the certificate. (In fact, a good fund raiser can get a framer to donate the frames, and then that framer gets a certificate too.)

Of course we mention, *prominently,* the recognition, in the mailing. And if we're especially bright that day, the recognition isn't for a donation; instead, the individual is appointed to the Board of Advisors or the President's Council or the Executive Circle. As long as we're passing out titles, let's not be stingy. Remember the personal psychology of the recipient, who now can be on the Executive Advisory Board and who may even be willing to give you an extra $25 because that puts him on the certificate-award level.

But we have a qualifier. The qualifier is the backbone of the recognition, and it's the core of Rule 4.

Rule 4: Be Sure the Recognition Expires.

This isn't a creative rule. It's a creative thinking rule, or a rule of psychological weaponry.

Visualize this: On the wall hangs a gorgeous certificate. Just one problem: Joe Doakes is on the Medical Advisory Board, but his appointment is for the year 1984. It's November, and every time he looks at that certificate Doakes is in a cold sweat. Let's see—maybe he can send the certificate to a photostat house and have the date changed. Of course he'll have to kill the artist who changes the date.

When a request for 1985 comes up, Doakes is relieved. He's legitimate for another year.

With a plaque, it's even easier. Some plaques have an indented slot into which you can position a mylar peel-off label with the year. For renewals you needn't send a new plaque, just a new label, something like a license plate.

Why is it important that the recognition expire? Because we need those psychological weapons. We aren't the only organization clamoring for money, and once we have someone captive, that person is seven to eleven times more likely to contribute than even the most carefully chosen cold-list name. We know the fertilizer to use to keep him green. It's a mistake not to sprinkle it.

Rule 5: Use Envelope Copy.

(The next chapter covers this subject in depth.)

Some fund raisers are so engrossed in their own dignity they forget the competitive nature of the mails. I'm not suggesting using tricky, elaborate, or phony phrases on the envelope. I do suggest that two types of envelope treatment tend to improve the pull.

Those two types are, (a) something official looking, such as a rubber stamp with "Your official credentials are enclosed"; or (b) a guileless handwritten message, such as the single word, "Help!"

At the very least, test envelope copy. And I beg you, don't test a blank envelope against a far-out envelope legend such as "Open if you dare!" What too many people in my end of the business make the mistake of forgetting, ignoring, or never learning is—

YOU DON'T HAVE TO PUT ON A CLOWN SUIT TO GET ATTENTION.

Rule 6: Match the Message to the Reader's Experiential Background.

This may be the toughest rule of all, because it means doing some homework. Whenever you go into the mails, you know something about the person who gets that mail. If from no other source, you have information on the list card. It's a mistake not to milk that information.

Undoubtedly, from the zip code and list source, you know what type of neighborhood you're reaching. You have a loose idea about age and income. I propose that you go further.

In the 1980s, this country is polarizing into a society of special-interest groups. Political candidates need every ounce of savoir-faire to appeal to each of these groups without offending all the others. I offer you this proposition for effective fund raising in the mid-1980s: Deal in the recipients' sociological, economical, and political prejudices.

Notice—I omitted ethnic and religious prejudices. Please, please, don't adapt this terrible weapon to those ends. It'll work, but you'll feed the worst aspects of this slow degeneration of the union that makes the United States united. Stick with the prejudices that will help raise money.

Metropolitan Opera Association
Lincoln Center
New York, N.Y. 10023

Non Profit Organization
U.S. Postage
PAID
Metropolitan Opera
Association

The 1983 Met Raffle

This is your chance to play a part in The Met Centennial. And win jewels, cars, vacations, or any of 3,333 prizes.

Figure 13.1 Once upon a time the Metropolitan Opera could raise funds by listing donors in the program book. Not during the Age of Skepticism! Contemporary fund raising must benefit the donor as well as the institution.

If you implore someone, "Feed the hungry," he may ask incuriously, "Feed 'em what?" If you tell him, "*You're threatened*," he'll keep reading.

Yes, you'll be guessing about those prejudices. If it's an educated guess, you'll be right far more than you're wrong. You'll send your Republican fund-raising mail to some Democrats, and 15 percent of your "No More Nukes" mail will hit officers of the power and light company, and some of your "Get the Filth off the Streets" literature will wind up on the dartboards of the Linda Lovelaces, and some of your C.A.R.E. mailings will reach xenophobes.

But think how much more intense, how much stronger your penetration into the proper targets will be. Pull will be way up, not only because you've matched the message to the reader's own experiential background but also because of Rule 7, which is far and away the most important of all the rules of communication I can list.

Rule 7: Emotion Outsells Intellect Every Time.

If you're raising funds by mail, the best advice I can give you is to reread chapter 3 before sitting down at the keyboard.

I can't think of a fund-raising campaign in which intellect might outpull emotion.

Rule 8: Dullness Doesn't Sell.

If anyone has ever coughed nervously or shifted in his seat or lit a cigarette (and you know he isn't a smoker) while reading your copy, reread the first part of chapter 9.

The Bore/Snore Effect infests a lot of fund-raising copy, especially when the writer or the person paying the writer is in love with equipment (hospitals are especially prone to this failing).

The other common source of fund raising dullness is violation of the Third Law—$E^2 = 0$ (when you emphasize everything you emphasize nothing).

A mailing tells me, "147 Ways Your United Fund Helps the Community." It's like a wet sponge compared with, "Because of You—She Can See the Flowers."

Rule 9: Never Forget You're Competing for Attention.

Your project may be all you do, but your envelope isn't the only piece of mail your prospective donor gets. You have to re-educate him every time you contact him.

Look at your own mail for the next week. Which envelopes—yes, even the nonprofit third-class envelopes—scream to be opened? Which messages do you read all the way through?

It's a mistake to take the reader for granted. Every time you send out a piece of mail, ask yourself: "If *I* got this would I open it? Would I respond to it?"

Rule 10: Test.

The most challenging aspect of direct response is also the most frustrating. We learn something, and what we've learned seems to work only for that particular project at that particular time.

Testing is a humbling experience. I've had one-page letters that outpulled four-page letters, I've had black-and-white brochures that outpulled color brochures, I've had #10 envelopes that outpulled 9 × 12 envelopes. Okay, I also have had mailings that tested exactly the reverse.

What this means to me is that *not* testing is a sad and costly mistake. You know some basic rules of the game or you can't compete, but the rules change and you constantly augment them with revisions. It's something like the IRS regulations.

What to test? I suggest testing envelope treatment; the number of enclosures; the name of the person signing the letter; a precancelled stamp against the standard third-class nonprofit indicia; various levels of excitement in the approach, to determine just how much emotion to pack into it; frequency of contact with previous donors; and, most of all, lists. List testing is the ultimate key to success. I might write a piece of copy that would double response from cold lists, but astute list selection might increase response by a thousand percent.

Rule 11: Make the Age of Skepticism Work for You.

In the Age of Skepticism, we no longer lionize celebrities. We know they're reading a script when they appear in television commercials for a cause or exotic disease they aren't themselves totally familiar with.

Remember the wallop of the William Talman anti-smoking spot? Talman was the man who played the role of Hamilton Burger on the Perry Mason television series, and the reason for the effectiveness of that spot was Talman's death, of lung cancer, before the spot began to run.

Surely it was more effective than an antismoking spot starring Tony Curtis, who while the spot still was scheduled was arrested in London for possession of marijuana.

Many celebrity users are finding it's a mistake to use celebrities alone. They have recognition value, yes. But if you want the televised appeal to have the appearance of truth, you don't use a celebrity alone. You use a victim.

I'm not drawing a gruesome comparison. I'm drawing a comparison based on the most powerful word in direct response—*verisimilitude*.

It's a paradox. Truth may or may not raise funds for us, because truth can appear to be *un*true. But verisimilitude, the appearance of truth, can't fail us.

Rule 12: Make It Easy for Them to Give.

I'm sure you've tested, as I have, an envelope with the legend "Place Stamp Here" against a business reply envelope.

You also may have tested panels of names who get a regular envelope with (gulp!) a first-class stamp pasted onto it. You may have tested what I call a "super legend" in the stamp area: "We appreciate your putting the stamp on this envelope, as we appreciate your generosity."

How else can you make it easy for them to give? I think it's a mistake to ignore the moment of response, the reason we mail in the first place. If we're giving a certificate, have a big tinted space with the instruction, "Your Official Certificate of Merit will show your name exactly as you indicate here."

Be sure the donor form is clear, easy to read, properly inspirational, and brief. Don't let any dereliction kill the donation at the moment of ultimate decision.

AMERICAN CANCER SOCIETY® FLORIDA DIVISION, INC., BROWARD COUNTY UNIT

1983 Crusade

Dear Neighbor:

As a Broward County resident and as one who knows the anguish and pain which cancer inflicts on those we love, I have come to understand the important work of the American Cancer Society. For this reason, I am pleased to serve as your Broward County Residential Chairman for the 1983 Crusade.

The facts about cancer are startling. One cancer-related death every 78 seconds. Nearly 1110 deaths a day from cancer. As the second leading cause of death in this country, cancer will touch the lives of 1 person in every 4.

Yet, there is hope. And more importantly there is a way you can help! You can make a generous contribution to this year's Crusade. Your tax-deductible donation will enable us to continue funding our life-saving programs of Research, Education, and Service.

Our goal is to eliminate cancer in your lifetime. We are not there yet, but we are getting closer everyday. Your financial support helps more than you will ever know. Please return the enclosed envelope with your gift of life made payable to the American Cancer Society.

You REALLY do make a difference. Thank you for caring.

Sincerely,

June Taylor
Residential Chairman
Broward County Unit ACS

1303 EAST LAS OLAS BLVD., FT. LAUDERDALE, FLORIDA 33301 305/467-3363

Figure 13.2 Can you find a motivator in this letter? Statistics are impersonal; tax-deductible status has no uniqueness. Fund raising is competitive; the impulse to give isn't easily stirred. Although the seed of a motivator is here ("... cancer will touch the lives of 1 person in every 4"), the word *touch* is too soft and the one-in-four possibility of disaster isn't arrowed at *me*.

Those are the twelve Rules. Violating any one of them can impede response the way a flat tire can slow the motion of a truck. Violating two of them can blow the truck's gaskets.

Since this entire tirade smacks of iconoclasm, one final iconoclastic suggestion: Advance all your deadlines for your next mailing by one day. Take that extra day to check every component for adherence to the twelve rules. In my opinion it'll be time well spent. I'll stake my pledge card on it.

14

The Telltale Envelope

Every expert has a different opinion about the value of copy on the outer mailing envelope. And everyone is an expert.

Some embrace the idea of exhortative copy on the envelope. Others suggest you're better off with envelopes that look like personal correspondence and don't have handwritten or typeset prereading messages on them.

My opinion: Use envelope copy.

I say this not only because the tests to which I've been privy back up my contention that outer envelope copy does indeed spur that indolent recipient to open the blasted thing, but also because I've never seen any evidence that having your envelope look like a conventional letter generates business; in fact, some companies report an increase in "white mail" because the recipient is subliminally annoyed by the masquerade.

(The inevitable result of any mass mailing, "white mail" is a message, usually unsigned, in the business reply envelope you enclosed, criticizing your company—sometimes to the point of mad ranting.)

The Deadly "Neatness Complex"

Some with whom I've discussed the matter have, I swear, a neatness complex. The decision to avoid envelope copy has nothing whatever to do with marketing; it's the result of a "neatness counts" attitude. I follow a different cry; sales are all that count. Any other scorekeeping technique is ego driven.

There are three formats for envelope copy: the handwritten note, the printed message, and the typewritten lead-in.

Deciding which to use without deciding what to say isn't a particularly bright move. The other indication of imaginative sterility is the "We've always done it this way" conclusion, which
gradually deadens the impact of the envelope copy.

There's a psychological rule of which we all should be
aware as we battle for sales in the Age of Skepticism:

**IT'S EASIER TO RENOUNCE THE OBVIOUS THAN TO
RENOUNCE THE TRADITIONAL.**

I had recent proof of this maxim when I noticed that
several successive mailings from one company had a sales
message on the envelope, reversed into an inch-wide color
band that ran horizontally from the left edge to the window. I
asked an acquaintance who works for that company why all the
envelope treatment was identical. "That's our style," he explained. "Our customers expect it."

To me, that corporate attitude swims in the comfortable
laziness of resistance to change; the customers never know the
anticipation factor of opening the mailing because of envelope
motivation. And the hole in the logic gapes widely if the same
technique encompasses cold-list mailings.

Rules for Writing Envelope Copy

Before attacking the specifics of what to say on the envelope, here are two opinions masquerading as rules. Envelope
Copy being as short and controllable as it is, I know of no rules
of direct response copywriting as easy to enforce, reject, or
check.

1. **WHAT YOU SAY IS MORE IMPORTANT THAN THE
FORMAT IN WHICH YOU SAY IT.**
2. **IN THIS AGE OF SKEPTICISM, THE PROSPECTIVE
BUYER'S MOST FAVORABLE FIRST QUESTION IS,
"WHAT WILL IT DO FOR ME?", NOT, "WHAT IS IT?"**

I might have added a cautionary rule: Keep it short. But
I have trouble with that rule. There's one huge exception.

Miami Business Journal
3785 N.W. 82nd Avenue • Suite 204 • Miami, Florida 33178

```
0001549                    XC4
H G LEWIS
COMMUNICOMP
BOX 15725
PLANTATION        FL  33318
```

Figure 14.1 What possible reason could there be for opening this envelope? It has a third-class mail indicium, an ink-jet label, and no imperative copy.

INTERNATIONAL MINT, INC.
390 Pike Road,
Huntingdon Valley, PA 19006.

On June 20, 1782, the Continental Congress selected the American Eagle as the official symbol of our great nation's eternal vigilance in defense of freedom. Now, you are invited to join in the bicentennial celebration of the great American Eagle...

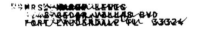

SATISFACTION GUARANTEED

Figure 14.2 Long envelope copy works if it motivates the recipient to open the envelope. This one doesn't. Why? It tells too much.

A handwritten envelope message shouldn't exceed a few words; a printed message shouldn't exceed two brief lines. But a typewritten lead-in message can be as long as the writer needs to draw the recipient into the golden aura of "Yes, my dear, your Rule 2 question is being answered. Here's what it will do for you."

I regard this as a superior piece of envelope copy. It's typed, to the left of the window in which the Cheshire label for cold-list name appears:

> Dear Philatelic Expert:
>
> I have information for you which is so far in advance of any announcement to the general public that I'm not even authorized to show you a picture . . . yet. But (CONTINUED INSIDE)

If someone were to say, "I'm putting 35 words on the outer envelope," terror would grip most of our hearts. But these 35 words, *typed,* not only don't appear to take as much space as a one-inch reverse band; they satisfy Rule 2 perfectly.

Examples, Good and Bad

Not so perfect is this copy, also typed in five one-sentence paragraphs along the left edge of a #10 window envelope:

> How do you start, strive and succeed with a small company?
>
> What 10 criteria tell you a stock is a "buy"?
>
> Anything more you should know about the changes ahead for the accounting profession?
>
> Have economists re-discovered free enterprise?
>
> May we send you the answers to these and other questions . . . FREE?

What's wrong here is that the copy goes too far. It not only uses the harsh word "strive"—which sounds like a lot of work; it also lapses into the final sell, right there on the envelope. The last paragraph is the giveaway: They're trying to sell

We're going to level with you...

```
EXPIRES   MAY 30, 1983
    AWARD #  3221X
MR/MRS H G LEWIS
9748 CEDAR VILLAS BL  00011
FT LAUDERDALE FL  33324
```

Figure 14.3 This is what I call, "Car dealer talk." Someone who says, "I'll be honest with you," suggests dishonesty. What saves this envelope is the clever wording on the label, with both an expiration date and the powerhouse word "Award" as impellers.

7237 Lake Street • River Forest, IL 60305

```
H. G. Lewis Pres.
Communicomp
PO BOX 15725
Plantation, FL 33318
```

**A year's worth of contacts
and 1,000 new ideas . . .
in just four enlightening days!**

REGISTRATION DOCUMENTS: DO NOT DELAY OR MISLAY!

Figure 14.4 What a shame this mailer didn't stop writing after the "Registration Documents" line! The three typeset lines to the right of the window are good arguments *against* opening the envelope.

me something. Shame, shame! There goes Rule 2. (Incidentally, one puzzling aspect is that this mailing, from a well-known business publication, was addressed to my wife, who handles our books but who isn't an accountant.)

A mailing from the AAA to cold lists: within a dotted line, the words, YOUR FREE MEMBERSHIP CARD IS ENCLOSED. Effective—good use of Rule 2.

We can compare one company's use of Rule 2 in two mailings. The first one didn't make it. This copy is set in script around a five-inch purple flower:

> Your Private Invitation . . .
>
> to return to the Romantic Past
>
> with The Language of Flowers

One cringes a little and hopes the postman didn't read that message. It's lyrical but not motivational, and it has a discomforting effect.

The same mailer, though, raises its batting average to .500 with this winner:

> This envelope contains
>
> actual currency.
>
> OPEN CAREFULLY!

A company whose mailings I usually respect struck out twice in a row, in my opinion, with a collectibles package. The first, mailed about two years before the second, had this envelope copy:

> "His talent is skyrocketing . . .
>
> A definite buy recommendation"

I objected to the mix: it wasn't his talent that was skyrocketing; they meant the value of his art. As I was collecting samples for this book, the same mailing rolled out. Same offer, same brochure, but this change in the envelope copy:

> His uniquely dramatic blending of fantasy and reality
> has rocketed him to the forefront of collectibles
> artists . . .

We still have the rocket's red glare, but confusion has been replaced by a textbook-quality violation of Rule 2.

One of the funniest violations of Rule 2 was in a mailing for a manufacturer of scientific equipment. The entire envelope was covered with a process-blue tint, with type either reversed in white or printed in black. On the face of the 6 × 9 envelope was this:

The

five words

every

teacher

would love

to hear . . .

(see other side)

Aha! I said. I know those five words! "School's out. I'm going home!"

Somehow I knew that even though my five words were logically correct, they wouldn't be the same five words chosen by the mailer. But cynical as I am, I still wasn't ready for the letdown when I flipped the envelope:

"THIS ISN'T SCIENCE . . . IT'S FUN!"

Clumsy Lies Don't Work

This brings me to Envelope Copy Rule 3 for the Age of Skepticism, and if you've read chapter 5 you already know how I feel about aberrations in copywriting:

DON'T LIE.

This has nothing to do with salesmanship nor with writing and communicative talent. Rather, the rule is based on *logic.* There are so many possible combinations of words for the envelope—far more than for any other component of the mailing—that lying doesn't make sense. Unquestionably you'll antagonize some recipients, and you'll do it for no reason since the desk drawer is full of equally powerful envelope copy.

An example:

You are cordially invited to celebrate the discovery of
one of the most remarkable artists of our times.

Who's the artist? Grandma Moses. The word "discovery" not only isn't apt; it's not true.

Here's another. The typical recipient opens the envelope looking for the "kicker," and he finds it quickly. On the envelope is:

The Membership Card inside entitles you to receive
genuine Emeralds, Rubies or Sapphires
FREE
There is no obligation to buy anything

Ah, but there is. One must buy a one-year membership for $6. Disclaimer copy on the order form explains it this way: " . . . but since your Emerald, Sapphire or Ruby alone is worth more than this your membership in effect costs you nothing."

One of the most effective pieces of envelope copy I know of in recent years also sold low-cost precious gems:

TO ADDRESSEE NAMED AT LEFT:
YOUR NAME HAS BEEN SELECTED BY
COMPUTER AS PART OF A NATION-
WIDE CORPORATE ADVERTISING CAM-
PAIGN, PURSUANT TO WHICH OUR FIRM
WILL SHIP YOU A GENUINE 1-CARAT
EMERALD FROM OUR VAULT FOR THE
SUM OF $5 IF WE RECEIVE YOUR
REQUEST NO LATER THAN MIDNIGHT
DECEMBER 15. THERE IS NO OTHER
MONETARY OBLIGATION. PLEASE SEE
INSIDE FOR SHIPPING INFORMATION.

See the motivators? Words such as "pursuant to which" normally are eschewed by good direct response writers because they smack of legalese. That's why they're so good here.

And the emeralds aren't just being shipped; they're being shipped "from our vault," suggesting value. Why must we open the envelope? "For shipping information." As I remember, this mailing of a few years ago was controversial, but it wasn't a lie. I wish I'd written it.

Some envelope lies are the result not of duplicity but of a wild and undisciplined search for superlatives, regardless of lack of a factual core: "We have to say something extraordinary or they won't open the envelopes," someone concludes. This conclusion has no relationship to the contents of the envelope; it's as though a sales organization assigned a high-pressure "closer" to reinforce the selling argument.

An example of this is a mailing that told me on the envelope:

> Inside . . . five great
> reasons for renewing
> your USTA membership
> *now.*

The USTA is the United States Tennis Association. Those who know my copy philosophy (and I'm chagrined the USTA doesn't) are aware of my objection to the word "great" as a nondescriptive exaggeration of superiority; but that's not the main problem with this envelope copy.

Instead, the problem is that the envelope promise is a lie. The "five great reasons," it turns out, are five continuing segments of my relationship with USTA which will expire if I don't renew: 1. " . . . your membership will continue without interruption . . . "; 2. "You will renew for another year your subscription to . . . "; 3. " . . . you'll continue to have the opportunity to participate in USTA sanctioned tournaments . . . "; 4. "You'll receive the official Membership Card . . . " (I already have one); 5. "In addition, you will continue to receive the many other benefits of membership . . . "

The lie on the envelope not only didn't "close" me; it generated a negative reaction since a promise, which I hadn't sought, wasn't kept.

Office of the President
Calhoun's Collectors Society
7275 Bush Lake Road
Minneapolis, Minnesota

BULK RATE
U.S. POSTAGE
PAID
CALHOUN'S
COLLECTORS
SOCIETY, INC.

Hundreds of charming characters in a dozen heart-warming scenes in a dozen heart-warming and exciting for an exciting! Prepare yourself for an enjoyable visual experience!

Figure 14.5 A classic case of overwritten envelope copy, this handwritten legend says nothing in too many words. The second sentence adds nothing to the sales argument.

Position and Technique

Should impeller copy appear on the left or the right? I prefer the left, because recently I read a scientific explanation of the brain hemisphere functions: The left hemisphere controls the right eye and the cognitive function; the right hemisphere controls the left eye and the emotional function. Since emotion swamps perception in head-to-head tests, I pay it more heed. (Many regard this whole concept as hogwash, and their viewpoint has merit too.)

More and more envelopes use a rubber stamp effect to suggest urgency. I suggest that if you want a rubber stamp effect, go to a rubber stamp company and have your words set into a stamp. Use the stamp on sheets of white paper until you have the effect you want; then paste it into the art. Notching and blotching straight typeset costs far more and doesn't have the verisimilitude of an actual stamp.

If your name is powerful enough, any additional copy on the envelope saps out strength. One of the best-pulling pieces I ever wrote had only this copy in the upper left corner of a 9 × 12 envelope:

Mr. Frederick Haviland

Limoges, France

The postal indicia were buried unobtrusively above the address window. I was reminded of this when a simple #10 cream-colored envelope arrived. In the upper right corner was a precanceled third-class nonprofit stamp. In the upper left were two words: Ronald Reagan.

Words that Work

Are there crutch words for the unimaginative and fearful? Are there catch phrases that can't miss?

Sure. Here are four words that should work in every circumstance:

Private

Advance

Invitation

Exclusive

Each of these four words underscores Rule 2. I'd guess, then, that "Private, exclusive advance invitation" should be a dynamite cliché!

"Free" always seems to work. "Now You Can . . . " is powerful provided the rest of the message doesn't violate privacy and embarrass the recipient.

The most electric motivator to open any envelope is the one that says to the recipient, "I'm thinking about you." I immediately opened a colorless mailing from a magazine to which I'd never subscribe, because the envelope had this single typed sentence:

Have I been misled about you?

How about you? Does your envelope copy burn through the dendrites right there at the mailbox, causing the target person to rip feverishly at the seam to fight his way inside the mailing? Or . . .

Have I been misled about you?

This child is missing.
Perhaps you might help us
find him.

He was playing in the yard,
and suddenly he wasn't there.
This isn't like Russell at all,
and his parents are frantic.

We need your help and that of
other concerned parents.

Mr. ᎡᎧᏂᏟᎢᏟᏜᎧᏟᏟᎧᏟᎡᏟᎧᏟᎡᏟᏜᏟᎡᎧᏟᏜᎡᏟᎧ
ᏯᏯᏯᏯᏟᎧᏟᏟᎧᏟᏟᏜᏟᎧᎧᏟᏜᎧᏟᏟ
ᏯᏟᎧᏟᏟᏜᏟᎧᏟᏟᎧᏟᎧᏟᏟᎧᏟᏟᏟᏚᏟᏚᏯᏜ

Figure 14.6   This is one of the best pieces of envelope copy you'll find. Who can resist opening it? (The mailing, from a nonprofit organization, promotes child fingerprinting.)

Figure 14.7 Do I have to open it, Mom? Knowing I'll wade through 14 reasons makes whatever is inside this envelope less than attractive; and the copy itself violates the Third Law of force-communication ($E^2 = 0$).

15

A Look to 1990 and Beyond

Human nature being as cantankerous as it is, we have no laws of probability.

What we do have is an apparent disintegration of the unity we now can call "our society" only on Flag Day, Thanksgiving, and Christmas. Groups splinter and then resplinter. Minorities are black, female, old, young, educated, uneducated, of every religious persuasion, of nonreligious persuasion, residents of a particular subdivision, drivers of small cars, drivers of large cars, truck drivers, railroad passengers, thieves and scoundrels, recent immigrants, old-line native-borns, police, firemen, rapers and rapees, and those with only a black-and-white television set in their cars.

As I've said throughout this book, a major advantage of direct response advertising is its ability to appeal to vertical-interest groups within the fields of interest they represent. No other medium can do that. The late-night news can't do it. The daily paper can't do it. Even special-interest magazines can do it only in part, and then only on a rigid and unyielding schedule in which no advertiser has dominance.

Can We See Any Trends?

How many times can a single person be astounded by the same lunacy? I'm constantly reastounded at the most common circumstance I see in the most enlightened practitioners of the noble art of direct response selling:

A meeting of six people, for half a day, results in the careful choice of lists and media. We choose this list because it has women 18 to 34; we choose that list because it has senior citizens who own cars that cost

$12,000 or more; we choose the next list because the
family has bought a Boy Scout uniform within the past
two years. . . .

Then what do we do? We create a single direct mail
package and mail it to all of them, figuring we'll sort out the
winners from the losers by analyzing the response.

On occasion, when we've dabbled with packages tailored to the supposed key interest of a particular group and
tested that package against the "standard" approach, the results have been encouraging. Why, then, don't we do it more
often? Time and economics are sensible restraints, but as we
approach 1990 economics probably (yup, I know I said we have
no laws of probability) will swing around to favor greater attention to the demographic/psychographic differences that caused
us to choose that market segment.

Other trends? I see strong movement to the vernacular
in copywriting, and I say Hurrah! By 1990 the last rusting iron
bastions of false dignity should crumble, because the principles
explored in chapter 3 are inviolable in a free society.

The survival of antique writing isn't due to its superiority as a means of communication; it's due to a truism unearthed
a generation ago by David Ogilvy: "What you say is more important than how you say it." As I write this chapter I'm looking at a piece of mail addressed to me, selling a doll with this
rhetoric:

> As befits a work of this importance, Kate Lloyd Jones'
> Strawberry Girl will be meticulously handcrafted with
> the same care, the same attention to detail as the great
> collector dolls of yesteryear.

You guessed it—the other verbiage is parallel. It's
larded with *for* instead of *because, diverse* instead of *different, you
will notice* instead of *you'll see*—a quill pen writing from the
past. Is this bad, considering they'll sell some dolls?

It *isn't* bad if they've tested this copy against communicating copy and found this approach superior. It *is* bad if the
writer fears the personalized relationship that separates copy
we *read* from copy we *note*.

Reading Time—Increasing or Decreasing?

Will the message recipients of 1990 spend more time or less time reading the mailings and space ads, and viewing the electronic bombardment, than they do now?

My opinion: more.

I'll justify that opinion with a quick reference back to the opening of this chapter. As we increase penetration into specific-interest groups, we logically can expect greater attention from those we reach, because their interest in what we say should be greater.

(This presupposes our ability to reach them on a level of their own interests, not ours.)

I'm not interested in the Strawberry Girl doll—*as presented in the mailing sent to me.* Now, a favor please: Reread the last sentence, because it's the core of this chapter: I'm not interested in it *as presented in the mailing sent to me.*

In an enlightened creative writing course a brilliant assignment might be having the students create a mailing that *would* appeal to me. Who am I? I'm old. I'm young. I'm rich. I'm poor. I'm macho. I'm a poet. I'm any of the 230 million special-interest groups who respond best to an appeal specifically tailored to them, not arrogantly aimed at "those people" out there.

Sure, I'm on special-interest mailing lists. When I get a mailing for scuba equipment I'm quite naturally more inclined to read it than I am the Strawberry Girl doll mailing. Don't you see? That's the challenge. If you know who I am, you hurl down the gauntlet. "You *are* interested!" you thunder. "And here's why. . . ."

This isn't selling refrigerators to Eskimos. It's creating a logical marketing appeal within my experiential framework.

Realistically, if I contributed $10,000 to the Republican National Committee during the last election, the Democrats will have a hard time raising money from me. If I'm the president of the Down With Dolls League, probably I'm a poor prospect for this mailing. That's the purpose of demographic selection—to avoid contacting me.

But you say, "This guy didn't give a dime to *any* political party. He's worth plenty. And he never bought a doll but he
bought figurines."

Now what?

Now you tailor your approach to me, not to you. Your
inbreeding tells you to disqualify yourself as a criterion for
what *I'd* like.

Yes, I'll read it. I don't play major league baseball or
football, but I read the sports pages. I did read your competitor's mailing, for, yes, a doll, all the way through. I'm not a
hopeless case; are you?

Learn Your Craft!

If you're using words to sell, play a game with yourself.
You're in a word store, a giant emporium, and you've won a
contest giving you the right to use any words in the store.

The store has hundreds of thousands of words in it, and
they're all yours, free. A game? Nonsense, it's exactly what we
have at our fingertips every day. We have the whole store, so
why do so many of us head for the bargain basement where the
selection is poor and full of cheap "seconds"?

Here's a product that deposits an antifriction coating on
my automobile engine. The copy says:

> This drastically reduces your friction and drag,
> consequently lowering your engine's operating
> temperature.

The word *drastically* is about as pejorative a word as the
writer could find. I don't want a product that drastically reduces *anything*. Come on, writer, ease my fears; don't create
more of them.

On occasion I run an ad for my own copywriting services in some of the advertising publications. The heading on
the ad is, "Call the Pro." I had a letter from someone who, after
telling me how much he admires my writing, asks, "Could you
not be more humble and herald 'Call the Man Who Wants to
Help Make Your Dollars More Money,' or, 'Call the Man Who
Has Had More Successes than Failures' "?

No, I can't. Humility doesn't enter into the mix. Weakening the statement does. If I'm called on to justify my position in the world of force-communication, I'll never use as credentials the statement, "I've had more successes than failures." If I did, would you buy a piece of used copy from that man?

A targeted message, delivered with force and clarity—what can beat it? I've kept as a sample an ad for a computer headed, "A computer that understands plain English for under three thou." The first paragraph has this subhead:

> The keyboard is as familiar as a tennis court.

A conceit? You bet, since the illustration shows a bearded egghead wearing mufti, not tennis clothes; he's pointing to a keyboard, not a tennis court. I play tennis every day, but familiarity isn't a word I'd associate with the court. Now read what's under that headline and subhead:

> Now, get a mega-return on your typing class. The
> revolutionary HASCI (has-key) keyboard is designed just
> like an electric typewriter. Everything is familiar and
> easy to operate.

It is, huh? Is HASCI familiar? I never heard of it before. And having a keyboard like a typewriter is about as un-unique a selling proposition as I ever read. The ad, in a daily newspaper, misses the point of its own argument.

To all of us, including me, a reminder: The body copy should verify the claims you make in your headlines.

Hail and Farewell!

Every time I write a book, I say to myself and to everyone within earshot, "This is the last one. I don't have anything left to say."

This time I might* mean it. I've emptied the basket.

To those on whose toes I've tromped by attacking copy over which they oozed honest sweat, I owe not an apology but a free lunch. To those who disagree with my opinions on what

---

*How better to end this book than with a weasel word?

works and what doesn't, I justify every word on the ground that they *are* opinions, clearly labeled.

To those who love words, who reach heights of ecstasy from polishing the gems of our trade, I salute you. You're my brothers and sisters, and you can swim in my pool any time, whether you agree with my opinions or not.

Appendix—
Forty Questions

We all know that "Why didn't you . . . ?" is worthless while "Why don't you . . . ?" may be invaluable. Questions asked *before* the fact are neither competitive nor derogatory; proof is that they're asked in time to make corrections.

Direct response companies face four crossroads without direction signs when they decide to sell something. Too often, we tend to fudge by asking and answering only two questions before spending money with minimal wisdom:

1. What are we selling?
2. Who's going to write it?

I'm not knocking those two questions, especially since my own professional existence depends on the second one. I do say that after this primitive decision making, answering each of ten questions within the four decision-making categories will absolutely, positively improve professionalism—and response.

The Categories for Decision Making

These are the four areas of direct response in which questions should be asked *before* promotional dollars are spent:

1. Determining the market
2. Determining copy slant and appeal
3. Determining lists to mail
4. Determining media buys

Of the four, *determining the market* is to me the most important. I was planning this book when a client asked my opinion about running space ads for a "sock wallet" that protects a passport and cash by concealing them in a pouch attached to the leg. Two problems: he was buying it not from the manufacturer but from a distributor, with a markup of only 50 percent; and someone else already had run ads in travel publications. His argument was based on personal enthusiasm rather than marketing logic: If that competitor had run the ad for the better part of a year, the product must be sound. My recommendation was to scrap the promotion. Neither the proper markup nor an open field was available.

Determining copy slant often is left to the writer. This can be for one of three reasons: respect for the writer's ability to mount a powerful selling argument; fear of making a mistake; or ignorance of who buys what and why. None of the three is valid, not even the first one. At the very least, the writer should be told: "The buyer we're trying to reach is . . . " That statement is the result of consideration of the next category:

Determining lists is the decision that will make the greatest difference in the pulling power of a piece of direct mail. Whoever first said that to whom you mail is more important than what you say has my admiration and agreement. Poor copy won't completely ruin a mailing the way poor list selection can.

Determining media buys is to many the finger exercise of flipping through the pages of Standard Rate & Data looking for ideas. The dynamic changes in ad sizes (such as standard ad units) and ways of spending less are subordinate to empirical decisions based on "what I like to read." Asking the right questions will avoid the wrong answers.

Since lists are supposed to come out even (astonishing, isn't it, how many people have a neatness complex and are uneasy when comparable lists are of uneven length?), here are exactly ten questions to ask yourself *before* making decisions.

Questions for Market Determination

1. Are you testing? What?
2. Will the test results help build sales?

3. Do you know who your logical buyers are?
4. What incentives to buy from you do you offer?
5. Do you offer the buyer solid evidence underscoring your claim that he or she should buy?
6. Is the thrust aimed at the proper target group?
7. Does the envelope appeal to the most logical buyers?
8. Is the quantity large enough to give you a reading?
9. Is the quantity small enough to leave you a universe of names for the rollout?
10. Is the markup adequate without overpricing the item to the buyer?

Questions for Copy Slant and Appeal

1. Have you motivated the buyer? Have you told the buyer what to do?
2. Is each component as strong as you can make it?
3. Are your testimonials and endorsements credible?
4. Is the buyer instantly aware what it is you're selling?
5. Are grammar and spelling flawless?
6. Have you broken up long, gray copy blocks?
7. Is the type as large as it can be within the space allocated?
8. Do dates, prices, deadlines, and facts all match?
9. Has someone unfamiliar with the offer read it and understood it?
10. Have you simplified pomposities, governmentalese, and obfuscations?

Questions for List Selection

1. Have you and your competition worked these same lists to death?
2. Has any list lain dead for more than six months?
3. Who else has used and profited from the lists?
4. Is the universe big enough to make testing worthwhile?
5. Are you merge-purging out duplications?
6. Have you included two or three speculative lists?

7. Are you choosing class before mass?
8. Have you included list rental in figuring a break-even point?
9. Are you set up to analyze results?
10. Within lists are you testing price and different appeals?

Questions for Media Buying

1. Have you bought space or time at the lowest rate?
2. Have you investigated remnants, standbys, and discounts?
3. Have readers or viewers responded to similar offers?
4. Are you testing copy with an A/B split before rolling out?
5. Is clarity more important to you than artistry?
6. Will you have merchandise on hand within 30 days after publication or air date?
7. Have you avoided locking yourself into noncancellable contracts?
8. Are you working far enough ahead to avoid Federal Express shipments of production materials?
9. Is production professional and is camera-ready art really camera ready?
10. Are your insertion orders unmistakably clear?

So What?

What's the benefit of being able to check your sales promotion against these questions and, without fudging, answer them with the right answer—either "Of course!" or "Of course not!"?

There's more than one benefit. Three separate benefits will caress you:

First, you'll enjoy the benefit of moving away from the knotted-gut approach to direct response marketing. When you think like a professional you act like a professional, which means you take risks knowingly instead of unwittingly; you're in command of Dame Fortune.

Second, you benefit from the learning experience. Because you control the variables, you'll gradually build a base of knowledge in which your guesses can develop into predictions.

Third, you'll probably save money and be more likely to make money. Is there any better way to keep score?

INDEX

Bradford Exchange, 89
Braggadoccio Syndrome, 150–155
Brooklyn Bridge, 184
Bugs Bunny, 150
Business Week magazine, 193, 195, 196

Calhoun's Collectors Society, 190
Callouts, 212–213
Caples, John, 113
Carriage Hill Collection, 31
Catalogs, 124, 199–216
    clarity, 211, 214–216
    copy length, 199–216
    hot-line offers, 208
    objective copy, 208
    personalizing, 207–208
    possessive copy, 208
    relationship, copy to illustration, 208–216
Cheating, in copy, 75–80
Chevron Travel Club, 239
Children (as target group), 36
Chrysler, 6
Citibank, 142
Cody, Sherwin, 112
Collector Investor, 148
Cologne Trade Fair, 93
Comparative advertising, 122–123
Conceits, 180
Conditional declension, law of, 45–48
Confusion Factor, 171–178, 180
Contemporaneous transmission, rule of, 55
Copy slant, determining, 247–249
Coupon, 175

Dakota Farmer magazine, 193, 194
Dannoe Enterprises, 181
D-Con, 6
DeLorean Motor Club, 77
Demographics, 206–207
Dior, Christian, 174
Dire warning, as sales technique, 189–191
Direct Marketing magazine, v
Dodge, vii, viii
Dull copy, 141–150, 222